La Pointe

VILLAGE OUTPOST ON MADELINE ISLAND

La Pointe

VILLAGE OUTPOST
ON MADELINE ISLAND

Hamilton Nelson Ross

Foreword by Thomas Vennum, Jr.

WISCONSIN HISTORICAL SOCIETY PRESS

Library of Congress Cataloging-in-Publication Data

Ross, Hamilton Nelson, 1889–1957.
   La Pointe: village outpost on Madeline Island / Hamilton Nelson Ross ; foreword by Thomas Vennum, Jr.
   p.cm.
  Originally published: St. Paul : North Central Pub., 1960. With new introd.
  Includes bibliographical references (p.) and index.
  ISBN 0-87020-320-7 (hardbound)   ISBN 0-87020-321-5 (paperbound)
   1. La Pointe (Wis.)—History. I. State Historical Society of Wisconsin. II. Title.

F589.L13 R6 2000
977.5'21—dc21   00-038799

TO

Dorothy

MY PATIENT AND DEVOTED

SOUNDING BOARD

Foreword

In the summer of 1999, La Pointers were astonished one morning to find a large German cruise ship at anchor halfway between Madeline Island and Bayfield on the mainland. Due to rough seas, the ship had been diverted from its intended stop some ten miles north on Lake Superior off picturesque Raspberry Island. As cash-laden passengers were shuttled back and forth to the mainland, Bayfield merchants enjoyed a brief economic bonanza—leading some to urge negotiations with the cruise line to include their town in future ports-of-call.

Hamilton Nelson Ross (1889–1957) would have been amused. As an accomplished amateur historian, he knew well the cyclical nature of events. A half-century earlier in his *La Pointe: Village Outpost,* Ross had reviewed the vacillations of the region's economy—from the fur trade to the commercial fishing business of the mid-nineteenth century and the sudden wealth arising from real estate taxes on timberlands in the late 1890s. He noted the temporary depletion in La Pointe's population following the discovery in 1844 of iron ore in the Marquette Range. But he pointed out that, long before Duluth, Superior, and Ashland were established, La Pointe still "retained its supremacy as the general receiving and assembly point for the commerce of the region...for all vessels arriving at the western end of the lake." As in the case of the German cruise ship, La Pointe was also regarded as a "harbor of refuge" in bad weather.

Ross was born in Beloit, Wisconsin, home of the college he attended. He spent a post-graduate year at the Massachusetts Institute of Technology to improve his engineering skills and better qualify him for work at the Beloit Iron Works where his father was part owner, building machinery for papermaking. Ross first visited Madeline Island as an eight-year-old and later became a lifelong summer resident, staying at the Ross family cabin. An adventuresome youth, fond of boating, he began to explore the region on his own. His excursions led him "into every nook, cranny and cave of the Apostle Islands....[including] the midnight experience of being washed ashore on a plank at Montreal River, from a wrecked sailboat...." He developed an abiding love for the natural beauty of the area as well as a fondness for the colorful citizens of La Pointe, but his curiosity about its history met with frustration. He encountered an almost total lack of written information or, at best, stories from locals, which conflicted widely. Wishing to set the record straight and provide the serious scholarship the area deserved, Ross embarked on his journey as a historical researcher and writer.

After years of informal interviews with area citizens, both Indian and white, Ross traveled extensively with his wife. They visited appropriate historical societies, pursued bibliographic references, and established personal acquaintanceships with such scholars as Grace Lee Nute (author of the classic *Lake Superior* [1944]). Once he had accumulated sufficient material, he decided to publish privately his earlier tract, The *Apostle Islands* (1951). But for Ross the topic was obviously too large and important to be contained in such a slender volume. Thus it became the basis for his much-expanded *La Pointe: Village Outpost* (first published in 1960, republished in 1971, long out of print, and now issued for the third time, by the State Historical Society).

The scholarship behind Ross's history is first rate, and his bibliography exhaustive even today. Little of the history of the western Great Lakes escaped him. Where there is controversy, Ross was careful to present conflicting evidence. He relegated most to footnotes—some lengthy enough to occupy more space on the page than his main text. For example, in a discussion of the origins of the name La Pointe and its first use, he begins, "There is no direct proof that the French had a post here earlier than 1692.... The theory is refuted by [Louise Phelps] Kellogg.... This, in turn, is contradicted by Francis Parkman...."

Ross's intimate knowledge of the topography and climate of the area, which he gained from years of navigating its waters, enables him to challenge previous assertions. For instance, his familiarity with the rough water off Washburn's Houghton Point ("The Charybdis to Chequamegon's [Long Island's] Scylla") leads him to take issue with the eminent historian Reuben Gold Thwaites regarding a purported Ottawa Indian fort on the Point in the late seventeenth century. Ross argues convincingly that the settlement *must* have been on Long Island rather than the mainland. His knowledge of the seasonal changes in Lake Superior's weather brings him to question accounts that the Jesuit Father Rene Menard was abandoned at the foot of Keewenaw Bay by fellow Frenchmen and spent the winter of 1660–1661 alone there.

Basing his disagreement on the report of Menard's French comrades leaving their winter quarters on April 19, Ross determines persuasively that they could *not* have been at Madeline Island, since the date is too early for the breakup of ice in Chequamegon Bay sufficient to permit safe canoe travel.

Where evidence is vague or lacking, Ross is confident enough to offer his own conjectures. Thus, the location of "la petite peche" (the little fish), where Jean Baptiste Perrault reports he camped in 1784, Ross guesses must be the present Siskiwit Bay, a popular Indian fishing ground. Perrault was en route to La Pointe, his next stop, "where le gros pied [big foot] and his family helped us out.". After searching, Ross admits there is no record of who "gros pied" was. The name "big foot," however, suggests an Indian family, *mangazid* (big foot) being a plausible Ojibwe surname. In another instance, converting the French "league" of the time to miles and using United States survey charts, Ross contributes his opinion on the true location of Father Claude Allouez's first chapel, which he places two miles south of Bono's Creek between Washburn and Ashland on the mainland.

Ross shows himself master of a number of topics, ranging from metallurgy to Indian nomenclature. Consider his detailed attention to the architecture, construction techniques, and histories of Madeline Island buildings he deemed important, such as the first Protestant mission in the Northwest, which was being used as a cow stable when he first visited it in 1897 as a boy. To provide the floor plan and elevation (figure 4), he personally took its measurements in 1951. Finding no description of its foundation, he nevertheless conjectures the construction techniques as those used for the fireplace: moistened local clay and stones, possibly tamped into wooden forms. Or take his detailed history of Treaty Hall, so called because of the disbursement in 1854 of government annuities from the building to all the Lake Superior Ojibwe. Or note the attention to detail in his discussion of the first Protestant church in the Northwest, which accommodated 150-200 parishioners. It was built with eight logs placed horizontally in slots of upright logs, the joints being chinked with local clay and moss, its exterior siding made of hand-sawn boards, its interior sealed with whitewashed clay plaster. Ross recorded other architectural data, including the design specifications of the 860-foot bridge over Silver Creek, and he relates the fate of a 408-ton brownstone monolith ("world's largest") which had been quarried locally for the World's Columbian Exposition of 1893 in Chicago. Because it was too heavy for transport by rail or ship, the monolith was eventually cut into building blocks.

La Pointe: Village Outpost is enriched by Ross's wealth of anecdotes, culled from a variety of sources. He relates stories surrounding visits of famous people to the region, such as the advice given in 1868 to Abraham Lincoln's widow, Mary Todd Lincoln, not to stay in the Island hotel: "...It's full of knotholes, and the men snore something awful." Eyebrows were raised sixty years later during a visit by Calvin Coolidge, when it was rumored that the president had used *worms* for bait while fishing nearby in the trout-rich Brule River.

One can imagine the relish with which Ross reported the arrival in 1902 of the first bathtub on Madeline Island, "an event of no historical importance, but one which caused considerable local comment." Because there was no running water on the island then, it had to be hauled by bucket from the lake and heated—a luxury beyond the imagination of locals, who are reported to have sneered "Snobs!" and "Down with the rich!"

Ross developed an ear acutely tuned to local gossip, and, though a member of the "summer folk," he was also a privileged outsider. He knew but did not divulge the identity of two island "Robin Hood" thieves who had stolen from railroad boxcars on the mainland and distributed their booty in La Pointe by night, leaving sacks of flour at the back door of "a certain kindly woman, famed for her baking [probably "Gram" Johnson]." Also surreptitious had been the nocturnal digging up of Indian skulls in 1900 by Beloit College students staffing the Old Mission Inn, which happened to be sited on a large former Indian cemetery. According to Ross, when upset local Ojibwe informed the amateur archaeologists that their ancestors had died of smallpox, the skeletal remains were quickly reburied, and the students hastened to get inoculated against the disease.

Despite its erudition, Ross's history is presented in a clearly written style, easily accessible to the average reader. Much of the book's charm is due to his frequent light-humored asides, some of them almost tongue-in-cheek. How intensely personal this history was to him is evident when Ross fits his own reminiscences into the recitation of historical facts. For example, regarding the naming of Hermit (or Wilson's) Island, Ross confesses, "There are a number of different versions to this tale. The author has chosen the one which most appeals to him." Lending verisimilitude to the experiences of summer visitors during services at the rather primitive bark-shingled Old Mission Church, Ross notes, "Numerous flies also attended," and, in a footnote, "So did the author." For his impression of River Bridge near Ashland, he comments that despite its being an engineering marvel, trains were always slow to cross it, and the bridge was said to sway. In fact, "The author, when a little boy, was quite sure that the sway was several feet."

Ross's clear style, combined with his gentle sense of humor, did not prevent him from lapsing occasionally into rich prose. To describe the glacial action which formed the Great Lakes region, Ross avoids a mere dry, scientific descriptionñopting instead for the following colorful passage: "Not content with moving parts of Canada into the United States, the glaciers began to recede under more powerful sun's rays and, like proper robbers caught with their ill-gotten wealth, dropped their loads of boulders, gravel, sand and silt, willy-nilly."

Ross regrets that the sights and sounds of his youth on the Island are part of the irrecoverable past. During his day, summer recreational life was vastly simpler. Most boats were non-motorized, some old birch-bark canoes still plied the waters, and exciting adventures would be sailing to another island to pick berries or scrambling aboard the annual hayrack ride to Big Bay. Long afterward, he clearly recalled the clanking of pots and pans as the wagon traversed a stretch of corduroy road, and the sounds of band music aboard boats arriving from Ashland for the annual clambake.

Change has been slow and gradual in the area since the publication of Ross's history. With the decline of the fishing industry, tourism has become the economic mainstay. Madeline Island's year-round population has in fact dwindled over time: in the 1830s it was near 600, today closer to 200. At the same time, the number of summer homes continues to increase as more city folk find a haven in its beautiful setting of northern pines bordering white sandy beaches or red rock cliffs. Like Hamilton Ross, many summer residents occupy the same modest family cabin for several generations. (Today Hamilton Ross II and his sister Mary Gordon Ross continue as year-round La Pointe residents.)

The topography of the area has changed somewhat, as Lake Superior continues to rise, causing land erosion. Even in Ross's day, wave action had reduced some of the original Apostle Islands to underwater shoals. Soldier's Rock, which he pictured (Plate 5), has long since vanished. Technical improvements have brought inevitable changes to island life, too. Wells have replaced the old "water trolleys" along the shore, although Ross felt it important to document their technology by creating a diagram (page 175) of a trolley first used in 1896.

A new sense of historical conservation among Islanders is in part attributable to Ross's history. The Madeline Island Historical Museum, opened in 1958, was acquired by the State Historical Society of Wisconsin in 1969, and then expanded in 1991. (Hamilton Ross's research was in fact the basis for the layout of the rooms as well as the Museum's "storyline.") The Madeline Island Historic Preservation Association was formed to save buildings unique to the Island's history ó the old Lake View schoolhouse on the island's north end, for example, was moved to downtown La Pointe. When the Old Mission Inn was torn down, one wing of its dining room was salvaged to serve as the town's post office. And the beauty and serenity of Madeline Island and the surrounding wilderness were forever preserved from development by the creation of the Apostle Islands National Lakeshore in 1970.

Although power boats were already coming onto the scene in Ross's time, recreational sailboats in profusion outnumber them today—enough to keep several marinas occupied in summertime. Some activities maintain an unbroken link with the past. Ross's colorful depiction of Colonel Woods preparing to leave the Island daily at 9 A.M. sharp in his powerboat *Nebraska*, even if it meant leaving family members behind, is paralleled by today's ferry line service, where one can still see passengers and cars scrambling to make departures. Despite the annual hunting season, overabundant white-tailed deer continue to plague the island, destroying gardens and any new growth of cedar, white pine, or hemlock. The large number of feral dogs formerly on the island have been replaced by domestic pets on leashes, although, said locals in the 1890s, the wild dogs, when not raiding citizens' larders, with help from hungry wolves reduced the deer population considerably. The annual clambake evolved into community "bring a hotdish to pass" picnics with accordian music by locals at Leona's Bar in the '60s and '70s, then into today's Fourth of July Parade and festivities.

Ross closes his book worrying that "the importance of the village has probably been overemphasized." Not so, Hamilton! The Island's role in the fur trade alone earns its place in history. Indeed, the exploration and opening up for settlement of the entire Upper Midwest depended on this far-flung "outpost." This reprint of Ross's history should serve future generations interested in the rich history of one small corner of the Old Northwest.

THOMAS VENNUM, JR.
Smithsonian Institution
February, 2000

Acknowledgments

As indicated in the front of this book, my wife, Dorothy, was the all-suffering person who gently led me away from many pitfalls of rhetoric into which I probably would have fallen. Next to her was my friend of many years, Leo Woods Capser of St. Paul, Minnesota, who furnished, by outright gift, many old and rare books bearing on the subject matter. Altogether, he has smoothed an otherwise difficult path to much valuable information.

In addition, he was kind enough to introduce me to the Misses Grace Lee Nute and Lucile Kane, of the Minnesota Historical Society. Miss Nute, the walking encyclopedia of all matters pertaining to Lake Superior, has been most generous in giving her time and many priceless leads, particularly in regard to the North West Company and to the Lake Superior fisheries. Miss Kane, probably through pity, offered to undertake the thankless task of editing my work and of rescuing me from a sea of semicolons which, if I ever knew their function (and I admit I didn't), I had forgotten in the years of pursuing matters other than writing.

Such Historical Societies as the Wisconsin, Minnesota and St. Louis County (Minnesota) have placed their facilities at my disposal with surprising graciousness. To Benton H. Wilcox of the Wisconsin Society, to Miss Cora Colbrath and Mrs. Josiah E. Greene of the St. Louis County Society and to the staff of the Minnesota Society I tender many thanks.

The Madeline Island Historical Museum, of La Pointe, Wisconsin, has given me unstinted access to its complete collections, as well as constant and enthusiastic encouragement in the compiling of this record.

I am also indebted, on many counts, to the following: Mrs. George W. (Sarah Wheeler) Bunge, my beloved first grade school teacher, for much information and many family sidelights concerning her grandfather, Leonard H. Wheeler, in his missionary labors at La Pointe and Odanah; Mrs. Daniel Angus, Jr. for access to old La Pointe Town records and official plats of the village; Joseph ("Dragi Joe") Gregorich for the loan of books and manuscripts concerning Bishop Baraga, along with much collateral information; Herbert P. Zimmermann of R. R. Donnelley & Sons Company's Lakeside Press, who for more than twenty-five years, has sent me *The Lakeside Classics,* among which were several volumes bearing on my subject; in addition to which he has loaned me several volumes of like nature; James B. Nash, Henry C. Capser and Einar Miller for the loan of many books; the late Jerod W. Day for the old survey records of LaPointe; Henry J. Wachsmuth, Mrs. Joseph Neveaux, Nelson E. Angus, Mrs. Clara Angus Gilbert, Miss Dollie Bishoff, Allan Born and Mrs. William S. Johnson for much local information; Joseph P. O'Malley for many old maps and local information; the late Dr. James S. Reeve for the gift of pictures taken in 1897; Alex Butterfield for his reminiscences concerning the old Bayfield Road and other contemporary information; Leigh P. Jerrard for maps and records concerning the Bois Brule River and the Bayfield Road; C. E. Schreiber, of the Wisconsin Public Service Commission, regarding old railroads of northern Wisconsin and the "Official Excavator;" "Al" Galazen, for unearthing sites of old forts, along with many artifacts.

Such organizations as the United States Coast Guard, the United States Engineers at Sault Ste. Marie, the Great Lakes Survey Office and the Lake Carriers' Association have been most responsive and courteous in furnishing much material.

Of considerable assistance in refreshing dates and occurences since 1895 have been the Thomas G. Grassie family's *Annals of Merrymeet,* and the *Ross Family Log* of my own folk.

H. N. R.

Contents

Foreword by Thomas Vennum, Jr.   vii
Acknowledgments   xiii
Introduction   xvii

I.   "AS IT WAS IN THE BEGINNING"   3
Gloria Patri ... B.C.? to A.D. 1615

II.   "SEEK, AND YE SHALL FIND"   17
Matthew 7:7 ... 1616 to 1677

III.   "KNOCK, AND IT SHALL BE OPENED UNTO YOU"   34
Matthew 7:7 ... 1678 to 1762

IV.   "SO I SAW THE WICKED BURIED"   58
Ecclesiastes 8:10 ... 1763 to 1816

V.   "I GO A FISHING"   73
John 21:3 ... 1817 to 1842

VI.   "THE FORGER—OF BRASS AND IRON"   108
Genesis 4:22 ... 1843 to 1877

VII.   "BEHOLD THE FIRE AND THE WOOD"   132
Genesis 22:7 ... 1878 to 1888

VIII.   "THERE GO THE SHIPS"   147
Psalms 104:26 ... 1889 to 1900

IX.   "OLD THINGS ARE PASSED AWAY"   162
II Corinthians 5:17 ... 1901 to 1957

Glossary of Ojibway Names   179
Bibliographical Note   185
Chronology   190
Index   195

Maps

1.	La Pointe-Chequamegon Territory and Lake Superior.	xvii
2.	La Pointe and the Apostle Islands.	xx
3.	Silver Islet and Environs.	5
3A.	The Keweenaw Peninsula.	6
4.	Lake Nemadji Stage of Lake Superior.	8
4A.	Lake Duluth Stage of Lake Superior.	8
5.	Lake Algonquin Stage of Lake Superior	9
5A.	Nipissing Great Lakes Stage.	9
6.	Chequamegon Bay. Probable Contours of 1620.	12
7.	Great Lakes and Route from Montreal to Lake Huron.	15
8.	Chequamegon Bay, 1659–1671.	21
9.	Southern River Systems of Chequamegon Region.	22
10.	Main Portage Routes from La Pointe to Mississippi River.	24
11.	Probable Trail of Early Sioux Indians.	26
12.	Brule River and Portage to St. Croix River.	36
13.	Brule-St. Croix Portage.	38
14.	Key Map to Madeline Island.	41
15.	First Location of La Pointe on Madeline.	42
16.	First Location of La Pointe. (Large Scale.)	44
17.	French Fort of 1718.	47
18.	Shoals Which Might Have Been Islands.	66
19.	Approximate Location of North West Company.	68
20.	Location of American Fur Company.	71
21.	La Pointe in the 1830s.	81
22.	American Fur Company Location in La Pointe.	82
23.	La Pointe and Environs.	92
24.	Missions of the 1830s.	94
25.	Old Trails and Roads, Bayfield Peninsula.	138
26.	Old Trails and Roads, Near Ashland.	140
27.	Anachronistic Map of Bayfield.	142
28.	Quarries in the Chequamegon Region.	150

Diagrams

A.	Plan and Elevation of Protestant Mission.	85
B.	Water Trolley.	175

Illustrations

A selection of photographs depicting scenes from the history of La Pointe follows page 122.

Introduction

There is a village in northernmost Wisconsin, little known today, which has experienced periods of prosperity, years of fame, and decades of somnolence. La Pointe was the home of the Ojibway. It was the haven of safety for that tribe and for subsequent posts of the French and English fur trader, from the hostile attacks of the Sioux and other Indians. Map 1. Here were planted the seeds of both the Roman Catholic and Protestant religions when the Northwest was unknown country.

It is possible that the La Pointe area was being explored when the Pilgrims landed at Plymouth Rock. Its development, one thousand miles inland, under the French regime, came at the same time as that of the English thirteen colonies on the Atlantic seaboard. In the La Pointe region a church was founded the year after the English took Manhattan from the Dutch, and the village was a thriving settlement when George Washington was born.

To the French, who were the first white arrivals, the terms La Pointe and Chequamegon (She-wam'-egun) were practically synonymous, although the latter was the first known and older name. To them the terms meant not a specific locale, but an area three times the size of the State of Massachusetts, bounded on the north by the south shore of Lake Superior between Baraga, Michigan, and Duluth, Minnesota; and on the south, by a line roughly running from Lac du Flambeau on the east to the Lac Court Oreilles country on the west.

All this territory will not be discussed in this book, except when incidents and personalities impinge on the affairs and inhabitants of La Pointe. I have confined myself to the south shore of Lake Superior, from the Montreal River on the east to the Bois Brule River on the west, with special emphasis on the old Village of La Pointe, and on the Apostle Islands. Map 2. The Apostle Islands occupy an area of approximately six hundred square miles in Lake Superior, although their actual land

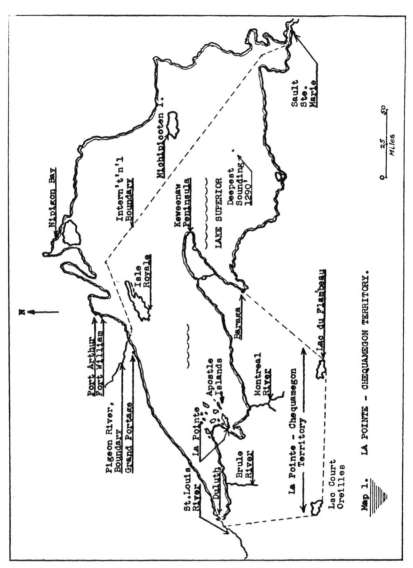

N

Nipigon Bay

Michipicoten I.

Sault Ste. Marie

Intern't'n'l Boundary

Keweenaw Peninsula

LAKE SUPERIOR

Deepest Sounding 1290

Isle Royale

Port Arthur Fort William

Pigeon River, Boundary Grand Portage

Baraga

Lac du Flambeau

La Pointe

Apostle Islands

Montreal River

St. Louis River

Duluth

Brule River

La Pointe – Chequamegon Territory

Lac Court Oreilles

0   25   50
Miles

Map 1.   LA POINTE – CHEQUAMEGON TERRITORY.

1. La Pointe-Chequamegon Territory and Lake Superior.

xviii

area is but seventy-seven square miles. La Pointe is toward the south-west end of Madeline Island, the largest of the Apostles.

Lake Superior and its surrounding basin have been the subjects of much study by famous geologists. In fact, one of the greatest of them said, "There is no region of equal area in North America, east of the great cordilleras [Rockies], that surpasses this in geological interest, whether we consider the magnitude of the formations involved, the difficulties in the problems offered for solution, or the unique character of one of its great rock systems." [1]

These men have furnished the answers to why huge chunks of virtually pure copper have been found along Lake Superior's shores and on Michigan's Keweenaw Peninsula. Only in Coro Coro, Bolivia, has this phenomenon been approached. The same geologists have explained the origin of a region which has produced, and is still producing, the major portion of the country's iron ore, when the nearby terrain belied the fact that there was ore in Minnesota's Mesabi Range. For many years, the old Cornish miners had denied that there could be this mineral wealth, because of the absence of the typical greenrock outcroppings. Long after many millions of tons of the "non-existent" ore had been shipped down the lakes, someone found the greenrock, and the Cornishmen then sank back in satisfaction.

Into this land of former geological mystery, into this region of Gitche Gumee, which the Ojibway had adopted as the home of their gods, came the traders, the members of the Society of Jesus, the French explorers, the voyageurs, the hunters and trappers, the fishermen, the miners, the loggers, the entrepreneurs and the summer tourists.[2]

It was as a summer tourist that I first entered the region in 1894, and from that time it has been, to me, a place of utter fascination. During this brief span, I have seen the destruction of the pineries, the disappearance of the old lumber hookers and the whalebacks, the practical extinction of the sturgeon, the conversion from sail to gasoline or diesel engine in the fishing boats; and today, view with nostalgia the few paltry representatives of the brook trout still extant.

I have also seen part of the major shifts of nationalities in the population, particularly in Ashland. Upon my first arrival in that city most of the inhabitants were Americans of English descent, having come from the Maine pineries by way of Michigan. A smaller number, comprising Swedes, Norwegians and Finns, had established themselves in farming, fishing and logging.

[1] Thomas C. Chamberlin, *Geology of Wisconsin* (Madison, 1880), 3:3.
[2] Gitche Gumee is the name which Longfellow popularized for Lake Superior. The Ojibway (Chippewa) called it Kitchi Gami, their name for Big Water. (Author's note.)

xix

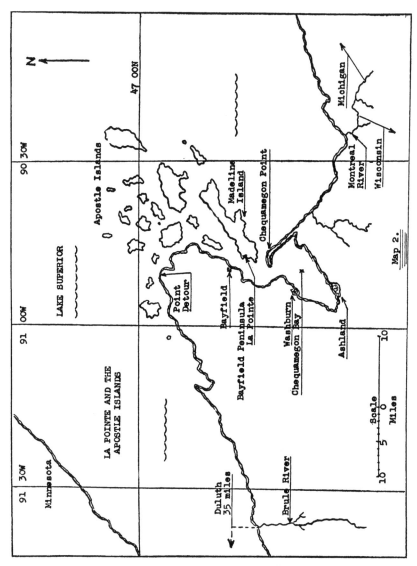

2. La Pointe and the Apostle Islands.

There was then a gradual exodus of the English-Americans, whose places were filled by more Scandinavians and a considerable number of Polanders, so that by 1957 the two latter nationalities were in the majority.

Through consanguinity and environment I have been especially fortunate in my contacts with the general region. My maternal uncle, the Reverend Mr. George William Nelson, was engaged in the home missionary field in Ashland in the early 1890s. This circumstance took me to Ashland in 1894 on a family visit. I was still more fortunate in marrying a granddaughter of the Reverend Mr. Thomas Gordon Grassie who was in similar work in the same city. My birthplace of Beloit, Wisconsin, brought me to know the Leonard H. Wheeler family, who had moved there in 1866, after the Reverend Mr. Wheeler had retired from his missionary work at La Pointe and Odanah.

Through these channels I became acquainted with La Pointe; and the later, disguised, blessing of hayfever, along with a most generous and indulgent father, took me there every summer from 1897. My wife, Dorothy, still lords it over me, as a rank newcomer, because she had been in La Pointe in 1895.

These yearly trips, combined with a love of boating, led me into every nook, cranny and cave of the Apostle Islands. Even the midnight experience of being washed ashore on a plank at Montreal River, from a wrecked sailboat, did not diminish my attachment for the region.

Although, during these years, the historical background of the area was near the bottom of my list of interests, the many conflicting stories concerning it gave me the desire to straighten them out, if possible. I was also a bit miffed at the attention given the Green Bay and Prairie du Chien districts, to the almost total exclusion of La Pointe. I felt that this older region should have its place in the sun if it were within my power to put it there.

After gaining a valuable insight into that season's conditions by spending two winters at Bayfield and La Pointe, I prepared a booklet, *The Apostle Islands*, which gave a brief resumé of the historical background of the area. *La Pointe — Village Outpost* is an expansion of the subject, giving details which are important to an understanding of the old village, and which could not be covered in the limited space available in a booklet.

La Pointe

VILLAGE OUTPOST ON MADELINE ISLAND

CHAPTER ONE

B.C.? As It Was in the Beginning 1615

Probably the Lake Superior region is the oldest of the known world, the first to emerge from a global ocean.[1] Because of its geological age, its subjection to some of nature's most violent treatment and to subsequent erosion, part of the earth's most profound secrets have been exposed here to human eyes.

Geologists say that northern Minnesota and Wisconsin, with the Laurentians of Canada, were the first bodies of land to appear above the waters, and that owing to their age and proven stability, they are possibly the most earthquake-proof regions of the world. During this rise, with its volcanic actions, the Vermilion Iron Range, in northern Minnesota, and some of the Canadian ranges, further east, were formed. Later on, during similar upheavals which might have made Hiroshima or Krakatao seem parvenu, the giant Mesabi Range was born, along with the lesser Michigan and Wisconsin ones.[2]

After this gargantuan travail, there was evidently a period of rest, during which sedimentary action laid down the slates and conglomerates. At this time, the region which was to become Lake Superior formed part of this height of land. But underneath the area was an immense pool of molten material, supporting what appeared to be solid ground. Then, either in another convulsion, or in a series of them, this pool was spewed out, principally toward the north and, to a lesser degree, to the south, bringing with it a mixture of silver, nickel, copper and cobalt, in varying quantities and combinations. These were forced out to the surface and jammed into the cracks and crannies of the earth's crust.[3]

[1] Thomas C. Chamberlin, *Geology of Wisconsin*, (Madison, 1883), 1:61–62.
[2] Mesabi is the Ojibway word for giant. Frederic Baraga, *A Dictionary of the Otchipwe Language*, (Montreal, 1878), 114.
[3] It is the contention of some geologists that pure copper and silver were not forced out to the surface from the subterranean pool of molten matter. They main-

3

East of the south end of Thunder Cape (map 3), which lies about thirty-five miles northeast of the international boundary between Minnesota and Canada, and slightly over fifteen miles from Port Arthur, Ontario, an outcropping was thrust which proved to be practically pure silver. The modern tale of how this was mined is no part of this story, but in its brief career Silver Islet produced over three and one-quarter million dollars' worth of silver.

The same series of convulsions brought up the copper of Michigan's famed Keweenaw Peninsula.[4] Map 3A. Here there were instances of such large pieces of the metal (up to five hundred tons) that they could not be mined with the facilities then available. Ordinary blasting methods had little effect on the pure copper on account of its ductility, and special means had to be devised to handle the problem. Old miners claimed that after a blast the hole stuck out. For about thirty years the Keweenaw furnished over seventy per cent of the country's supply of copper.

With this supporting mass of molten material gone, the upper regions began to sink, forming a gigantic trough, portions of which today are more than six hundred feet below sea level. At some time in this geological history, a lofty mountain range which covered all of northeastern Wisconsin and part of the Upper Michigan Peninsula was pushed up, subjected to centuries of erosion, forced down to be submerged, and then again uplifted. This was followed by more centuries, during which activities known only to modern geologists took place.

Came the glaciers with more physiographical mystery — monstrous bulldozers which hacked and chewed vast territories, and moved them bodily southward, not once, but a number of times.[5] Each time smaller bulldozers, or lobes of the parent ones, went off on side excursions of

tain that metal particles were occluded in the igneous rocks, and that later leaching or chemical action precipitated the pure metal. However, the author has followed Charles R. Van Hise and Charles K. Leith's *The Geology of the Lake Superior Region*, (United States Geological Survey, Government Printing Office, 1911), not only in this instance but also in all of the major geological matters touched upon in the text.

[4] Keweenaw is the Ojibway word for "The way made straight by means of a portage." L. R. Masson, *Les bourgeois de la compagnie du nord-ouest*, (Quebec, 1889), 2:161. Portage Lake with its nearby rivers offered a portage route which saved many miles in skirting the south shore of Lake Superior. This natural passage has since been converted into the modern Keweenaw Waterway which found great use before the days of radar and larger ships. Today, the latter avoid the canal for the most part because of slower progress. (Author's note.)

[5] Chamberlin, Ibid, 1:261–274. European geologists maintain that there were five glacial epochs, but American authorities do not agree. They set the number at not less than three nor more than four. Chamberlin believed that only two were responsible for the glacial action in the area under discussion. (Author's note.)

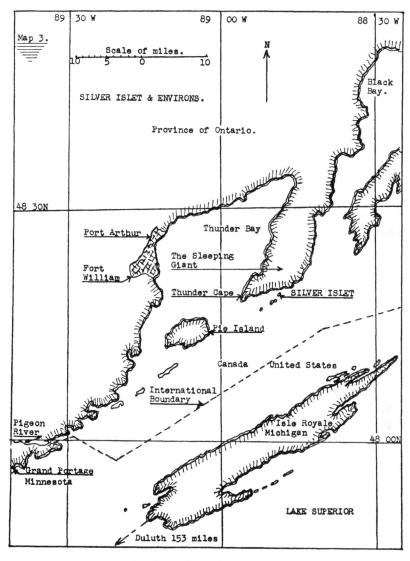

Map 3.

Scale of miles.

10   5   0   10

SILVER ISLET & ENVIRONS.

Province of Ontario.

N

Black Bay.

48 30N

Port Arthur

Thunder Bay

The Sleeping Giant

Fort William

Thunder Cape

SILVER ISLET

Pie Island

Canada   United States

International Boundary

Pigeon River

Isle Royale Michigan

48 00N

Grand Portage Minnesota

LAKE SUPERIOR

Duluth 153 miles

3. Silver Islet and Environs.

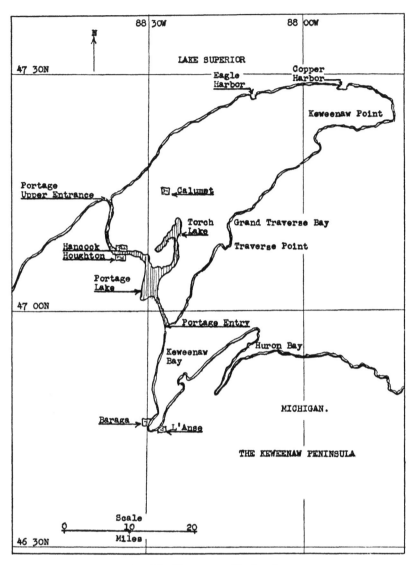

3A. The Keweenaw Peninsula.

their own, staging their peculiar raids, and mixing up the landscape, apparently in pixy moods to bewilder and bemuse, but not entirely to hoodwink, the modern geologist.

Not content with moving parts of Canada into the United States, the glaciers began to recede under more powerful sun's rays and, like robbers caught with their ill-gotten wealth, dropped their loads of boulders, gravel, sand and silt, willy-nilly.

Some of this fallen loot formed the gentle hills and eskers of southern Wisconsin. Other masses were dropped in enormous dikes which impounded vast areas of water from the melting glaciers. The Lake Superior trough, for the most part, was filled with ice, leaving the comparatively small glacial Lake Nemadji held back by one of these gigantic barriers. The shore line of this ancient lake is visible at Duluth, about five hundred feet above the present lake. With further melting of the glaciers, this body could only overflow, and it broke through the then weakest point — southwest from Duluth via the Kettle and St. Croix Rivers to the Mississippi. Map 4.

Another potential outlet, approximately 50 feet lower, existed about twenty-five miles further east in the present valley of the Bois Brule River. During the Lake Nemadji Stage this outlet was blocked with ice, but as this melted, the lake began to drain southward to the Mississippi by way of the St. Croix River which forms the face of the Wisconsin Indian who peers across that stream into Minnesota. This is known as the Lake Duluth Stage. Map 4A.

With further recession of the ice sheet, the Great Lakes entered their geological Lake Algonquin Stage, with the water flowing down the Illinois River past the present City of Chicago. It also ran down the Mohawk River where it joined a further discharge from geological Champlain Sea. These two made their ways to the ocean by means of the Hudson River. At this stage Lake Superior was drained toward the east instead of at its western end. Map 5.

In another period, the former channels were largely deserted. The upper lakes drained by the Ottawa River from Lake Huron, by the Hudson River from Champlain Sea, and also by the St. Lawrence River from the same sea. This was called the Nipissing Great Lakes Stage. Map 5A.

After untold centuries, during which the Great Lakes assumed their present forms, Lake Superior emerged with a north shore which is indeed a stern and rockbound coast. Here the granites and other igneous rocks predominate, with harbors few and far between. Seemingly to make amends for this cold and repellent rim, nature created the south shore with many and lengthy sand beaches, and, with the exception of the Keweenaw Peninsula, which resembles the northern coast, en-

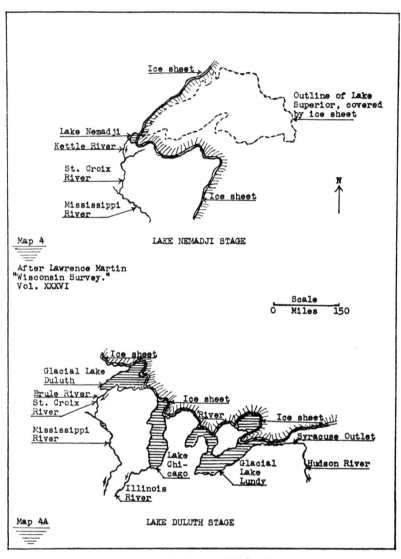

Map 4

After Lawrence Martin
"Wisconsin Survey."
Vol. XXXVI

LAKE NEMADJI STAGE

Scale
0   Miles   150

Map 4A

LAKE DULUTH STAGE

4. Lake Nemadji Stage of Lake Superior.
4A. Lake Duluth Stage of Lake Superior.

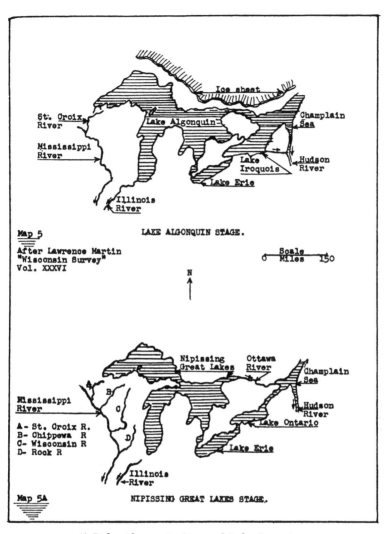

Map 5

After Lawrence Martin
"Wisconsin Survey"
Vol. XXXVI

LAKE ALGONQUIN STAGE.

Scale
0   Miles   150

N

Map 5A

A- St. Croix R.
B- Chippewa R
C- Wisconsin R
D- Rock R

NIPISSING GREAT LAKES STAGE.

5. Lake Algonquin Stage of Lake Superior.
5A. Nipissing Great Lakes Stage.

9

deavored to seduce the traveler with more gentle hills and a greater number of harbors. Here, the sandstones and other sedimentary rocks are in evidence.

Of the south shore area, nature lavished her bounty on the Chequamegon region. In the diaries and reports of the early Jesuits and explorers, many references are made to the natural beauties of this country, the apparently endless forests with trees of magnificent stature growing down to the water's edge, the lofty hills with their perpetual greenery, the whiteness of the sand beaches, and the extensiveness of the wave-formed caves and grottoes in the sandstones of both the mainland and the adjacent islands. All of these, in combination with the red cliffs and the blue lake, caused even the rough and hardy voyageurs and coureurs de bois to pause and to drink in their majesty.

Although the district was probably rough and unfriendly at some stages of its development, glaciation knocked off many of the high spots, with erosion and vegetation smoothing the remainder. There were valleys gouged out by the torrents from the melting glaciers. Geologists believe that these streams formed the valleys between the various islands of the Apostle Group. Then, in a sinking period, which is still in action, these valleys were flooded, and the islands formed. It is estimated that the whole south shore of the lake is sinking at the rate of five inches per century, although some geologists believe that it is as much as ten inches.[6] In some thousands of years the lake may again seek the Mississippi.

With this brief summary of the creation of the region, the era of man is reached. Since the tribes of Indians who roamed the district left only myths and uncertain legends passed on from one generation to the next, what occurred before the advent of the white man can only be surmised. Among the almost staggering duties of the Indian women was the responsibility of acting as historians, and handing down the lore of their people. Whenever it has been possible to check these stories, it has been found that they have been amazingly accurate.[7]

From estimates of the Indian's rather vague conception of time, it is believed that the Ojibway left their former home on the Gulf of St. Lawrence, and after a trek consuming several years, arrived in the Chequamegon region about 1490.[8] The legends of the tribe attribute the migration

[6] Lawrence Martin, *The Physical Geography of Wisconsin*, (Madison, 1916), Bulletin XXXVI, 424.

[7] This was done by means of checking known solar and lunar eclipses against the Indians' estimates of the same phenomena. (Author's note.)

[8] William Whipple Warren, "History of the Ojibways," *Minnesota Historical Collections*, (St. Paul, 1885), 5:90. Although the modern and popular name of the tribe is Chippewa, introduced by the English, the author, at the risk of adverse criticism, is using the older and original name.

to the mysterious conduct of a great white shell, Megis, which gave warmth and light to the tribe. When it disappeared from the eastern waters of the gulf, and reappeared in the St. Lawrence River, the tribe concluded that the omen should be followed. It successively appeared further and further westward, until it led the tribe to Chequamegon, where it has remained to this day.

During this hegira, various parts of the tribe split off from the main body, and either remained at selected places along the line of march or branched off, seeking sites on which to settle. One group, which the Ojibway later called the Ottawa, took up its home along the river which discharges into the St. Lawrence above the present City of Montreal. The word Ottawa was the Ojibway for Trader. It was applied because these Indians performed that function between the western and eastern tribes. In due course, the river was given the same name.[9]

From Sault Ste. Marie westward, the main body of the tribe was beset by the Fox Indians to the south, and the Sioux to the west, whose territories they were invading. They finally arrived at the comparative safety of Chequamegon Point (map 6) where they were able to ward off these attacks more easily. To insure their security, they moved across the one and one-half mile channel to Madeline Island, their Moningwunakauning — The Home of the Golden Breasted Woodpecker.[10]

It is estimated that they lived on the island for one hundred twenty years. The shaded portion of Madeline Island on map 6 is where they might have settled, but it is extremely doubtful if such is the case.[11] There are some conjectures that their population ran as high as twenty thousand. However that may be, there were evidently so many of them that the island could not support them. In a severe winter, when food ran short, their medicine men resorted to cannibalism, selecting as their

[9] Warren, Ibid, 82. Also Frederic Baraga, A Dictionary of the Otchipwe Language, (Montreal, 1878), 267.

[10] Warren, Ibid, 96. Colaptes Auratus. Flicker, Yellowhammer or High-holder. In some respects the Indian name was a misnomer since the bird did not make the island its home. However, it appeared in almost unbelievable numbers in the spring and fall on its migratory flights. In the early 1900s it was highly prized by the local inhabitants for yellowhammer pie, and hundreds were killed for that purpose. (Author's note.)

[11] Philip Ainsworth Means, Miscellaneous Smithsonian Collections, (Washington, 1916), 66: #14. Warren, Ibid, 96, believed the settlement was located at the southwest end of the island, and this belief is borne out by the extensive burying ground on the end of the point. The author accepts Warren's belief in preference to Means'. The latter spent but a very short time on Madeline Island which, for some strange reason he called La Pointe Island although it had not gone by that name for over one hundred fifty years. Furthermore, he apparently accepted hearsay evidence from persons not qualified to give it. His attempted survey in 1916 failed owing to the difficulty in digging, and to the reported resentment of the local French-Ojibway. (Author's note.)

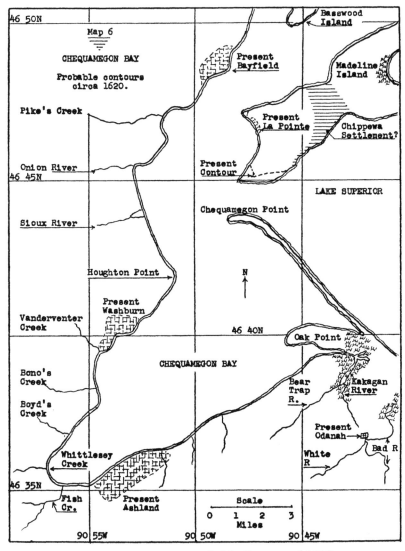

6. Chequamegon Bay. Probable Contours of 1620.

victims young children, preferably female. They continued the practice for a number of years until the enraged tribe, overcoming its fear of the witch doctors, put them to death.

Despite this remedy they imagined that the spirits of the dead victims stalked forth at night, and they considered this an omen for them to leave the island. Whether an omen or plain fright, it resulted in their departure about 1610, to take up their abode for the next one hundred fifty years near the Sault, although fragments of the tribe remained in the general Chequamegon region and along the south shore of the lake. Upon the advent of the French, the tribe was called the Saulteurs or Sauteurs.[12]

Later traders and missionaries noticed that the Ojibway shunned the whole Apostle Group, and it was not until the nineteenth century that an Indian would remain over night on Madeline Island, unless under the protection of French or British guns. They especially feared present day Devil's Island, which they named after their evil god or devil, Matchi-manitou.[13]

Those who have heard, even on a calm day, the muttered gurgles of the water in the extensive cave formations of that island, can appreciate the Indians' feelings. When the lake is rough, and the waves surge into these openings, the mutterings rise to roars of awful proportions. Today it is sometimes whispered among the descendants of the tribe that balls of fire over a certain slough on Madeline Island betoken the wandering spirits of the youthful victims. Up until recent years it has been considered unhealthy to live near this place on account of its nightly 'vapors and miasmas.'[14]

The departure of the Ojibway from Madeline Island might have occurred at about the same time as the founding of the first permanent French settlement in Canada, but there might have been preliminary explorations by whites before that time. One of these, still controversial, was the possible trip of Norsemen to Minnesota in 1362, when the Kensington or Minnesota Rune Stone was supposed to have been left.[15]

[12] A quotation from Allouez's journal. Louise Phelps Kellogg, *Early Narratives of the Northwest*, (New York, 1917) 135.

[13] Baraga, Ibid, 72. Also Chrysostum Verwyst, "A Glossary of Chippewa Names," *Acta et Dicta*, (St. Paul, 1916), 4: #2, 259.

[14] The balls of fire which many of the older inhabitants of Madeline Island claim to have seen, might be attributed to St. Elmo's fire, ignition of marsh gases or by some phosphorescent phenomenon. The 'vapors' are due to the frequent fog banks which hover over the slough at night. (Author's note.)

[15] The authenticity of this stone has been alternately confirmed and denied. In 1957 the whole affair is considered a hoax. Part of the theory relates to the route followed by the Norse into Minnesota. If the stone proves to be genuine, it would appear that the area in which it was found was approached from Hudson Bay rather than by the Great Lakes. (Author's note.)

The actual French settlement, however, was initiated by the early explorations of Jacques Cartier who discovered the Gulf of St. Lawrence in 1534. On this trip, fog prevented him from finding the river of the same name. Upon his second voyage in 1535 he located and investigated the river as far as Montreal, where further progress was halted by the Lachine Rapids.

These quests were undertaken in an effort to disclose the legendary Northwest Passage to China and the East Indies, and whatever was unearthed en route was merely incidental to the main objective. This accounts for Cartier's name of Sault de la Chine — The Rapids of China.

Cartier made another trip in 1541 which failed because of the hostility of the Iroquois Indians who blocked his progress above the rapids.[16] Discouraged, Cartier returned to France in 1543, but on the strength of his revelations, Francis I laid claim for France to the entire basin of the St. Lawrence. From this time, for a period of sixty-five years, the French made no effort to capitalize on their discoveries, and it was not until 1608, upon the arrival of Samuel de Champlain, that the City of Quebec was founded.

In their efforts to establish a northwest passage, as well as to open the western country to fur trading, they attempted to follow the route essayed by Cartier, but met with the same hostile reception from the Iroquois. The Ottawa Indians, from whom they had first obtained furs, informed them not only of the existence of large inland bodies of water, but also that the Ottawa River was a means of access to them.

They therefore explored and opened this shorter but more difficult route by traveling almost due west up this river, and, by a system of portages on it and the Mattawa River, reached Lake Nipissing. Map 7. From here, via the French River, it was only about fifty miles to the upper reaches of Georgian Bay in Lake Huron. Champlain personally conducted one of these trips, and while he ventured no further west than Lake Huron, he learned from the Indians of still another and larger body of water to the west.

It is generally accepted as fact that the first white man of record to see Lake Superior was Etienne Brule, in about 1622.[17] However, the

[16] The Iroquois remained an almost continuous stumbling block to the French. (Author's note.)

[17] There is considerable doubt as to the exact date. Gabriel Sagard-Theodat, *Le Grand Voyage du Pays des Hurons* (Paris, 1865), 74. This edition is a reprint of his Paris book of 1632. Sagard was a Recollect scribe, and in 1623 he recorded that Brule *had* been on Lake Superior. Thus Brule might have made his trip in 1622 or earlier.

Edward D. Neill, *Neill's History of Minnesota*, (Minneapolis, 1885), 399–400. This states that Brule reported the location of the lake in 1618, and that he brought back some copper. Milo M. Quaife, *Lake Michigan*, The American Lakes Series,

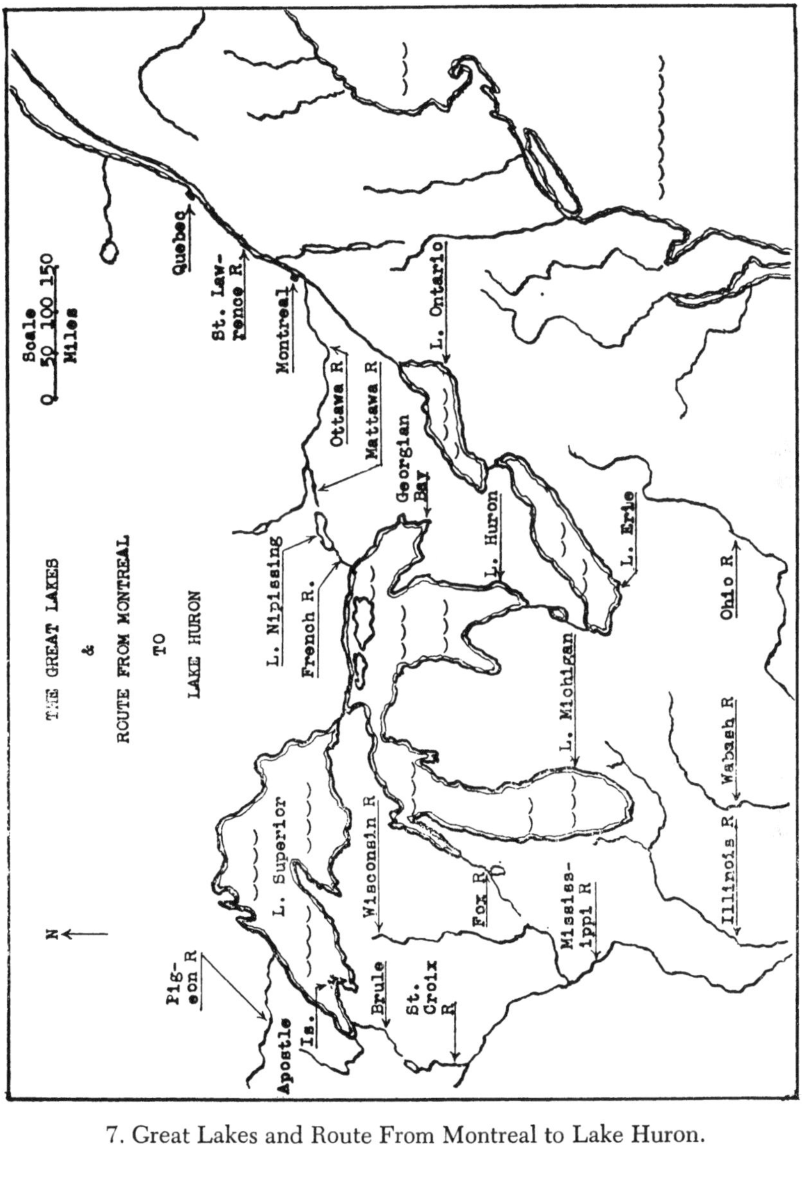
THE GREAT LAKES
&
ROUTE FROM MONTREAL
TO
LAKE HURON
Scale
0 50 100 150
Miles
N
Quebec
St. Law-rence R.
Montreal
Ottawa R
Mattawa R
L. Ontario
Georgian Bay
L. Huron
L. Erie
Ohio R
L. Nipissing
French R.
L. Michigan
Wabash R
Illinois R
Mississ-ippi R
Fox R
Wisconsin R
L. Superior
Pig-eon R
Apostle Is.
Brule
St. Croix R

7. Great Lakes and Route From Montreal to Lake Huron.

diary of Grenolle, who accompanied Brule, shows that upon their arrival at the Sault, the Ojibway were calling the rapids Sault de Gaston, after the brother of Louis XIII.[18] This would seem to prove that some unsung white had been there before that time.

It is believed that the map which Champlain published in 1632, and which is fairly accurate save in respect to Lake Superior, was the result of Brule's explorations.[19] This map called the lake Grand Lac.

An Ojibway legend which may bear considerable weight, because of its supposed hieroglyphic record on a somewhat mythical copper plate, indicated that there were two white men on Madeline Island about 1610, and there are other legendary references to traders who might have been there before 1622.[20] The thought occurs that the two might have been Brule and Grenolle.

(Bobbs-Merrill, 1944) footnote 1, 27 stated that Brule *might* have been on Lake Superior in 1615, but that nothing is certain regarding the exact date.

[18] Kellogg, ibid, 59. Also Gabriel Sagard-Theodat, *Histoire du Canada*, (Paris reprint, 1866), 716. The author has followed Sagard in the spelling of Grenolle's name, although ibid, 328, Sagard calls him Crenole. Kellogg, ibid, 91, and others called him Grenoble. None gives his first name.

[19] Kellogg, ibid, 62.

[20] Warren, ibid, 90.

CHAPTER TWO

1616 Seek, and Ye Shall Find 1677

On Brule's first trip or possible subsequent ones, he and Grenolle visited some place on the lake where Indians were working copper mines. It is not known whether these were on Isle Royale, the Keweenaw Peninsula, or on the Ontonagon River.[1]

It is possible that Brule found and explored the Bois Brule River, by which later explorers and voyageurs made their way to the St. Croix and Mississippi Rivers.[2] If this is so, he preceded Duluth whom historians credit with opening this route. His own diaries were lost, and Grenolle's were extremely sketchy. Also since Brule and Champlain were at loggerheads, except when Champlain needed Brule's services, it is questionable whether Champlain would credit Brule with important discoveries, even though Brule might have made them, and later given Champlain a verbal account.

In contrast, there are well confirmed records of the next visitor. In 1634, one year after the first settlement in Connecticut, Jean Nicolet saw Lake Superior from the Sault, but ventured no further west on the lake. His arrival was incidental to his main objective of exploring upper Lake Michigan and then proceeding to Green Bay. While never proven, some historians believe that Nicolet might have gone up the Fox River to the portage to the Wisconsin, and thence to the Mississippi.[3]

[1] Isle Royale is part of the present State of Michigan, and is but a short distance from Port Arthur, Canada. The Ontonagon River flows northward into Lake Superior about fifty miles east of the present Wisconsin-Michigan boundary. (Author's note.)

[2] The Bois Brule name has posed the question: Was it named after the explorer or because there were burned-over woods nearby? Proponents of both claims can summon convincing arguments, but the supporters of the latter alternative have won out, and the official name is Bois Brule — Burnt Wood. If Mr. Brule could have had some other name, the solution might have been easier. (Author's note.)

[3] Reuben Gold Thwaites, Editor, *The Jesuit Relations and Allied Documents,* (Cleveland, 1896–1901), 23:275–279. Benjamin Sulte, *Wisconsin Historical Col-*

Since Nicolet was licensed to trade in furs, and was undertaking the trip under the auspices of the Company of the One Hundred Associates, he set out with the approval and blessing of Champlain.[4]

After the arrival of Nicolet and before the advent of the next explorers, it is possible that other persons had come to the lake, and had traded with the Indians.[5] It is difficult to believe that the region lay dormant while reports circulated in Quebec of the riches available in furs and copper. It is more than probable that some hardy souls, unlicensed and therefore not of record, slipped off to investigate the reports, and to capitalize upon them. This theory is confirmed by Radisson's later observations. (Page 20.)

Two men who might have been the instigators of later quests and expeditions came to the lake in 1641. The Jesuits, Charles Raymbault and Isaac Jogues arrived at the Sault, and are credited with the naming of the rapids in the St. Mary's River, where the waters of Lake Superior take their twenty-one odd foot drop on their way to Lake Huron.[6] In typical Jesuit fashion, they affixed the name of Sault de Sainte Marie – The Rapids of St. Mary.

From the report in the *Jesuit Relations*, it was at the Sault that they learned of another tribe of Indians, called the Nadoussis, who, they learned, lived eighteen days further west. It was said that one traveled nine days to reach the other end of the lake and another nine days to ascend a river leading to the tribe. It was at this time that the lake was being called Grand Lac du Nadouessiou.[7]

Possibly the estimate of nine days to reach the west end of the lake, some four hundred fifty miles by canoe, may have been on the optimistic side, for one might observe that the lake would have to have been in one of its less tempestuous moods for a canoeist to have averaged fifty miles

lections, 8:188–194. Louise Phelps Kellogg, Editor, "The Journey of Jean Nicolet, 1634," *Early Narratives of the Northwest*, (Scribner's 1917), 12. (This Fox River rises near the present City of Portage, Wisconsin, and flows northeastward into Lake Michigan's Green Bay.) (Author's note.)

[4] H. P. Biggar, *Early Trading Companies of New France*, (Toronto, 1901), (University of Toronto Series), 94–98, 115, 119, 134. The Company of the One Hundred Associates was the fifth of the so-called Companies of New France.

[5] Father Mercier, in a letter of September 21, 1654, alludes to a flotilla of canoes, guided by two traders, loaded with furs, belonging to Indians who had come "400 leagues from the west." He stated that if "Thirty Frenchmen could be sent in that country they would gain many souls for God," as well as "—generous profits from furs." Thwaites, ibid, 40:11.

[6] Thwaites, ibid, 23:223–227. Pierre Margry, *Decouvertes et Etablissements des Francais dans l'Ouest et dans le Sud de l'Amerique Septentrionale*, (Paris, 1879–1886), 1: chapter 1.

[7] The Ojibway called the Iroquois Nadowe (or Naudowaig), implying Enemies,

per day.[8] The river in question might have been the Bois Brule or the St. Louis, either of which would lead to the Mississippi, although it is probable that the report referred to the St. Louis.[9]

The reports of these missionaries, along with the probable and unlicensed visits of the coureurs de bois, excited the interest of others who envisioned great opportunities in the fur trade. Among these were two men who probably had as much to do with France's loss of Canada as the later corruption in the courts of the Louis, and the peculations and graft of local officers. Medart Chouart, Sieur des Groseilliers, and his brother-in-law, Pierre Esprit Radisson, were well known in New France. Both had made trips to the Huron country, and while Groseilliers had acquired some standing with the Jesuits, Radisson was generally considered a coureur de bois by that society.[10]

In making their plans for a trip west, they applied for a trading license, but were told that unless they were accompanied by certain officials, as well as by a Jesuit priest, the license would not be issued.[11] The resentment created by this edict, plus Radisson's hatred of the Jesuits, caused the partners to steal off on their expedition without a license. Upon their trip along the south shore of Lake Superior they used the portage route across the Keweenaw Peninsula in order to save about one hundred miles of paddling around that point. It was here that Radisson recorded that the portage paths were well worn from the passage of earlier "commers and goers." The partners arrived at Chequamegon Bay in the fall of

but literally Adders. Upon their contact with the Sioux, who were also bitter enemies, they applied the name Nadouessiou (or Naudowasewug) — Like Unto Adders. Warren, ibid, 72, 83.

[8] There are many records to show sustained canoe travel of from 90 to 100 miles per day, and there are probably more to indicate delays of from one to ten days. The delays were termed Dégradés, which meant Windbound. (Author's note.)

[9] The St. Louis River flows past the City of Duluth, but its natural outlet then was further south, at the present City of Superior, Wisconsin. (Author's note.)

[10] Pierre Francois Xavier de Charlevoix, History of New France, (John Gilmary Shea's translation, 1866–72), 2:71. Charlevoix's account stated, "They were nick-named Hurons from their manner of wearing their hair: 'Quelles hures!' — 'What boars' heads!' said they; and so they got to calling them Hurons." (The Hurons had originally lived along the St. Lawrence River. They had called themselves Wendats, later corrupted into Wyandottes, and in spite of their Iroquoian ancestry, were deadly enemies of that tribe. The more powerful Iroquois gradually drove them westward until, at the time of the early French explorers, they had settled around the south end of Georgian Bay, near Lake Simcoe, in the Province of Ontario, Canada.) (In Radisson's time the term coureur de bois was virtually synonymous with rogue.) (Author's notes.)

[11] It is estimated that the Jesuits controlled nearly 90% of the fur trade in Radisson's time, and consequently were very watchful in the matter of licenses to trade. That they exerted a tremendous influence on the colony is indicated by Francis Parkman. The Jesuits in North America in the 17th Century, (Boston, 1894).

1659.[12] Here they built a log cabin, the first structure of the sort on this bay, and possibly the first on the entire lake.[13] Map 8.

Of their arrival, Radisson wrote, "In that bay ther is a chanell where we take great stores of fishes, sturgeons of a vast bigness, and Pycks seaven feet long. At the end of this bay we landed."[14] After completing their log cabin and making preparations for the coming winter, they went on, possibly to Lac Court Oreilles, probably following the route which later fur traders used.[15] This was up Fish Creek with a portage to the White River and thence to Lake Owen. From here, another portage took them to the headwaters of the Namakagan River and thence to Lac Court Oreilles.[16] Maps 9 & 10. Plate 2.

During the winter of 1659–60, the partners, nearly starving to death, not only cultivated a band of Ottawa whom they found there, but also, after the famine was broken, held a great feast at which "eighteen sever-all nations" partook. After the feast, in response to an invitation of the Sioux, they went "to the nation of ye beefe [Sioux] wch was seaven small Journeys from that place [the rendezvous]."[17]

Returning to Lac Court Oreilles, the explorers found that the Ottawa had left, and later discovered that the natives had gone to Chequamegon Bay where they had built a village of sorts. This was located at the

[12] Radisson, *Voyages of Pierre Esprit Radisson*, (New York, 1943), Peter Smith edition, 175.

[13] An aluminum plate with a text of about one hundred words, commemorating the event, was erected in 1952 at the junction of highways U.S. #2 and Wisconsin #13, west of Ashland, Wisconsin, not far from the supposed site of the cabin. (Author's note.)

[14] At the time of his trip, Radisson kept no journal of record. In 1669, he wrote an account, and that record, still later, was translated into the English of the time. (Author's note.)

[15] In later years this lake was sometimes called Ottawa Lake. The name Court Oreilles evolved from the French nickname for that tribe — Lake Short Ears. In local parlance, it is now called Lake Couderay, and sometimes even Lake Corduroy. (Author's note.)

[16] David D. Owen, *Geological Survey of Wisconsin, Iowa and Minnesota*, (Philadelphia, 1852), 157–158. Owen's party followed this route and described it in considerable detail. (While a person who is familiar with present-day conditions of these streams may question their navigability, even with a canoe, it should be remembered that up through the 19th century the whole region was heavily timbered, and that all these creeks were much larger than now. In fact, many of the smaller brooks have entirely dried up. In the early 1900s there were many springs in the region which no longer exist.) (Author's note.)

[17] Grace Lee Nute, *Caesars of the Wilderness*, (New York, 1943), 64. This book is a most comprehensive and thorough study of the Radisson-Groseilliers story. (The Ottawa were in this part of the country due to two factors. The first was the French policy of eliminating them as intermediary traders along the Ottawa River. The second was the constant and hostile pressure of the Iroquois. In 1669, the Ottawa had not yet concentrated in any one locality, and the tribe was split up into more or less roving bands.) (Author's note.)

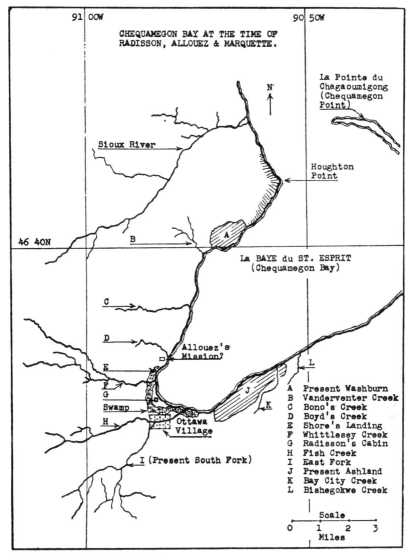

The map text includes:

CHEQUAMEGON BAY AT THE TIME OF
RADISSON, ALLOUEZ & MARQUETTE.

91 00W

90 50W

La Pointe du
Chagaoumigong
(Chequamegon
Point)

N

Sioux River

Houghton
Point

46 40N

B

A

La BAYE du ST. ESPRIT
(Chequamegon Bay)

C

D

Allouez's
Mission?

L

E

F

G

Swamp

H

J

K

Ottawa
Village

I (Present South Fork)

A   Present Washburn
B   Vanderventer Creek
C   Bono's Creek
D   Boyd's Creek
E   Shore's Landing
F   Whittlesey Creek
G   Radisson's Cabin
H   Fish Creek
I   East Fork
J   Present Ashland
K   Bay City Creek
L   Bishegokwe Creek

Scale

0   1   2   3
Miles

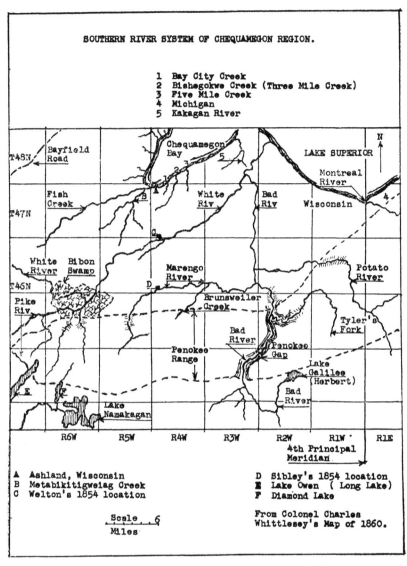

9. Southern River Systems of Chequamegon Region.

junction of Fish Creek and its tributary, South Fork, not far from present Ashland Junction. Map 8.[18] The site has been determined by excavations.[19]

In the spring of 1660, Radisson and Groseilliers built a fort on the end of Chequamegon Point.[20] From Radisson's record it is not clear just when or why it was built, because he made no further reference to it. It is possible that the name La Pointe du Chagaoumigong was applied to the peninsula at that time, but there is nothing to confirm that conjecture, although it seemed to be well known at a little later date.

Also, probably very early in the spring, or else before the explorers' return to Chequamegon from Lac Court Oreilles, the Ottawa had built a fortress of some sort on Houghton Point, across the strait from Chequamegon Point.[21]

[18] Fish Creek was known to the Ojibway as Gigonsi Sibiwishe — a Small-fish Creek. Verwyst, ibid, 260. South Fork was known as Metabikitigweiag — probably Small River Running into a Larger. Baraga, ibid, 214, 299. (The name frequently appeared in old records and maps, and is shown as late as 1906 on Bayfield County plats.) (Author's note.)

[19] Joseph Stephen LaBoule, "Claude Jean Allouez," Parkman Club Publications, #17, June 8, 1897, 196. (Milwaukee).

[20] Radisson, ibid, 193.

[21] Thwaites, "The Story of Chequamegon Bay," Wisconsin Historical Collections, (Madison, 1895), 13:403. Also Kellogg, The French Regime in Wisconsin and the Northwest, (Madison, 1925), 109–110.

Both of the above construe Radisson's statement of ". . . received word that the Octanaks [Ottawa] had built a fort on a point that forms that bay, which resembles a small lake . . .," to mean that the Ottawa had built their fort on Chequamegon Point, and that if Radisson had built any fort it would have been on Houghton Point.

The author does not agree with these conclusions for a number of reasons:

A. Radisson stated: "That point should be very fitt to build and advantageous for the building of a fort, as we did the spring following." That he meant Chequamegon Point is most evident, since, in the sentence before, he calls Houghton Point, ". . . a cape very much elevated like piramides." Radisson, ibid, 193.

B. Houghton Point is also one, ". . . that forms that bay, . . . " It would have been much more reasonable for the Ottawa to have built a fort there than on Chequamegon Point, because their only enemies at the time were the Sioux who followed a rather classic route from the west in their approach to the Ottawa village. (See 'F' below.) The Sioux were not equipped with canoes to by-pass a land fort. Therefore an Ottawa fortress on Houghton Point would be of greater strategic value, and would be entirely useless if erected on Chequamegon Point.

C. If Radisson's estimates of distances were correct, his statement that he traveled four leagues over the ice, from the Ottawa village on Fish Creek to the fort, would confirm the Houghton Point location since Chequamegon Point was five leagues from the village.

D. Radisson recorded (ibid, 222) that after reaching the Ottawa fort over the slush-covered ice, and there suffering great torture from strained leg muscles (cured with the "hot oyle of bears"), he set out on a two-day march to the west, but made no mention of any return over the ice. If the Ottawa fort had been on Chequamegon Point he would have been forced to negotiate the ice again or to have taken the

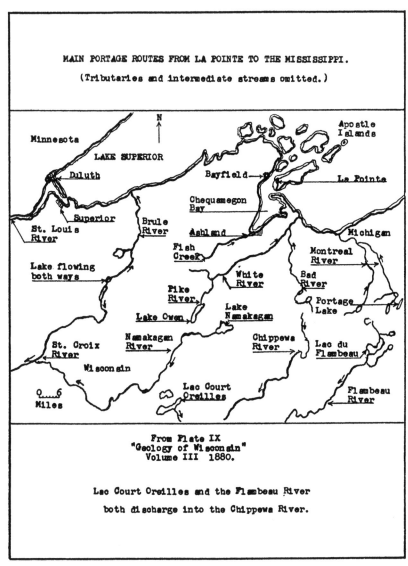

MAIN PORTAGE ROUTES FROM LA POINTE TO THE MISSISSIPPI.

(Tributaries and intermediate streams omitted.)

From Plate IX
"Geology of Wisconsin"
Volume III 1880.

Lac Court Oreilles and the Flambeau River

both discharge into the Chippewa River.

10. Main Portage Routes From La Pointe to the Mississippi River.

Upon concluding their trading operations, Radisson and Groseilliers returned to Quebec in 1660. According to Radisson's account, the value of their furs may have been $120,000, but other sources fix greater amounts.[22] In any event, owing to their extra-legal status as coureurs de bois, the authorities confiscated all but $20,000 worth of their cargo.

It was at this time that Radisson staged his hoax concerning a trip to Hudson Bay. While he was at Chequamegon, a number of Cree Indians, from Hudson Bay, arrived with great packs of furs which the partners procured. These furs were of such prime quality that Radisson became convinced of the potentialities of that northern district. His belief was further confirmed on his return to Quebec where he met the Jesuit priest, Father Gabriel Druillettes, who told him, in considerable detail, of the story related to him by an Indian named Awatanik. The native, according to the priest, had made a trip to the bay, and was greatly impressed with the wealth of furs obtainable there. Radisson adopted the tale as his own. However, in spite of his attempted deception, he must be credited with the vision of realizing that access to the territory was more practicable by sailing directly into the bay from the North Atlantic Ocean than by any other means.

arduous and circuitous route via the Kakagan sloughs. He did not mention the latter alternative.

E. From the French standpoint, a fort for them on Houghton Point would have been virtually useless. Since they were on a trip of exploration and trading, their means of travel was by canoe which presumed a convenient and reliable site from which to launch, and on which to land their craft. Because the shore line about Houghton Point is composed of sandstone cliffs which rise from twelve to twenty-five feet out of the water, canoes could not be launched or landed save in a dead calm. Plate 3. On the other hand, Chequamegon Point afforded long sand beaches and convenient lees from which canoes could be launched in practically any wind. Thus, protected on three sides by water, and on the fourth by an easily defended narrow neck, they were safe from Indian attacks. Since the French considered any Indian as a potential enemy, any fort erected by them on Houghton Point could easily have been surrounded and isolated.

F. This route was used well into the 19th century, and followed the barrens, west of present Washburn, to the headwaters of the Sioux River, thence along that stream to the lake, and then southward via Houghton Point. Map 11. The Sioux River acquired its name through this circumstance. (The only authorities to substantiate the name and route were a number of French-Ojibway in their 80th and 90th years, who claimed that their ancestors as far back as their great-grandfathers had so stated.)

This round-about route was used in order to avoid the tangle of thickets which lay on the lower ground, west of the Ottawa village, and to make use of the high barrens where there was little undergrowth.

[22] Father Thomas J. Campbell, *Pioneer Laymen of North America*, (New York, 1915), 2:61. This sets a value of $400,000. Douglas MacKay, *The Honourable Company*, (Toronto, 1938), 18, sets a value of $300,000. (Radisson's account is such a mixture of pounds, pounds Sterling and pistoles that it is difficult to judge the true value of the cargo.) (Author's note.)

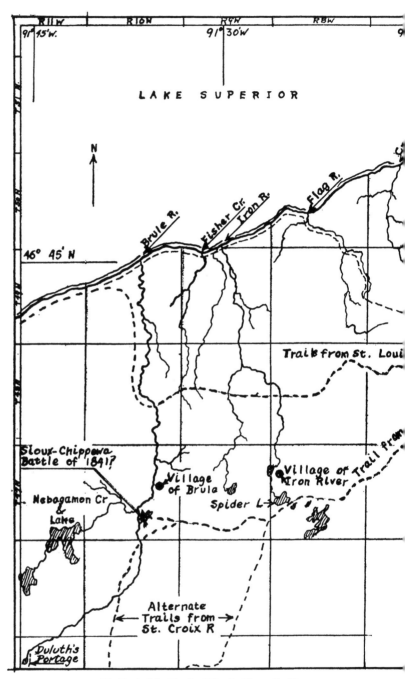

11. Probable Trail of Early Sioux Indians.

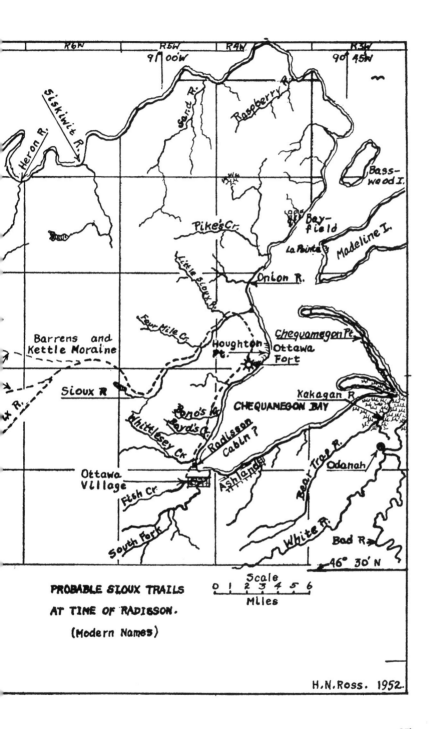

PROBABLE SIOUX TRAILS
AT TIME OF RADISSON.
(Modern Names)

Scale
0 1 2 3 4 5 6
Miles

H.N.Ross. 1952.

Although the confiscation of the furs probably saved the colony from bankruptcy, the authorities placed little credence in Radisson's story, and refused to grant the partners a license to trade in Hudson Bay.[23] After repeated and futile efforts to convince the local officials, they finally gave up, and Groseilliers sailed for France to protest at court on the action of Governor D'Argenson in confiscating their furs. Since this was of no avail, Groseilliers returned to New France, and the partners sought help in the New England Colonies. After this effort failed, they tried to get merchants in France interested in their schemes, but these men proved indifferent. At last they went to England where they were successful in interesting that "Company of Adventurers" who formed the Hudson's Bay Company in 1670.

Thus, flanked on one side by the British Colonies, and on the other by an aggressive English Company which disregarded France's territorial claims, the Colony of New France found itself in a position which would eventually result in its severance from the mother country.

In the meantime, interested in the partners' stories of the Indian village on Chequamegon, the Jesuit, Father Rene Menard, began his trip there to spread the gospel, and made his start on August 28, 1660.[24] Other members of the party were Jean Guerin, Adrien Jolliet (the elder brother of Louis Jolliet, the explorer), Antoine Trottier, Jean Bellecourt, Claude David, Pierre Lavasseur L'Esperance *dit*, — Lafleche and one other whose name is uncertain. Although the trip was nominally under Menard's command, the priest seemed to have been the victim of insults and hardships at the hands of rather vicious coureurs de bois and their Indian companions. This might serve as another example of the hatred which the coureurs de bois bore the Jesuits in general but not necessarily Menard in particular, for one might infer from the priest's letters that he was a kindly and retiring individual.

En route, because of an accident to the canoe in which he was traveling, Menard, who was very feeble, was left behind with a few Indians and possibly with his French companions.[25] The party spent the winter

[23] Radisson, ibid, 241, 243, 252, 254, Also Grace Lee Nute, *Lake Superior*, The American Lakes Series, (Bobbs-Merrill, 1944), 21–22.

[24] Thwaites, *The Jesuit Relations and Allied Documents*, (Cleveland, 1896–1901), 45:163. Although this account states that Father Charles Albanel accompanied Menard, it is believed that at the moment of departure, Albanel was forced out and refused passage. Kellogg, ibid, 146. There have been some reports that Radisson went with Menard, but there is conclusive evidence that he did not, since the Three Rivers, Quebec, parish register has an entry dated September 18, 1660 recording that "Radisson stood godfather to a little 'Trifluvian' in Three Rivers." Again, Gagnon, *Essai de bibliographic canadienne*, 2:333 states that Radisson was in New France on October 28, 1660.

[25] Thwaites, ibid, 46:141. Some accounts state that Menard was heartlessly left

at the foot of Keweenaw Bay. Menard named the bay Ste. Therese since he had arrived there on October 15, the day of that saint. In spite of the jeers of his companions, he built an altar and performed his daily offices. After suffering many winter hardships, he made his way to Chequamegon in the spring of 1661 where he rejoined the remainder of his party.[26]

The trip was ill starred for Menard and his lay assistant, Jean Guerin. Upon hearing that a band of Hurons, toward the headwaters of the Black River, was starving, Menard, still enfeebled, set out with three canoe-men and guides to render aid.[27] In a short time two of the party deserted him, and at some portage, possibly on a tributary of the Chippewa River, Menard fell behind his leader and was never heard of again. One report stated that his cassock and breviary were found the following year in the possession of some Hurons. Shortly afterward, Guerin was accidentally shot and killed.

Menard's party had intended to return to Montreal in the fall of 1661, but their plans were disrupted by a band of raiding Sioux. The Frenchmen had procured so many furs that their own crew was unable to transport the cargo. Before the Sioux attack the traders had engaged some of the Ottawa to act as canoe-men, but the raid held the latter in camp for its defense. The departure was delayed until the following year.

While the trip of Menard's party had not been financially successful,

behind by his fellow Frenchmen, and there is a possibility that such was the case. However, in the *Relations*, supra, Menard wrote, "We decamped from our winter quarters on Easter Saturday [April 19, 1661], to proceed . . . ." ". . . so we left the savages and nine of us Frenchmen embarking in three canoes, we continued our navigation." This would indicate that either the Frenchmen stayed with Menard all winter or had returned from Chequamegon to pick him up. The latter eventuality might have been possible, but to get to Keweenaw Bay from Chequamegon in time to leave the former place by April 19 would presume a very early break-up of the ice in Chequamegon Bay.

[26] Chequamegon meant Soft Beaver Dam according to the Ojibway. Warren, ibid, 102. The Ojibway claimed that Chequamegon Point was built by their demi-god, Nanabazhoo, to impound a giant beaver which he had unsuccessfully chased at great length, over a considerable part of the lake. His dam extended to the western mainland, but in an unwary moment on his part, the beaver broke through, and thus formed the present opening to Chequamegon Bay.

Baraga believed that the Indian word Shagawaumikong (which he spelled Jagawamikong) meant A Low Sandy Point Like a Needle. A number of other definitions have been advanced, with a variety of meanings, but the author has followed Warren who was 7/16 Ojibway. Warren was born on Madeline Island, spoke the language fluently and was employed as the official interpreter for the later American Fur Company. In addition, he made a study of the Ojibway lore and legends.

[27] Although there are two Black Rivers in Wisconsin, it seems reasonably certain that Menard was bound for the larger one which flows into the Mississippi at present-day La Crosse, Wisconsin. The smaller Black River flows into the Nemadji River near Superior, Wisconsin. The highest waterfall in the State is found on this river, where it plunges over the escarpment of the southern Lake Superior rift. It is one hundred sixty-four feet in height. Plate 3A. (Author's note.)

its members had seen enough of the potential wealth of the Chequamegon region to excite their enthusiasm for subsequent trips. Their report, in combination with the known returns of Radisson and Groseilliers, inspired others to such an extent that thenceforth there was a steady stream of adventurers heading westward.

In addition, the information concerning the Indian village on Chequamegon Bay revived still more, the interest which had originally prompted the Jesuits to send Father Menard. Accordingly, Father Claude Jean Allouez was appointed to carry on missionary work, and he set out from Three Rivers, Quebec, on August 8, 1665 with six traders and more than four hundred Indians, with Chequamegon as his objective.[28] A considerable number of the natives had left the party by the time Allouez reached the Sault, and probably very few went the entire distance with him.

When he arrived at Chequamegon he found that there were two Indian villages; the first was the Ottawa at the Fish Creek location, which Allouez described as having some "eight hundred fighting men," and the second, Hurons who had settled near present Bono's Creek, about four miles north of the Ottawa.

Allouez reported: "This section of the lake shore, where we have settled down, is between two large villages." Map. 8. Here he built his crude, bark-covered chapel, the first house of worship west of the Appalachians except those in French or Spanish territories to the far south and southwest. It seems probable that his chapel was erected on or near present Boyd's Creek.

The Ottawa had cleared a considerable acreage on their site, and were engaging in rudimentary agriculture. Allouez had hoped to find some evidence of Christianity among the Huron; thinking that the work done by earlier Jesuits, when the tribe lived near Georgian Bay, might make his own task easier. In this he was disappointed, and recorded that both tribes were primitive pagans. The Ottawa had been joined by parts of several other tribes whose members had probably never seen a white man.[29]

After about a year at his first location, he wrote: "Thus, little by little, this Church was growing; and as I saw it already imbued with our mysteries, I deemed the time had come to transfer our little chapel to the midst of the great village [of Ottawa], which lay three-quarters of a league from our abode, and which embraces 45 to 50 large cabins of all nations, containing fully 2,000 souls."[30]

[28] Thwaites, ibid, 49:163, 50:249–311, 51:21–69.
[29] These were the Potawatomi, Illini, Sauk, Fox and Gree. (Author's note.)
[30] Thwaites, Ibid, 50:301. Although there has been considerable doubt as to the

While this excerpt might indicate a degree of optimism in the conversion of the Indians, later entries show evidences of discouragement, particularly after the Ottawa staged a riot in which his new chapel was destroyed, and from which he barely escaped with his life. After a two-year struggle which convinced him that he needed more help, he left for Quebec on May 6, 1667. It was on this trip that he completed his circumnavigation of Lake Superior, going first to the west end of the lake, skirting along the north shore and then ascending the Nipigon River to the lake of the same name. His band of traders, while not accompanying him, left Cheqaumegon the same season. After their departure, the Indians began to regret their resistance to Allouez's spiritual advances, principally because they were deprived of the trade goods upon which they had become dependent.

Upon reaching Quebec, Allouez enlisted a number of assistants, most of whom were unable to return with him on account of the canoe-men's refusal to transport them. This might be another example of the hatred the coureurs de bois bore the Jesuits. However, he was able to secure passage for himself and another Jesuit, Father Louis Nicolas. His choice of the latter was unfortunate, since Nicolas was appalled, not only at the rampant paganism of the natives but also at the conditions under which he was forced to live.

Although Nicolas was of little or no help to Allouez when they arrived at Chequamegon, the natives turned out en masse for baptism. We may speculate on whether he truly understood the Indians' desire for trade goods or was convinced that they had suddenly seen the light.

After putting in a dreary winter, Nicolas started eastward in the spring of 1668 as soon as the lake was open to canoe travel. Later in the same year, Allouez also left but with the promise to the natives that his place would be filled by another priest — and another group of traders.

During Allouez's stay at his Mission of the Holy Ghost, as his station

true location of Allouez's first chapel, his statement that it lay between two Indian villages and that it was three-quarters of a league from the larger, or Ottawa, village, would seem to give a very close approximation as to where it was located.

Knowing the site of the Ottawa village (supra), and allowing 2.52 miles to the French league of the time, Allouez's three-quarters of a league is equivalent to one and seven/eighths miles. See Joseph Steven LaBoule, "Claude Jean Allouez," *Parkman Club Publications*, (Milwaukee, June 8, 1897), #17, 197, The official U. S. Lake Survey chart #961 of 1948, from which map 8 was prepared, scales almost exactly this distance from the Ottawa village to Boyd's Creek. This creek is close to the local Shores' Landing — a name persisting from the logging days of the early 1890s.

In view of the above, the Huron village might well be presumed to have been on Bono's Creek, about two miles further north from the site of Allouez' first chapel. (The creek was named after an old Bayfield family. In 1942, the U. S. Geological Survey, by intent or by mistake, named this Bonus Creek on its official map.) (Author's note.)

was known, active fur trading was being established in the neighborhood, not only by his own band but also by an ever increasing number of
coureurs de bois. The presence of the latter is indicated only by references to them by the Jesuits, by licensed traders and by the admission
of the Quebec authorities that about eight hundred of the younger
habitants had deserted the colony to take up this wild and carefree life.
While these independent traders could not dispose of their furs through
regular channels, they did so in Quebec and Montreal black markets,
and to English traders.[31]

In this era the lake was given the dual name of Lac Superieur au Lac
Tracy. The latter was in honor of Alexandre Prouville, marquis de Tracy,
who arrived in Quebec in 1665 as lieutenant-general for all French
possessions in North America. The name Superieur originated from the
French concept that it was the uppermost lake in the Great Lakes chain.
The later English retained it on account of the lake's size.

In 1668, the French were able to negotiate a temporary peace with
both the Iroquois in the Lake Ontario region, and the Sauk and Fox
Indians in Green Bay and along the Fox River. This opened an easier,
though longer, route westward, and for the first time the French discovered that Lakes Erie and Huron were connected, providing a continuous waterway from Quebec to Lake Superior and Green Bay. Since
the route from the latter to the Mississippi had become known, and since
that river's immense territory was rich in furs, the bulk of the fur trade
for the next twenty years was carried on by this avenue.

Despite this shift to the Fox River route, a few independent traders
stayed on in the Chequamegon region, maintaining contact with the
Indians, and taking what furs were available. The Jesuits, too, persisted
in their missionary efforts. In 1669, Father Jacques Marquette came to
the mission of La Pointe de St. Esprit.[32]

The year's absence of Allouez had not furthered the cause of Christianity among the Ottawa, and Marquette found that his efforts were of little
avail. Moreover, either he or the nearby villages had, in some manner,
incurred the enmity of the Sioux who, by their continuous raids, disrupted his labors. Marquette left the mission in 1671 and probably in
that same year the Sioux forced the natives of the two villages to aban-
don them and to retreat eastward. This also ended all missionary efforts
in that region for one hundred sixty years.

These same raids also interrupted the work of the traders, and it is
possible that they might have moved to the west end of Chequamegon

[31] Frederick J. Turner, "The Character & Influence of the Fur Trade in Wisconsin,"
Wisconsin Historical Proceedings, (Madison, 1889), #36, 66.
[32] Thwaites, Ibid, 54:169–175. Kellogg, Ibid, 158.

Point at this time. There is no confirmation of this move, and it may not have taken place until some years later. There is also an unconfirmed report that a band of French traders built a small fort of the palisade type, mounting a small cannon, on Madeline Island in 1671, at the lagoon near the present Indian cemetery. Whether they came from the Indian village at the foot of Chequamegon Bay, or from Chequamegon Point, or from either, is not known. At least the story was embroidered to the extent that at the end of one year the post was abandoned and the cannon pushed into the slough. Map 17.

Despite the paucity of records, it is fairly evident that among the explorers or the Jesuits were cartographers of considerable skill. A map published by the Jesuits in 1672 shows Lake Superior with amazing accuracy. A notation on it claims that the survey had been made in the years 1670 and 1671, and the work has been generally attributed to Allouez.[33]

[33] Kellogg, Ibid, 154.

CHAPTER THREE

Knock, and It Shall Be Opened Unto You
1678 — 1762

After Marquette's departure from Chequamegon, there followed a period of eight years during which the only fur trade carried on was done by unlicensed traders.[1] Toward the end of this time, Daniel Greysolon, Sieur Dulhut, fitted out an expedition, with the object of making peace with the Indians of the western country, reopening the lakes to commerce, exploring the country beyond Lake Superior and locating the much-talked-of copper mines.[2] His plans for carrying out his venture were more or less clandestine since, technically, he rated as a coureur de bois. However, the current governor, Louis de Baude, Count de Frontenac, was so anxious to recoup not only his own fortunes but also those of New France that he probably encouraged Duluth.[3]

Duluth set out from Montreal on September 1, 1678 with "3 slaves [Indians] and 7 Frenchmen."[4] Besides himself, his party comprised the two brothers Pepin (after whom Lake Pepin was named), Sieur le Maistre, Paul de Vigne, Sieur Bellegarde, Sieur de la Rue, his interpreter, Faffart, as well as one Ojibway and one Sioux who were to act as guides.

He spent the winter of 1678–79 at the Sault where he made firm friends with the Ojibway. In fact, during his entire trip, he built up a reputation as an outstanding negotiator with, and ambassador to, the Indians.

In the spring of 1679, he started on what proved to be a most successful peace mission as well as one of important exploration. On July 2, 1679, he visited a great village of the Sioux, probably on Lake Mille Lac, Minnesota, where he ". . . set up the arms of his Majesty . . .," and claimed

---

[1] Edward D. Neill, *History of Minnesota*, (Minneapolis, 1873), 117–119.

[2] Kellogg, Ibid, 202–209. (Enemies of Duluth accused him of fur trading on this trip. He not only denied the charge but also there is no evidence that he engaged in the trade.) (Author's note.)

[3] Ibid, the common form of Duluth will be used hereafter. (Author's note.)

[4] Kellogg, "Memoir of Duluth on the Sioux Country," *Early Narratives of the Northwest*, (Scribner's, New York, 1917), 330.

all of the surrounding territory in his king's name. It is believed, although there is no authentic confirmation, that he also met a gathering of Assiniboin in the general neighborhood of present Duluth.

He spent the winter of 1679–80 on Chequamegon Bay, making friends with the mixed tribes of Indians who had returned to their villages after having been driven away at the time of Marquette. From this as a base he conducted side trips of exploration.

In June of 1680, he set out with ". . . two canoes, with a savage who was my interpreter, and with four Frenchmen . . ."[5] He followed the shores of the Bayfield Peninsula and coasted along the south border of the lake until he came to the Bois Brule River. From his interpreter he learned that the river was called the Nemitsakouat, the Sioux name. In later years the Ojibway called it Newissakode — Burnt Wood Point, and Wisakoda Sibi — Burnt Pine River.

He ascended this river, tearing out an estimated one hundred beaver dams which impeded his progress. After reaching its headwaters he negotiated the two-odd mile portage to Upper St. Croix Lake. The portage lay in swampy terrain which has an elevation of about 425 feet above Lake Superior.[6] A phenomenon of the time was the small lake, one end of which discharged into Lake Superior by way of the Bois Brule, and the other into St. Croix Creek and thence to the Mississippi.[7] Map 12, shows the general area in respect to modern townships, and map 13, on an enlarged scale, gives the course of the old portage trail.[8] From Upper St. Croix Lake, Duluth descended the river of the same name, and reached the Mississippi. His record of this pathway westward popularized the route for later travelers. This highway was established one year before William Penn founded his colony in Pennsylvania.

When Duluth reached the Mississippi he was informed by a village of Sioux of the capture and enslavement of Father Louis Hennepin and the latter's two companions, Antoine du Gay Augel and Michel Accault. Leaving two of his Frenchmen at the Sioux village, he set out with the others to meet and free Hennepin.[9]

[5] Kellogg, Ibid. (Duluth did not mention where he had lost some of the "Frenchmen" with whom he had started.) (Author's note.)

[6] Chamberlin, Ibid, 3:314.

[7] The small lake has since been captured by St. Croix Creek.

[8] Leigh P. Jerrard, (Winnetka, Illinois, 1943), Map.

[9] Kellogg, Ibid, 332. Father Louis Hennepin, *A New Discovery of a Vast Country in America*, Edited by Reuben Gold Thwaites, (Chicago, 1903), 1:293. Here, Hennepin stated that when he was rescued by Duluth, the latter was accompanied by five men. The rescue took place on July 25, 1680. Again, ibid, 299, when he was about to return to Canada with Duluth, Hennepin stated that there were ". . . eight Europeans of us in all." The return trip was made via the Wisconsin and Fox Rivers to Green Bay. (Author's note.)

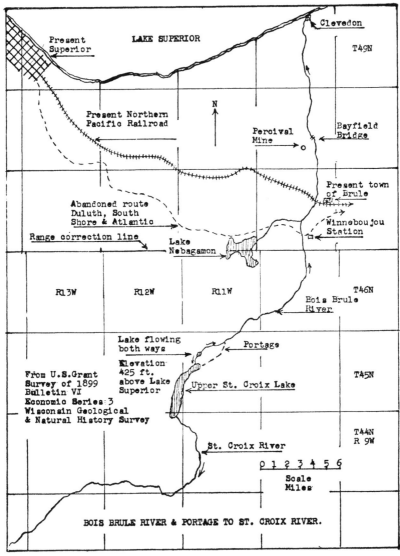

12. Brule River and Portage to St. Croix River.

While much could be written about Duluth's later travels, it is scarcely within the scope of this account, except the fact that all he accomplished did not bear fruit until after his death in 1710. This delay in immediate results was brought about by the English-French War of 1689. (King William's War.) In it the Iroquois sided with the British, forcing the French to give up the Lake Ontario route, and resort to the older and more difficult way via the Ottawa River. Simultaneously, through the machinations of English agents, the Sauk and Fox sealed off the Green Bay district, again leaving Lake Superior the principal source of supply for the fur trade, and making it the only highway to the upper Mississippi.

The incoming traders, particularly near the west end of the lake and at Chequamegon, still met with the annoying incursions of the Sioux, although Duluth's peace efforts had temporarily held that tribe in check. To overcome this situation, the traders moved their establishment to the entrance of the bay, on the end of Chequamegon Point. It was at this time that the new location definitely assumed the name of La Pointe. The date of this move is indeterminate, but it was probably about 1690.[10]

At this new site, the only way in which the raiding Sioux could reach the new post was to circle the bay, and approach from the south-eastward. Since this tribe's natural habitat was the woods and prairies, it was not equipped with canoes suitable for the lake, and therefore was not in a position to essay an amphibious landing. Its only alternative was to skirt the south end of the bay with its extensive swamps at the mouth of the Kakagan River (locally pronounced Kaw-kaw'-gun, and meaning The Home of the Wall-Eyed Pike). Chequamegon Point is only a few rods wide, and it was, therefore, comparatively easy to defend. Nevertheless, the Sioux did attack via this route, and while they never succeeded in overpowering the settlement, they were such a nuisance that it was often-times impossible to conduct trade.

In 1693, Frontenac, in spite of the war, urged his traders to resume

[10] Edward D. Neill, *Minnesota Historical Collections*, (St. Paul, 1885), 5:408. There is no direct proof that the French had a post here earlier than 1692, with the exception of Radisson's temporary one in 1660. However, there are allusions to it in contemporary records which might support the theory of an earlier one. Vide Francis Parkman, *Half Century of Conflict*, (Boston, 1894), 1:11–14. Steven S. Hebberd, *History of Wisconsin Under the Dominion of France*, (Madison, 1890), 52–55, 71–72. William W. Warren, Ibid, 5:125, 417. Frederick J. Turner, Ibid, 66. The theory is refuted by Kellogg, *The French Regime etc.* Ibid, 219, who stated that all the coureurs de bois had returned to Montreal and Quebec under the terms of a general amnesty. This, in turn, is contradicted by Francis Parkman, *Count Frontenac & New France Under Louis XIV*, (Boston, 1894), 252–253, who held that in 1690, 55 canoes manned by French traders arrived at Montreal laden with furs. Also, ibid, 315–316, he stated that in 1691, 200 coureurs de bois were known to have been at Mackinac or in the wilderness thereabout, and that they came to Montreal with 200 canoes.

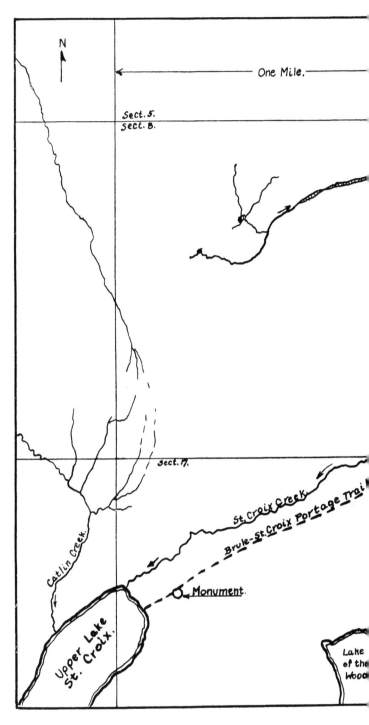

13. Brule-St. Croix Portage.

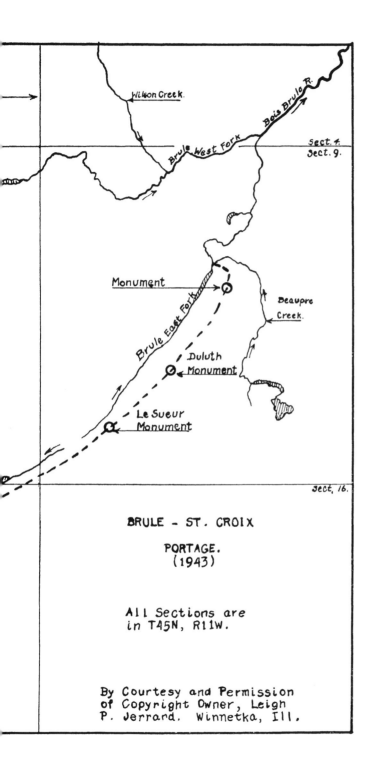

BRULE - ST. CROIX

PORTAGE.
(1943)

All Sections are
in T45N, R11W.

By Courtesy and Permission
of Copyright Owner, Leigh
P. Jerrard. Winnetka, Ill.

business, not only to replenish his coffers, but also to maintain contact with the Indians in the hope of enlisting them as allies in his war against the English.[11] He appointed Pierre Le Sueur as commander of a detail of soldiers to proceed to the La Pointe-Chequamegon region with a company of traders, and establish there, as well as at points further west, posts for conducting trade with the Indians.

Upon Le Sueur's arrival, he saw the conditions existing both at the foot of the bay and on the end of Chequamegon Point. He decided to locate his fort across the channel from the latter, on the south point of Madeline Island. This is present Grant's Point, and the Moningwana Neiasha – Golden Breasted Woodpecker Point – of the Ojibway. He thus pursued the same tactics which the Ojibway had, nearly two hundred years before. This move practically insured the post against the forays of the troublesome Sioux.

The new center, with its small fort, probably of the palisade type, was located almost due north of the present La Pointe lighthouse of Long Island. The key map, 14, shows the townships, ranges and sections of Madeline Island, according to the U. S. Government Survey. Maps 15 and 16 show the site of the fort in respect to the sections.[12] Thenceforth

[11] Thwaites, "The Story of Chequamegon Bay," Ibid, 13:408.

[12] The author was shown this site in 1898 by the Reverend Mr. Edward P. Wheeler, a son of the 1841 missionary at La Pointe, Leonard H. Wheeler. Unfortunately, Wheeler did not cite his authority for his statement that Le Sueur had built his fort at that particular spot. In 1898, corner and fireplace stones were still in evidence. (These have since been used by nearby enthusiastic dock builders.) Excavations in 1951 have disclosed a large fireplace foundation, made of sizeable boulders, laid up in clay, in an otherwise sandy terrain, the typical French method of fireplace building.

However, some confirmation, by allusion, exists. Thomas L. McKenney, *Sketches of a Tour to the Lakes*, (Baltimore, 1827), 265, stated that while at Michel Cadotte's house on Madeline Island, in 1826, he wished to have visited the seat of the Jesuit mission but was told that there were no remains of it; that it was northwest of Cadotte's house, and about ¾ mile away. Since the location of Cadotte's house is fairly well known, toward the south end of Madeline Island, a distance of ¾ mile in a northwest direction would bring one into the lake. Moreover, there is no extant record to prove that the Jesuits ever had a permanent structure on the island. Mass might have been celebrated there by a passing priest when the Le Sueur fort was in existence, but this was only about five hundred feet due west of Cadotte's house. (Author's note.)

Again, ibid, 267 et seq., upon leaving Cadotte's house on the way to Fond du Lac, his course took him around the southern end of what he called Michel's Island. (Present Grant's Point of Madeline Island.) After rounding this, ". . . we were opposite the ancient missionary establishment . . . ." Maps 16 & 19. Plate 4.

These allusions would seem to confirm the site, because Michel Cadotte would certainly have known that the principal French post of later years had been located at the so-called Middle Fort, a distance of nearly one and one-half miles from his home. While Cadotte might have believed that the Le Sueur site had been a Jesuit mission, he might not have known about the fort, built nearly one hundred years before his time. (Author's note.)

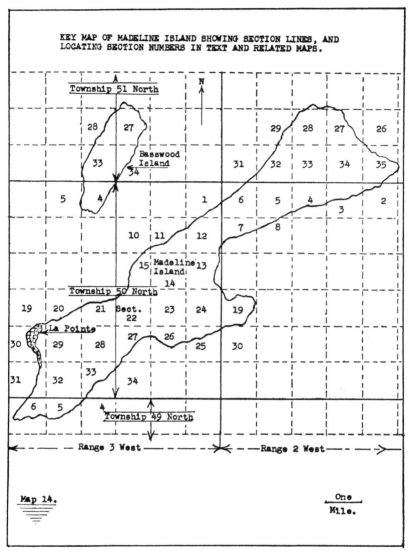

14. Key Map to Madeline Island.

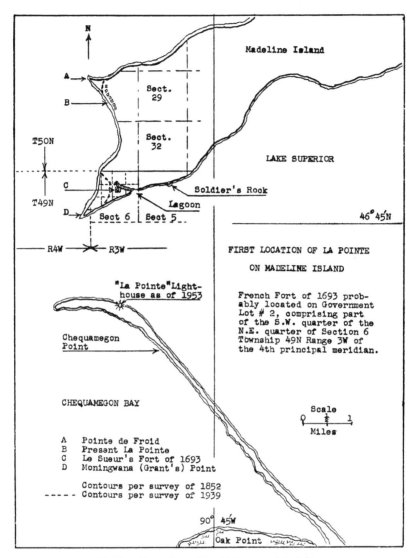

N

A → Sect. 29

B →

T50N
T49N

C →

D →

Sect 6 | Sect 5

R4W ⟶ R3W

Sect. 32

Madeline Island

LAKE SUPERIOR

Soldier's Rock

Lagoon

46° 45'N

FIRST LOCATION OF LA POINTE

ON MADELINE ISLAND

French Fort of 1693 prob-
ably located on Government
Lot # 2, comprising part
of the S.W. quarter of the
N.E. quarter of Section 6
Township 49N Range 3W of
the 4th principal meridian.

"La Pointe" Light-
house as of 1953

Chequamegon
Point

CHEQUAMEGON BAY

Scale
0   ½   1
Miles

A   Pointe de Froid
B   Present La Pointe
C   Le Sueur's Fort of 1693
D   Moningwana (Grant's) Point

Contours per survey of 1852
- - - - - Contours per survey of 1939

90° 45'W

Oak Point

15. First Location of La Pointe on Madeline.

La Pointe was located on Madeline Island, although the name was used well into the 1870s to denote the entire surrounding area.

The site of the fort is about one hundred feet from the water at present, but the shoals in front of the location and the Government survey of 1852 lead one to believe that in Le Sueur's time the post was at least twelve hundred feet from the lake. It was on low, sandy terrain of the barrier-beach type. Assuming that present flora had their counterparts at the time of the fort, this wide beach was probably covered with low juniper and yew bushes with a scattering of deciduous plants which were able to secure a foothold in the sand. Also there might have been a spring enclosed in the stockade or else close by.[13]

Immediately back of the fort was the lagoon which served as a harbor for the canoes of the Indians and traders. Thus the post was protected by water at its front and back, while wide, open spaces at the sides offered little cover to potential enemies.

On high ground at the north were hemlocks and pines, many of which were over four feet in diameter and one hundred fifty feet in height.[14] Again, assuming that these forests were similar to those of later years, it was probable that there was little or no undergrowth, and that the pine-needle-covered ground was mottled with the rays of any sunlight which was able to filter through the cathedral-like reaches of the trees.

Any cabins of the settlement were probably placed on level and higher ground to the northeast. Here, too, was ample room for the Indians to erect their lodges when they arrived for trading. Both cabins and lodges were across the lagoon from the fort.[15]

At this time, the French named the island St. Esprit, after the earlier calling of Chequamegon Bay and Allouez's mission. Until the arrival of the English it was successively called Isle Detour, La Pointe, La Ronde, St. Michael's and Montreal.

Le Sueur's project was not confined to the post on Madeline Island.

[13] The matter of the spring is speculative. In 1953, a phenomenon was noted in the bottom of the lake, about one hundred yards off shore to the west and slightly south of the fort. An old crib about twelve feet square, with its top even with the lake bottom, was discovered in about seven feet of water. Inside the crib, the water was about twelve feet deep with an accumulation of debris. Since, under ordinary conditions, the crib would have been filled with sand, it was deduced that a spring of sufficient size to clear out any collection of sand in the crib must exist at the bottom. Because means were not at hand to clear out the debris in order to see the spring proper, a test was made with a thermometer. The latter read 48 degrees Fahrenheit when lowered to the bottom of the crib. At the same time, the temperature of the water a few feet away from the crib and on the lake bottom, read 64 degrees. This seemed to prove that there was undoubtedly a spring inside the crib.
[14] The author is comparing these with later virgin timber which he has seen.
[15] This may be speculative, but many evidences of ancient habitations have appeared in widespread excavations. (Author's note.)

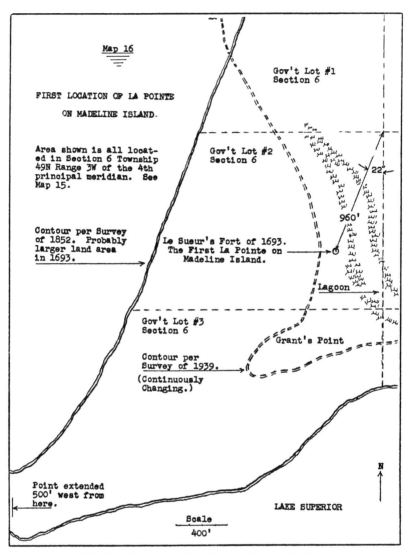

16. First Location of La Pointe. (Large Scale.)

To enhance the supremacy of France, he proceeded westward, following Duluth's route up the Bois Brule River. To command the portage between this and the St. Croix Rivers, he erected a small fort, not far from Upper St. Croix Lake, Map 12. He also descended the St. Croix River to the Mississippi where he built another fort on Prairie Island, about nine miles below present Hastings, Minnesota.[16]

With the closing of the Green Bay route, the La Pointe center was a most important one in the fur trading schemes of the French. It was chosen as the assembly point for furs, and served much the same function, to a lesser degree, that the famous Grand Portage post later did for the English.[17]

To La Pointe came the furs from the territory served by the St. Louis River and its tributaries, via Fond du Lac (present Duluth) and the south shore of the lake; from the vast reaches of the upper Mississippi by both the St. Louis and Brule Rivers; from the southwest, via both the Namakagan and Chippewa Rivers into Chequamegon Bay by Fish Creek; from the south by the Bad River, through the fabled Penokee Gap — the route allegedly followed by legendary Indians of the South and Southwest, in their quests for Lake Superior copper; from the East via the Montreal River and its trail to Lac du Flambeau, from the Ontonagon River and its tributaries, and also from still further east, as far as Baraga, Michigan, east of the Keweenaw Peninsula.[18]

It is probable that the same technique was used as at later Grand Portage, with the big forty foot canoes, paddled by the mangeurs de lard, arriving from Montreal with their loads of trade goods, to return with furs. No doubt the same kind of rendezvous was held every year, with the Indians assembled from all directions, the coureurs de bois from their lonely stations of the interior, the important men from Montreal and the soldiers of the post. Here the lesser lights lazed, hunted, gamed and made merry while the big men decided policy and prices of furs. Then, upon the departure of the large canoes, the rendezvous would break up, leaving only the skeleton command and some itinerant Indians.[19]

It might have been at this time that the local legends concerning

[16] Present Pélee Island. Kellogg, *French Regime*, ibid, 252.

[17] Grand Portage lies in Minnesota, on the north shore of Lake Superior, about five miles from the International boundary. (Author's note.)

[18] This Fond du Lac is about thirteen miles up the St. Louis River from present Duluth. They are associated here to differentiate this Fond du Lac from the one in Wisconsin. The Montreal River-Lac du Flambeau trail is shown on Franquelin's map of 1688. The Indian names for the Bad River were Mushkeego Sibi or Mashki Sibing — The Swamp River. The French called it the Mauvais. (Author's note.)

[19] The furs were pressed into ninety pound bundles, one of which was considered the proper load for one man when the canoes arrived at a portage. (Author's note.)

Soldier's Rock originated. This rock was located about one mile east of the post, and jutted out into the lake. Map 15, Plate 5. Although the elements have shattered this big monolith of red sandstone, so that parts of it are only visible at low water, it was at least twenty-five feet high in the 1870s.[20] It was about twenty feet long, twelve feet wide and six feet thick in 1905, and was probably much larger approximately two hundred sixty years ago, at the time of Le Sueur.

One story was to the effect that a deserting French soldier met a fellow conspirator at this spot, and was ferried away. Another, more romantic, legend had this as a trysting place for a soldier and an Indian maid. The latter tale was expanded into a story which recounted that the maid, after repeated solitary visits, realized that she had been jilted, and threw herself into the lake to perish.

Another reasonable conjecture for the origin of the name is that the rock was a very definite landmark, and stood out on the shore considerably higher than the neighboring terrain. It might have been likened to a sentinel on guard.

The life of this La Pointe post was short. In 1698 it was abandoned because Le Sueur and the commandants of other trading posts had virtually swamped both Old and New France with the volume of furs they had procured. Prices sank to ruinous levels. One Montreal merchant bewailed the fact that he had a "ten year supply" in his warehouses. This caused King Louis XIV to issue a royal decree cancelling all trading licenses and forbidding the shipment of trade goods to the west. This action, in effect, was the beginning of the end of French domination in Canada and the northwest.

During the twenty-year life of this decree, the Hudson's Bay Company consolidated its position by the installation of new posts and by the promotion of good will among the Indians. This was brought forcibly to France's attention by the treaty of Utrecht in 1713, which gave the Hudson's Bay Company the exclusive right to trade in territory which France had considered her own. This did not affect Lake Superior. The region in question lay further to the north and northwest.

In a desperate attempt to recover her prestige, if not her lost territory, France established new posts on Lake Superior, and revived the one at La Pointe. For the next forty years La Pointe was to enjoy the high water mark of French activity in the fur trade at the west end of Lake Superior. From the standpoint of the historian it was also to be sterile ground for information regarding the times, the customs and, to some

---

[20] Chamberlin, Ibid, 3:74.

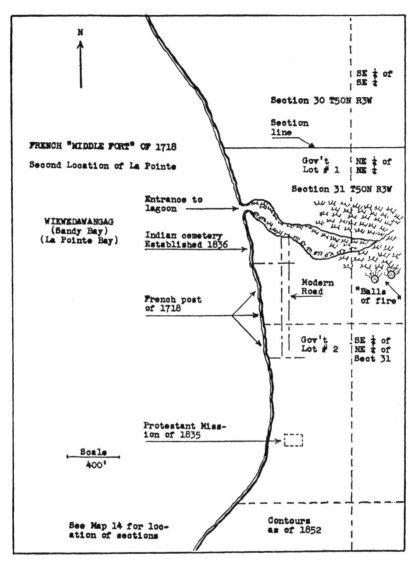

N

SE ¼ of
SE ¼

Section 30 T50N R3W

Section
line

FRENCH "MIDDLE FORT" OF 1718

Second Location of La Pointe

Gov't
Lot # 1

NE ¼ of
NE ¼

Section 31 T50N R3W

Entrance to
lagoon

WIKWEDAWANGAG
(Sandy Bay)
(La Pointe Bay)

Indian cemetery
Established 1836

Modern
Road

"Balls
of fire"

French post
of 1718

Gov't
Lot # 2

SE ¼ of
NE ¼ of
Sect 31

Protestant Miss-
ion of 1835

Scale
400'

See Map 14 for loc-
ation of sections

Contours
as of 1852

17. French Fort of 1718.

47

extent, the events. During the French Revolution practically all reports originating at La Pointe were destroyed.[21]

In 1718, Paul le Gardeur, Sieur de St. Pierre, was sent to La Pointe as commandant of the revived post, with the rank of captain. He was the son of Jean Baptiste le Gardeur, and a grandson of Jean Nicolet, the explorer. During Le Sueur's regime in the district, the Indians had become dependent upon the French for such articles as needles, blankets, shirts, axes, kettles and the almost endless variety of trade goods which were offered them. During the twenty year absence of the French, these items had worn out or become lost, and the natives, in that time, had forgotten their old arts of making substitutes. Thus, upon St. Pierre's arrival, he found the Indians in desperate straits, all half starved and poorly clad. He hastened to remedy this condition by advancing trade goods against the future take of furs.[22]

At the same time he selected a new site for his establishment. The lagoon at the old Le Sueur location was beginning to fill with sand, and harbor facilities were not of the best.[23] He built his new fort in Wikwedawangag — Sandy Bay — present La Pointe Bay, midway between the present Indian cemetery and the Old Mission. Maps 15 and 17, pp. 42 and 47. In later years, this would be known as the Middle Fort.[24] The new settlement not only possessed a larger lagoon than the old, but it also had the advantage of the protected bay. In addition, the post was surrounded on three sides by several hundred acres of level land suitable

[21] At this time the commandants were under the French Ministry of Marine, and while the reports passed through Quebec, they ended up in Paris. The Ministry of Marine seemed to have been the special target of the Revolutionists. While the building is still in existence, the contents were scattered and destroyed. What little information there is today has been gleaned from the works of contemporary writers whose manuscripts have remained in Quebec, Montreal or Three Rivers. Another source has been the papers and records of private individuals in France, saved as family heirlooms. Much information has come from allusions in these manuscripts rather than from direct statements. Some knowledge has been gained from Dutch and English records, preserved in New York and neighboring states. These, for the most part, express opinions and describe events through eyes of persons unfriendly to France. (Author's note.)

[22] Thwaites, "The Story of Chequamegon Bay," *Wisconsin Historical Collections*, (Madison, 1895), 13:409–412.

[23] In 1957 the location of the lagoon was dry land, except for a few marshy places. It has dried up considerably within the author's memory.

[24] Thwaites, Ibid, called this the Middleport. The author believes this name to be a misnomer. In the scant records of the post, neither the names Middle Fort nor Middleport appear. The fort is referred to as La Pointe, or, more generally, as the current name of the island. The "Middle" names must have been the product of later times when the site was midway between the old and new posts of the American Fur Company. It is unlikely that during its existence it could have been the middle of anything save the bay on which it was located. It was called Middle Fort by Baraga, Verwyst, Vincent Roy III and the Jean Baptiste Cadotte of the early 1900s.

for agricultural purposes. Like Le Sueur's original post at the south end of the island, the new fort was located on a low stretch of barrier beach with the latter's typical lagoon.

In the early 1900s, the summer visitors found many beads, arrowheads and a few tomahawks imbedded in the sand where the post had been. There was an active flurry in the sieve market, and the entire area was well screened. After the recovery of the original and authentic items, a local wag was discovered planting modern beads as a lure to budding archaeologists.

St. Pierre's principal task was to promote the fur trade with the Indians and to forward as many furs as possible to Montreal. In order to accomplish this he found that he would have to act as arbiter between the Ojibway and Fox, who were engaged in a series of hit-and-run assaults against one another. Through rounds of negotiations he persuaded the two tribes to hunt furs, rather than each other.

Another obstacle which he had to overcome was the discrepancy in prices between what he could offer and what the English were paying for peltries. This is illustrated in the following table:

	THE INDIANS PAID IN BEAVER SKINS	
	TO THE	
	English	French
For		
8 pounds of powder	1	4
1 gun	2	5
40 pounds of lead (for bullets)	1	3
1 blanket (red or white)	1	2
6 pairs of stockings	1	2
4 shirts	1	2

The English would also give six quarts of rum for one beaver as against the French one-fifth gallon of brandy.[25]

Only by exercising the utmost diplomacy was he able to win the Indians' grudging willingness to trade. In this he was aided by his geographical position. The Indians would have had to cross the lake and undertake many difficult portages to have reached posts of the Hudson's Bay Company, or would have had to run the gantlet of the hostile and terrifying Iroquois to have traded at Orange (present Albany) New York.

After St. Pierre's tour of duty ended in 1720, his place was taken by

[25] *New York Colonial Documents*, 9:408. What the above table does not show is that the French powder was much superior to the English product. The same was true of the French blankets. (Author's note.)

Rene Godefroy, Sieur de Linctot.[26] Linctot had originally come with
St. Pierre as an ensign. He was the scion of a well-known family which,
for over one hundred years, had been associated with the development
of Three Rivers, Quebec. Groseillier's wife had spent a number of years
in the Godefroy home when her husband had been absent on his trips
of exploration. Although considerable is known about Linctot both
before and after his term at La Pointe, information is lacking concerning
his six year stay. Inasmuch as he had commanded for this length of time,
it would seem that he had discharged his duties in an efficient and satis-
factory manner.

Linctot was succeeded by a commandant about whom more is known
than any other French officer at La Pointe. Louis Denis, Sieur de la
Ronde, took charge of the post in 1727. He had been well known in
Quebec and Montreal before he came to La Pointe. This fact, plus his
penchant and ability for writing to his friends and relatives in those
cities, has provided a great deal of information concerning the La Pointe
post. While his official reports went to France, and were probably destroyed, much of his correspondence was preserved in Canada.

La Ronde was probably La Pointe's most active and famous commandant. Upon his arrival in 1727, his aggressive spirit found an
outlet in spurring on the normal course of the fur trade and in administering to the welfare of the Indian inhabitants. He was the first to
encourage agricultural interest among the natives on the island. This
resulted in their building up a back log of food for winter, and also
furnishing the garrison with fresh vegetables.[27]

In his general curiosity about the surrounding territory, he was much
impressed with the Indians' tales of the floating island of copper. Indian
legend associated Michipicoten Island with this phenomenon. It is also
possible that they referred to Isle Royale where copper mines had been
worked for many years. However, he centered his efforts on investigating
their stories in an area nearer the post. Hearing their stories of free copper in the Ontonagon River district, he made the seventy-odd mile trip,
and found many rich samples.[28] So far as is known, he did not see the
Ontonagon boulder.[29]

La Ronde found a large number of promising specimens on both this

[26] Kellogg, The French Regime, Ibid, 301.
[27] Ibid, 351–354.
[28] Ibid, 353.
[29] The Indians considered this boulder as sacred, and it was not until the advent
of the English that they, with considerable reluctance, showed the latter its location.
There are estimates that the boulder must have weighed about five tons at the time
of La Ronde. Alexander Henry, Alexander Henry's Travels and Adventures, (Chicago, 1921), Lakeside Press Series, Milo M. Quaife, editor, 197. (A thirty-two inch
cube of the metal would weigh about this amount.) (Author's note.)

and nearby streams, and sent them to France for assay.[30] Judging from the later copper boom of the 1840s, it is probable that these specimens comprised nuggets and chunks of copper rather than the amygdaloid and conglomerate ores which required stamp mills for processing. At the same time he realized that transporting the metal via canoe or batteau was out of the question. He therefore went to the Sault, constructed a boat yard there, and in 1731 built the first sailing vessel on Lake Superior.[31] It might also rate as the first ore boat.

The craft was of about forty tons burden, and its iron work and rigging were brought from Montreal by canoe. He also considered fabricating another and larger vessel for Lake Huron, to transport the metal to the lower lakes, after it had been portaged past the Sault rapids. The Lake Huron boat was never built, and the Lake Superior one was used, almost entirely, to carry freight between the Sault and La Pointe. There is no record of the fate of this ship, although there is a reference to the foundering of a French vessel in 1763, during the first year of the British regime.[32]

The richness of La Rònde's copper specimens so impressed the French ministry that two experienced miners were sent to advise him on the most suitable locations for mines. Through some misunderstanding in communications, La Ronde did not meet the miners at the Sault, and the men went prospecting in another direction. By the time La Ronde contacted them, the season was so far advanced that the experts hesitated to remain longer, but La Ronde, by offering them more money, induced them to make a rapid trip to the Ontonagon, where several sites were chosen by the now enthusiastic specialists.

In 1732 La Ronde arranged for a number of men to accompany him, and opened a promising mine on what he termed the Ste. Anne River.[33] It is interesting to note that while La Ronde was seeking copper in this

[30] Kellogg, Ibid, 353.

[31] James Davie Butler, "Early Shipping on Lake Superior," *Wisconsin Historical Society Proceedings*, (Madison, 1895), 87.

[32] *Calendar of Canadian Archives*, (1888), 64. Also Grace Lee Nute, *Lake Superior*, (Bobbs-Merrill, 1944), 117.

[33] Edward D. Neill, *Macalester Historical Contributions*, (First Series #3, St. Paul, 1890), 194. Here, quoting La Ronde's journal, "They [the miners] entered St. Anne's River six leagues westward from the Tonagane [Ontonagon]." This would disprove some of the statements that the stream was the Iron River of Wisconsin. Michigan's Iron River is about twelve miles west of the Ontonagon. There is some discrepancy between La Ronde's estimate of the distance and that shown on modern Government charts, but the location seems to be further confirmed by a letter which the Governor of Canada wrote to France in 1736, concerning a trip of certain Indians enroute to La Pointe, ". . . they will pass by the Riviere au Fer, from which has been taken the lumps of copper . . . ." Neill, *Minnesota Historical Collections*, (St. Paul, 1885), 5:46.

district, a man was born who would later suggest that an expedition be sent to the same country on the same quest. George Washington, as President of the new United States, foresaw another war with England, and desired to build up a reserve of this vital metal.[34]

Although La Ronde's mining schemes apparently had an optimistic start, pressure of his other duties prevented him from closely supervising operations, and they were finally discontinued. The principal reason for his inability to carry on with his mining was the outbreak of hostilities between the Ojibway and the Sioux. The ancient enmity between these two tribes flared up, and was carried on so relentlessly that the collections of furs fell off to an alarming degree. All his diplomacy and friendship with both tribes failed to quiet them. Still confident of his influence over them, he set off for Quebec in an effort to revive interest in his copper ventures. It is not known what success he had there. On his way back to La Pointe he fell sick at Mackinac. His illness was of such serious nature that he retraced his steps to Quebec, and died there in 1741. His service of fourteen years was the longest of any commandant at La Pointe.

To review his accomplishments and some of the major events which took place during his regime: in addition to the agriculture which he fostered, he had imported a number of horses, built a dock, and had a mill for the grinding of grain. A new era was also ushered in because of the war between the Ojibway and Sioux. He did not live to see the final outcome, but it resulted in the Ojibway driving the Sioux away from Lac du Flambeau and Lac Court Oreilles and holding those areas thenceforth: a demonstration of the power of firearms over bows and arrows.

Another item of modern interest was the naming of the islands. During his time the Apostle Islands name became official, although it had appeared on some of the old French maps in earlier times.[35]

It is believed that La Ronde's son, Philippe Louis Denis La Ronde,

[34] So far as is known no expedition was ever sent. (Author's note.)

[35] It has often been assumed that the name was taken from the number of islands in the group. The author does not agree with this line of reasoning. First: twelve islands are not visible from any possible approach (save by air). Second: as soon as one arrives fairly among them, many more than a dozen may be counted. It seems logical to credit the Jesuits with the name, simply because they were in the habit of attaching holy names to new localities, such as St. Ignace, Sault de Ste. Marie and La Baye de St. Esprit. There is another legendary source for the name. This avers that a band of pirates, calling themselves The Twelve Apostles, had headquarters among the islands or on the nearby mainland. Whenever canoes, laden with furs or trade goods, passed by, these raiders would sweep down on them, and hi-jack the cargoes. Another fantasy, with an attempt at rather embryonic documentation, enlarges upon the above legend. This appeared in a pamphlet prepared by George Francis Thomas, *Picturesque Wisconsin*, (Milwaukee, 1899), 13–15.

attempted to continue his father's mining ventures, but since there are no records of any outstanding strikes, one may assume that he was forced to drop them in order to attend to the fur business of the post. About the only information concerning him is that he remained in charge for two years (1741–1743), and in later years was killed in the French and Indian War against the British.[36]

One of the most anomalous situations which one might imagine in connection with a frontier and primitive fur trading station occurred after Philippe La Ronde's tour of duty: an outpost in charge of a woman! When Philippe La Ronde left La Pointe in 1743, he was succeeded by his mother, who was given the position as a pension in reward for her husband's services. During her term, she received one-third of the gross receipts of the post. It is not known to what extent she was in command nor how much authority she delegated to some minor assistant or officer. In any event, it is notable that a woman should have been charged with the responsibility of administering such an important post in those times.

Madame La Ronde had been born in France in 1690, the daughter of Rene Louis, Chartier de Lotbiniere, a counselor of Louis XIV, and a Lieutenant General of New France for a period. After leaving La Pointe in 1748, she retired to Montreal where she died in 1760 — the same year that the city fell to the British General, Lord Jeffrey Amherst.[37]

In 1749, Joseph de la Margue, Sieur Marin, was appointed to the La Pointe post. He had held similar positions at Green Bay and Lake Pepin where he had established his reputation as a friend of the Indians. Both he and his father, Paul, had the names of being large-scale grafters. The father was deep in the political chicanery of New France. The younger Marin, who was commonly called Marin Fils, persuaded the Marquis de la Jonquiere, the governor, to abolish the old leasing system which had been in force since Le Sueur's time, and substitute for it the still older licensing method. The governor lent a sympathetic ear since he would receive a generous cut. The licensing system was, therefore, restored. Although Marin later left to fight the British and acquitted himself in notable fashion in the bloody defeat of General Edward Braddock in 1755, yet he and his kind were largely responsible for the rotten core which spelled the downfall of the French in Canada.[38] Marin left La Pointe in 1750 to take charge of the Green Bay post.

Until very recently, nothing had come to light regarding Marin's immediate successor. All of the old records indicated that the next commandant was Beaubassin. These also showed that Beaubassin did not

[36] *Wisconsin Historical Collections*, 17:351, 433, 444.
[37] *Wisconsin Historical Collections*, 17:444, 447–8, 498–9, 18:13–14, 35, 124.
[38] Kellogg, *The French Regime*, Ibid, 379–381, 429.

arrive at La Pointe until 1756. This left a gap of about five years which was totally unaccounted for. There were some conjectures that the post had been abandoned during this time, but these were dismissed on account of the recognized policy of the French to maintain La Pointe and two other posts at all costs.[39]

Strangely enough, this blank was filled by the information contained in an old diary of Marin which has recently been discovered.[40] The diary reveals that Joseph Gaultier, Chevalier de la Verendrye, was the commandant from 1751 to 1755. While it does not shed a great deal of light on affairs at La Pointe, it does confirm the belief that the station was a going concern during this period. The reason that Marin mentions La Verendrye is that the two were in a constant wrangle over their respective rights on the upper Mississippi. Marin stated that during the winter of 1753-54 he procured seven hundred sixty packs of furs for his Green Bay station, and "If Laverandrie [sic] had not stopped my people, I should have made 'un coup' such as Green Bay never made before." [41]

Marin had built a fort which he called Fort Duquesne, probably at the confluence of the Crow Wing and Mississippi Rivers. It was near here that La Verendrye stopped Marin's 'people' and confiscated their trade goods. Marin had also built another fort at the junction of the St. Croix and Mississippi, probably near present Hastings, Minnesota. In the charges and counter charges of the two men, it is difficult to decide just where the respective limits of their territories lay. According to the Marin journal, La Verendrye's official southern boundary on the St. Croix River ended at the Snake River. This flows into the St. Croix from the west, about ten miles east of Pine City, Minnesota. To determine La Verendrye's southern limit on the Mississippi is another matter, and it is doubtful whether it had been settled at that time. Possibly if one were to draw a line westward from the junction of the Snake and St. Croix to the Mississippi, it would meet the latter about thirty miles below Fort Duquesne, and a little way west of present Royalton, Minnesota, and also fix the southern limit of La Verendrye's territory. The

[39] Ibid, 312. One of these posts was at Green Bay, and the other, changed from time to time, was on the Mississippi.

[40] Journal de Monsieur Marin fils -Commandant pour le Roy etc. (Loudoun papers), Henry E. Huntington Library and Art Gallery, San Marino, California. Manuscript # LO 461. This manuscript was brilliantly reviewed by Grace Lee Nute, "Marin Versus La Verendrye," Minnesota History, (St. Paul, 1951), 32, #4, 226–238.

[41] Ibid. (Marin's 'people' followed the customary route from Green Bay to the Mississippi by way of the Fox and Wisconsin Rivers. La Verendrye's traders reached there via the Fond du Lac (Duluth)-St. Louis River-Sandy Lake course which brought them to the Mississippi about thirty miles northeast of present Aitkin, Minnesota.) (Author's note.)

limits of the La Pointe district would not be exactly defined until the advent of St. Luc, several years later.

La Verendrye was the youngest of Pierre Gaultier de Varennes de Verendrye's four sons. Pierre had distinguished himself in the annals of New France by having carried her flag to, and established forts on, Rainy Lake, Lake of the Woods and Lake Winnipeg. He had also explored and traded as far west as the Rockies.[42]

The last commissioned officer at La Pointe was Pierre Hertel de Beaubassin who assumed his duties there in 1756.[43] Born in Acadia, he had entered the army of New France, and had eventually become a Captain. He left La Pointe in 1758 with a company of Indians which he had trained, to aid the hard-pressed French forces against the English. After the fall of New France, he could not bring himself to remain as a British subject, and sailed for France.

After Marin's scheme to return to the old licensing system, the leasing arrangement was restored on the advent of Sieur Corne de la St. Luc in 1758. There are a number of unexplained factors concerning his arrival at La Pointe. He had held a commission in the army of New France, but his status at La Pointe was that of a civilian. Furthermore, with New France in desperate straits, it seems strange that an apparently capable officer was allowed to follow personal pursuits at a distant post. There is a possibility that he had been temporarily banished on account of the fiendish work of the Indians under his command, upon the surrender, by the English, of Fort William Henry the year before.[44] It has been reported that even the none-too-squeamish French regulars had been aghast at the insane butchery which had taken place.

St. Luc paid the Government eight thousand francs for the La Pointe concession. In normal times this might have been considered a bargain, but in view of existing conditions it would appear that he was overly optimistic. It has been estimated that the La Pointe post's annual shipment of furs in about 1750 amounted to two hundred fifty bundles.[45] However, from Marin's description of the limits of the post during St.

[42] Kellogg, *The French Regime*, Ibid, 336–337.

[43] Ibid, 384.

[44] In a letter to John Page, dated October 13, 1775, Thomas Jefferson wrote: "This St. Luc is a great Seigneur amongst the Indians, he has been our most bitter enemy, and is acknowledged to be one of the greatest scoundrels: to be assured of this I need only mention to you that he is the ruffian, who during the later war [The French and Indian War] when Fort William Henry was surrendered to the French and Indians, on condition of saving the lives of the garrison, had every soul murdered in cold blood." *The Writings of Thomas Jefferson*, (Washington, 1904), Andrew Lipscomb, Editor, Monticello Edition, 4:248–249.

[45] Harold A. Innis, *The Fur Trade in Canada*, (New Haven, 1930), 103.
Guy Burnham, *The Lake Superior Country in History and in Story*, (Boston, 1930), 87.

Luc's regime, it would appear that this estimate was much too low. Marin recorded that when La Pointe's trading territory was fixed, it included all of the south shore as far east from La Pointe as Au Sable Point which is about sixty miles west of Whitefish Point, one of the portals of Whitefish Bay at the east end of the lake. It also included the west end of the lake and the north shore as far as what he called "Roche Debout." The latter was probably Palisade Head of the Sawtooth Mountains, near the mouth of the Baptism River and about sixty miles northeast of Duluth.[46] It is assumed that the territory included the entire watershed within the above limits.

Even if St. Luc had been able to collect a minimum of two hundred fifty bundles, it is doubtful if he could have shipped them all, or have received a reasonable price. The English had sealed off the St. Lawrence waterway, and there was little or no communication with France. Thus, little is known concerning his venture at La Pointe. The value of the furs is also problematical. They might have been worth from ninety to four hundred fifty dollars per bundle, depending on the state of the market.[47]

Aside from the record of St. Luc's marriage on September 3, 1757 to Marie Joseph Gaultier, the widow of Jacques le Gardier, Sieur de St. Pierre, the last information about him shows that he commanded a band of Indians, under Burgoyne, at the Battle of Saratoga.[48]

Thus, with St. Luc's departure from La Pointe in 1762, the French regime in that part of the country came to an end. We may well speculate on a number of factors which, if altered here and there, might have changed the whole course of history in Canada and in the United States. What if Radisson had not disclosed the secret of Hudson Bay to the English? What if the courts of the Louis had been less venal, and the

[46] Nute, "Marin Versus La Verendrye," Ibid, 236.

[47] Neill, *Minnesota Historical Collections*, (St. Paul, 1885), 5:446. This record gives two hundred dollars per bundle as the value in 1791.

Innis, ibid, recorded that an Albany statement dated August 10, 1761 gave an estimate of eighty thousand livres as the value of beaver from La Pointe in an average year under the French regime.

Alexander Henry, Ibid, 183–184 quoted the beaver price at Mackinac as about ninety dollars per bundle.

Neill, *Macalester Contributions*, 2nd Series, #1, 1892 quoted a price of four hundred fifty dollars per bundle in 1835.

[48] Neill, *Minnesota Historical Collections*, Ibid, 428. This St. Pierre was the son of Paul who founded the Middle Fort at La Pointe in 1718.

Charles Neilson, *Burgoyne's Campaign*, (Albany, 1844), 196. While called the Battle of Saratoga, Burgoyne was actually defeated at Bemis's Heights, on the John Neilson farm, and forced back to his camp on the Freeman farm, both a short distance up the Hudson River from Stillwater, New York. The surrender took place at present Schuylerville, New York, which was called Saratoga at the time. It should therefore not be confused with the modern City of Saratoga Springs.

Intendants of New France more honest? What if the French had devoted their energies to colonization instead of to exploitation?

So we leave our La Pointe post to three decades of destruction, decay and neglect; a jousting ground for French renegades and English adventurers, but still possessing a vital seed for another era to germinate.

A Summary of French Commanders at La Pointe.

Pierre Le Sueur	1693–1698
Paul Le Gardier, Sieur de St. Pierre	1718–1720
Rene Godefroy, Sieur de Linctot	1720–1726
Louis Denis, Sieur de la Ronde	1727–1741
Philippe Louis Denis de la Ronde	1741–1743
Madame La Ronde (Wife of Louis)	1743–1748
Joseph de la Margue, Sieur Marin	1749–1750
Joseph Gaultier, Chevalier de la Verendrye	1751–1755
Pierre Hertel de Beaubassin	1756–1758
Sieur Corne de la St. Luc	1758–1762

CHAPTER FOUR

1763 So I Saw The Wicked Buried 1816

Former New France now experienced a period which Louise Phelps Kellogg termed The Interregnum. The World War II adjective Fluid might well be applied to the confusing series of events which were about to take place.

In 1759, the year after St. Luc took over his post at La Pointe, General James Wolfe captured Quebec. Montreal fell to General Jeffrey Amherst in 1760, but it was not until 1762 that all of the details of surrender had been arranged and that the former vast territory of the French came into British hands. Even then, the ministers of Louis XV were trying to find some method by which New France might be restored to the crown. The Indians, too, were not reconciled to the change.[1] The Ojibway, in particular, were hostile to the English, and on June 4, 1763, they captured the British fort at Mackinac and killed or abused the entire garrison. They accomplished this under the guise of staging a la-crosse game outside the gates of the fort. The garrison, relaxing its vigilance, in watching the game, paid but little attention when the la-crosse ball, in an apparently accidental manner, was thrown over the palisades, and the players stormed after it through the open gates. When they were inside, they produced their tomahawks and overcame the military.[2]

Also during these years, Pontiac, an Ottawa, conspired with the western tribes to push back the westward march of the English colonists.

[1] Kellogg, *The British Regime in Wisconsin and the Northwest*, (Madison, 1935), 25. The treaty was signed February 10, 1763, but virtually all details had been agreed upon in 1762.

[2] Alexander Henry, Ibid, 86–87.

The original Mackinac was located at Pointe St. Ignace, on the north side of the Straits of Mackinac. From 1712 until 1781 it was on the south side near modern Mackinaw City. In 1781, Governor Sinclair moved his British garrison to Mackinac Island. Thus the massacre occurred on the southern mainland. Milo M. Quaife, Editor, Alexander Henry, Ibid, footnote page 37.

There was, too, the alleged plot of Major Robert Rogers of Rogers' Rangers fame, to make war against the English. This created considerable turmoil at Mackinac, and although Rogers was acquitted before a court martial there in 1768, many still believed that he was guilty of the plan to form an Indian empire, of which he could be the head.

With all these shifting tides of human relations, it was not until 1765 that trade was resumed on Lake Superior. In this year, which marked the passage of the Stamp Act by the British Parliament, and the fury of the American colonists' reaction to it, an English subject from the Colony of New Jersey, named Alexander Henry, secured the concession on Lake Superior.

Henry had been a trader who had followed General Amherst's army on its expedition against Montreal. One might judge, from his written account, that Henry made such a nuisance of himself before the military governor of Montreal, General Thomas Gage, in requesting permission to trade in the old French territories, that the General finally granted it in order to get rid of him.

With considerable foresight, Henry had been preparing himself for his future ventures by trading, on a small scale, in and about Mackinac and the Sault. In these years he had made the acquaintance of Jean Baptiste Cadotte who had acted as an interpreter for the French at the Sault. He was the son of a Frenchman named Cadeau who had come to the Sault in 1671 with Sieur Daumont de St. Lusson, and had married the daughter of an Ojibway.[3]

The son, in turn, had married into the tribe.[4] The canny Henry, appreciating the high regard in which Cadotte was held by both Indians and French-Canadians, enlisted his services by taking him in as a partner, a relationship which would endure for many years.

The concession which Henry secured gave him exclusive trading rights on Lake Superior for three years. He immediately negotiated for a stock of goods at Mackinac on a twelve-month credit basis, and set out on July 26, 1765 for Chequamegon Bay. His cargo, carried in four canoes, weighed five tons, and he hired his crew of French voyageurs at the rate of one hundred pounds of beaver skins per year per man, plus found.[5]

[3] J. Fletcher Williams, "Memoir of William W. Warren," *Minnesota Historical Collections*, (St. Paul, 1885), 5:10. Also Kellogg, *Early Narratives*, Ibid, 6.

[4] Parish Register at Mackinac. This not only records the marriage but also shows that the birth of their two and one-half months-old daughter, Marie Renee, was legitimatized. The marriage occurred October 28, 1756. In addition to the daughter, two sons, Jean Baptiste, Jr. and Michel had been born to the couple in 1761 and 1764, respectively.

[5] The 'found' was the standard ration, adopted by the French traders many years before and existing well into the 1830s. It comprised one bushel of corn and two

Henry's canoes were thirty-six feet long, four and one-half feet wide, and each capable of carrying four tons, including the weight of the eight-man crew.

En route to Chequamegon he met a body of about fifty Indians who were suffering from near-starvation. He persuaded them to accompany him to assist in trapping during the ensuing winter. He issued them goods on credit with the necessary rations. Upon his arrival at Chequamegon, he found an Indian village of fifty lodges. Here, too, the natives were in precarious circumstances, and he made the same sort of agreement with them.

The crew of voyageurs set to work, building a cabin for him, quarters for themselves, and making preparations for the coming winter. The Indians set out on their hunting and trapping expeditions. During the winter he and his companions subsisted almost entirely on fish, caught through the ice.[6] Here, as he had previously learned at Mackinac, the most reliable diet, from the standpoint of health, was the whitefish.

In the spring of 1766, awaiting the return of his Indian hunters, he put up a supply of maple sugar, a procedure he had learned at the Sault. The ice in Chequamegon Bay broke up on April 20, and his hunters returned on May 15 with fifty canoes, all well laden with furs. In fact, they brought more than he could pay for, and after he had settled accounts which netted him fifteen hundred beaver, and two hundred fifty otter and martin, he set out for Mackinac. He was accompanied by fifty Indian canoes which carried an additional thousand beaver skins. En route he stopped at the Ontonagon River where, through the intercession of Cadotte who allayed the superstitious fears of the Indians, he was allowed to inspect the Ontonagon boulder. He reported that he had hacked off a piece of the copper with his axe.

Despite his apparent success at Chequamegon, Henry had greater plans in mind. These, for the most part, did not include La Pointe or Chequamegon, and so are not included in this story. However, his later activities and successes, while not responsible for the founding of the North West Company, probably encouraged the formation of that company which later played a part in the rejuvenation of La Pointe.

In the meantime, the hostility of the voyageurs and Ojibway toward

pounds of fat per man per month. The corn had been leached into a sort of hominy which had been washed and dried, so that it resembled rice in appearance. The fat was generally tallow although, at times, salt pork, beaver fat or bears' grease was substituted. When the daily ration was doled out, the crew put it into a kettle, added water and any fish or game available, and boiled the concoction over a fire. (Author's note.)

[6] Henry described the method used in threading the nets under the ice. It is interesting to note that exactly the same scheme is used today in that region. (Author's note.)

the English still existed. With the exception of Henry, who was more or less under the protective wing of Cadotte, these voyageurs and Indians did all in their power to resist the advancing British traders. Thinking that the old Middle Fort on Madeline Island might serve as a focal point for armed resistance, the English dispatched a detachment of soldiers there in 1765, with orders to destroy the former French post. This was accomplished.[7]

With this action on the part of the British, and Henry's interest centered in other directions, any trade which might have been conducted, with La Pointe as a base, was probably minor in character. There is some hearsay evidence that at least one trader was stationed there, but Jean Baptiste Perrault recorded: "We reached there [La Pointe]on the 1st of november [1784], all saints day, about noon. Messrs. Laviollet, Caillarge, and Graverot were wintering there. Everyone was drunk, as it was a fete." Again, he wrote: "We set out the next day [June 16, 1785, from the Bois Brule River], and we made a good day's journey. We camped a la petite pêche [fishing ground] on this side of la pointe. — We left that place [petite pêche], and made la pointe where le gros pied and his family helped us out."[8] It is difficult to imagine that the locale lay fallow after the French concept of its importance and the later English and American exploitation of it. Thus Perrault's account would indicate that there was some activity there before the advent of the British.

By 1768, Grand Portage was assuming prestige through its access to the great Northwest. It was possible to proceed from there, via the Pigeon River and a whole series of lakes and streams, with their respective portages, to the Pacific Coast.[9] This allowed the traders to tap an immense territory.

Also, in that year, Henry's franchise expired, leaving the Superior country open to other traders. The latter were not slow in moving in, many of them adopting the same scheme which he found so successful: that of taking a French-Ojibway as a partner.

[7] *Wisconsin Historical Collections*, 8:224–226.

[8] Jean Baptiste Perrault, "Narrative of the Travels and Adventures of a Merchant Voyageur etc.," *Collections of the Michigan Pioneer and Historical Society*, (Lansing, 1909–10), Edited by J. Sharpless Fox, 37:518, 535. There seems to be no record of the identity of le gros pied. La petite pêche might have been present Siskiwit Bay, a popular fishing ground of the Indians. (Author's note.)

There is a record of a Joseph Laviolette who was in charge of two canoes and twelve men for Pierre Gaultier de Varennes de Verendrye in 1743. Innis, *The Fur Trade in Canada*, Ibid 100. Also, a Beaubien and a Laviolette came into the Red River from the south in 1794. Ibid, 258. Whether the 'Laviollet' mentioned by Perrault was either of the above, or a relative, is not known. (Author's note.)

[9] Nute, *Lake Superior*, Ibid, 305.

So the trade boomed in spite of the 1773 Boston Tea Party and its portent of war. The declaration of hostilities in 1775 had little immediate effect on the fur trade. In the midst of the fighting, independent traders realized that there was unnecessary competition and duplication of facilities. They therefore organized a type of cartel in order to reach a concerted agreement about prices.

This association had the financial backing of a number of Montreal Scotsmen. These men, viewing with some jealousy the success of their ancestral enemies in the English Hudson's Bay Company, saw an opportunity to harass that organization and, at the same time, to feather their own nests. Thus, in 1779, the North West Company was formed, but Henry did not enter it at this time as one of the partners, since he seemed to prefer his independent status. That he worked in close harmony with the company appears fairly evident, for he had spent his first winter at Cumberland House on the Saskatchewan with the Frobisher brothers, Benjamin and Joseph, who, with Simon McTavish, were the acknowledged heads of the association.[10]

The company, including the majority of the more powerful former independents, was now in a position to present an united front against the older Hudson's Bay Company. Though never incorporated, the new combine maintained a vigorous existence throughout its entire lifetime and built up a remarkable esprit de corps among its personnel.

In about the year 1782 there was at least a recorded stir of life in the La Pointe neighborhood, although it would require another decade to nurse it into any virility at La Pointe proper. At this time, Michel Cadotte, Jean Baptiste's younger son, arrived in the region as factor for the Henry- Jean B. Cadotte partnership.[11] It is probable that he spent little or no time on Madeline Island. The French Middle Fort had been destroyed, and the Indians still shunned the legendary ghosts of their ancestors' children.

However, there were villages of Ojibway at Lac du Flambeau and at Lac Court Oreilles, and he spent virtually all of his time at or near these places. Since there was no object in using La Pointe as a gathering place for his furs, this function was probably performed at Montreal River. This was the lake end of the old Flambeau trail, and was accessible by trail and canoe from Lac Court Oreilles.

If the period between the fall of New France and the end of the Revolutionary War could be called confused, the following one, lasting nearly thirty years, might be termed chaotic. Upon the signing of peace,

[10] W. Stewart Wallace, *Documents Pertaining to the North West Company,* (Toronto, Champlain Society, 1935), XXII:4.
[11] Warren, Ibid, 5:111.

the new boundary lines between the United States and Canada were not immediately settled. There were no restrictions about who should trade where, and the North West Company operated very much where it pleased, including in the United States.

The whole northwest situation was fluid. The Indians had come to respect the English as they previously had the French, and resented the victorious Americans, their Kitchimokoman or Long Knives. The English bribed the Indians to maintain this hostility. They supported the wide Indian uprising which required an American military expedition under General Anthony Wayne to suppress. In an effort to retain their influence and power in the Northwest, they tried to persuade the Americans to form an Indian buffer state, comprising all territory to the west and northwest of Lake Michigan. Fortunately for the Americans, they did not fall into this trap.[11A]

In about 1787 or shortly thereafter, the Henry-Cadotte partnership was absorbed by the North West Company, and at that time Henry became a full-fledged Nor'wester. This ended Henry's active participation in the fur trade, and he remained a more or less silent partner in the company.[11B] This combination resulted in Michel Cadotte's being brought into the North West Company, and serving it as a factor in the upper Wisconsin area.

The year 1791 supplied some knowledge about La Pointe; the seed still lay dormant but received a little sunlight and mulching. It ushered in a Scotch-Irishman by the name of John Johnston who not only provided an historical character of interest, but also, through his published reminiscences, furnished minutiae concerning topography and events of the times.

Johnston had been born in Craige, Antrim County, Ireland in 1762. Finding his family's financial condition in precarious circumstances, he decided to seek his fortune in Canada. He arrived in Montreal with excellent letters of recommendation which he presented to the managing directors of the North West Company. They suggested that the old La Pointe location, vacant at the time, might be profitable for him.

Johnston's reminiscences concerning his trip to La Pointe are most revealing. He went into rhapsodies over the Pictured Rocks near present Munising, Michigan, the metallic-appearing formations of the Keweenaw Peninsula where magnetic ore stopped his watch, and the heavy stands of timber which reached the water's edge as he approached La Pointe.[12]

[11A] Kellogg, *The British Regime*, Ibid, 216.
[11B] Wallace, Ibid, 84, 456.
[12] Louis R. Masson, "Mr. John Johnston — An Account of Lake Superior 1792–1807," *Les Bourgeois de la Compagnie du Nord-Ouest*, (Quebec, 1890), 2:138–168.

He named the island on which La Pointe was located Montreal. He also introduced a new name for not only the sand beach near Fish Creek, at the foot of Chequamegon Bay, but also the entire Bayfield Peninsula. He called the whole locale Netoungan. There is a possibility that he confused this name with the old Indian one, Nantouagon – present-day Ontonagon.

He arrived on Madeline Island in the fall of 1791 with a number of voyageurs and a supply of trade goods. His initiation there was rather grim. He encountered some French-Canadian trappers who were definitely hostile to him and his venture.[13] These men induced his voyageurs to desert him, and with their departure they took all of his food supplies and some of his trade goods. His later experiences he likened to those of Robinson Crusoe, even with a parallel Friday who had refused to desert him. He described the construction of a log cabin and his struggle for food. However, there is no information as to where he placed his cabin, except that it was near the south end of the island, and probably on or near present Grant's Point.

While at La Pointe, Johnston fell in love with Shagowashcodawaqua – The Woman of the Green Glades – the daughter of Waubojeeg, Chief White Fisher.[14] Upon asking the chief for her hand, he received the reply that Waubojeeg, like Laban, thought Johnston should wait, for the patriarch had seen too many white men take Indian women for wives and then desert them. Business required Johnston to return to Montreal in 1792, and the chief thought that if he were in earnest he would return. He did come back in the spring of 1793, and unlike Jacob did not have to wait for seven years. The marriage took place immediately.

Johnston made a statement which brings up an interesting conjecture to the minds of the curious. He wrote of having ascended an high bluff, which we assume to have been toward the end of the Bayfield Peninsula. From this eminence, he claimed to have seen twenty-six islands; many of them, according to him, never having been visited by the Indians.

It may seem presumptous to question his statement, but it would appear most unlikely that he could have counted even the present twenty-three islands from any one height on the mainland. Even from the modern fire tower, northwest of Bayfield, which commands an excellent view of many of the islands, it will be discovered that Oak Island, near the peninsula, is so high that it screens out a number of the outlying

[13] The presence of trappers on the island at that time would further confirm its use by free lance traders. (Author's note.)

[14] Another spelling of the girl's name is Ozhawguscodaywayquay. Osborn and Osborn, *Schoolcraft-Longfellow-Hiawatha*, (Lancaster, Pa., 1942), 91. (The author opines that with this formidable name the girl might have been very glad to have changed it.) Waubojeeg belonged to the Reindeer clan. Warren, ibid, 5:52.

islands. However, he might have traveled among them, or have taken the word of an Indian guide.

In Johnston's time there was no Long Island, but there was at least one other, no longer in existence, known as Steamboat.[15] This would leave twenty-three as we know them today. In the area bounded by Devil's, Bear, York and Sand Islands, there are Bear, York and Sand Island Shoals. Map 18. These are covered with sixteen feet of water, on the average. From the experience of Steamboat Island, which today is reduced to shoals under ten feet of water, one might assume that the above three could have been islands in Johnston's time. It is to be regretted that Mr. Brule did not take aerial photographs at the time of his possible visit.

Johnston mentioned something which should whet the appetites of the modern lake troller. He recorded that lake trout, weighing up to fifty-two pounds, were taken off the northeast end of Madeline Island. He claimed that they were, "Just as good as the ones caught off Mackinac Island." Lake Superior enthusiasts would assert that this comparison was distinctly odious.

Johnston's stay at La Pointe was of short duration. In 1793 he settled at the Sault where he raised a family of four sons and four daughters.[16] Here, maintaining his status as an independent trader, he achieved considerable success until 1814, when a band of American raiders visited the Sault, to burn his home and his extensive warehouses. This not only caused him serious financial loss but also seemed to discourage him in his later undertakings. He died at the Sault in 1828.

During these times, another bit of romance occurred which resulted in the naming of Madeline Island. In making his rounds in the Chequamegon region, Michel Cadotte met Equaysayway — Traveling Woman — the daughter of Waubijejauk, Chief White Crane. The chief's home was on the mainland near present Bayfield. Equaysayway yielded to the suit of Cadotte, but since there was no priest in the locality, they journeyed to the Sault to be married. The princess was baptized there, and was given the name of Madeleine. After the marriage, they returned to La Pointe, and upon their arrival Chief White Crane decreed that thenceforth the island should be called by her new name. A later attempt was made by Henry Rowe Schoolcraft to change this to Virginia Island, but the French name persisted.[17]

[15] U. S. Lake Survey Office, *Bulletins of the Great Lakes,* (Detroit, 1903 and 1904), Bulletins Nos. 13 and 14.

[16] Osborn and Osborn, Ibid, 96–97.

[17] J. Fletcher Williams, Ibid 5:11. Since the Crane Clan was considered the highest in the Ojibway clan system, Waubijejauk's decree bore great weight. Warren, Ibid, 47, 48, 88.

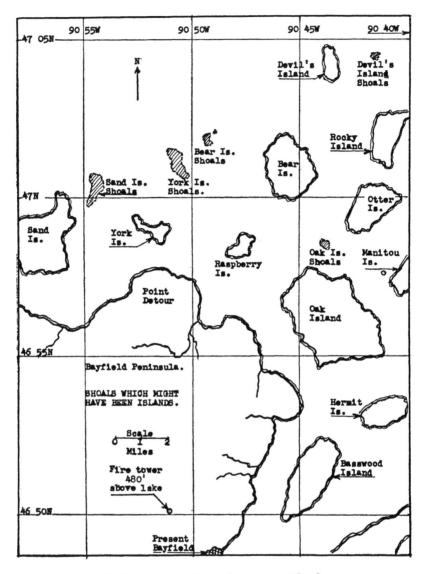

18. Shoals Which Might Have Been Islands.

In 1793, Michel was put in charge of trading at La Pointe by the North West Company, re-sprouting the seed of habitation, and opening a new era of which there would be a continuous record, more or less complete, up to modern times. For the company's post, Cadotte chose a site on the south end of Madeline Island, a short distance east of the original French fort built by Le Sueur in 1693. Map 19. Plate 6. Also from that time until his death, the island would be his home.[18]

In addition to the complications incident to the transfer of territory after the Revolutionary War, conditions in the fur trade became more confused by the developing opposition of two competitors of the North West Company. These two did not appear at La Pointe, but their effects were felt there as much as at other North West posts. Before 1796, the two had not encroached too seriously on the North West's preserves, but with the Americans moving into Mackinac and Detroit in that year, and putting into effect the heavy import duties on trade goods destined for foreign fur companies operating within the United States, the two had no place to turn except toward the Northwest.[18A]

In about 1797, this competition became serious to North West from Forsyth, Richardson and Company, a subsidiary of Phyn, Ellice and Company of London, and from Parker, Gerrard and Ogilvy, both competitors from Montreal. On October 28, 1798, Forsyth, Richardson and Company joined forces with the Detroit firm of Leith, Jamieson and Company, to call themselves, rather brazenly, The New North West Company.

For one or two years, a triangular struggle went on in the Northwest, but in 1800, a union was effected between the New North West and John Ogilvy with John Mure of Quebec, which became known as the XY Company. In 1802, the New North West (and/or XY) Company received the re-enforcement of Sir Alexander Mackenzie. Mackenzie had withdrawn from the original North West Company in 1799, disgruntled with its management. He reorganized the combine under still another name, i.e., Sir Alexander Mackenzie and Company.[18B]

This new Mackenzie company vigorously sought sites in the Northwest, and frequently built stations near those of the older company. Here, it offered the Indians more for their pelts in the way of trade

---

[18] Thwaites, "The Story of Chequamegon Bay," Ibid, 415–416. *Michel Cadotte's Account Book, 1793–1823,* Privately held. Photostat copy with Bishop Baraga Association, Marquette, Michigan. This book has an entry dated May 11, 1793, showing the list of trade goods with which Cadotte started at La Pointe. The list is typical of the times, and its total value amounted to six shillings over eleven hundred pounds, Sterling.

[18A] Wallace, Ibid, 16, 17.

[18B] Ibid, 18.

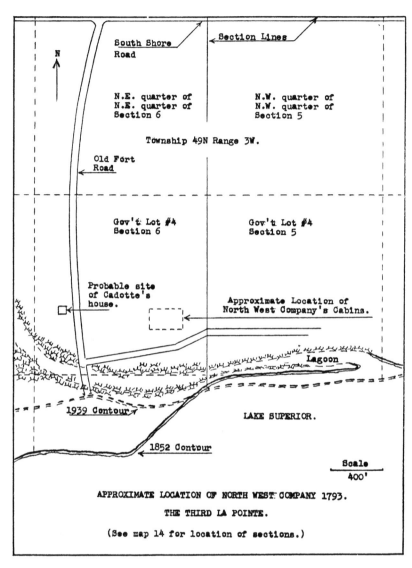

19. Approximate Location of North West Company.

goods. At the same time, it cut prices in the sales market to almost ruinous levels. Finally, in 1804, seeing that it was accomplishing nothing but its own ruin, the XY Company arranged a merger with North West, and the two thenceforth conducted their affairs under the name of the older company. The merger, in effect, was really a rather harsh absorption of the XY Company by North West. Mackenzie took North West shares in the transaction, but "was excluded from any interference." [19]

Other factors tended to confuse matters. England and France were engaged in the Napoleonic Wars. English merchant ships, carrying furs, were seized by the French. The North West Company, to avoid this loss, had its shipments carried in American bottoms, consigned by John Jacob Astor to English ports. Because the United States was considered a neutral ally by France, her ships were able to reach England without molestation. We thus see an early trend of events which would lead Astor into the La Pointe region. [20]

In the decade 1796 to 1806, American traders were pushing further and further into territory of the United States which the North West Company had previously exploited. In an effort to protect its own traders, the United States enacted stiff tariff laws on all foreign goods entering the country. Thus, the North West Company was subjected to taxes to which its American competitors were not. Since North West's chief port of entry into the United States was at Mackinac, the company re-routed its imports through the Canadian Sault, allowing goods destined for Lake Superior ports to enter duty free. However, imports for Green Bay, still a most important fur outlet, were subject to the taxes.

In 1806, the Michilimackinac Company was organized. [21] It would appear that the only reason for its corporate existence was its sub rosa intention of smuggling goods past the United States' ports of entry. On the day of its official incorporation, it contracted with North West to take over all of the latter's posts east of the Mississippi, except the one at Fond du Lac (Duluth). Thus, La Pointe fell under the jurisdiction of a new company, but the old personnel remained the same, under Michel Cadotte. The smuggling operations were carried on under the supervision of a Robert Dickson, and none, to this day, knows how he accomplished them. In a short time the Americans became aware of this subterfuge, but did not learn the method. They therefore not only

---

[19] Wallace, Ibid, 19, 20, 474–5.

Kellogg, Ibid, 239.

[20] Ibid, 265–268.

[21] Ibid, 259–260. (The company's name was pronounced Mish-il'-e-mack'-e-nah, with a slightly nasal nah, and in the Ojibway it meant The Great Turtle. Mackinac and Mackinaw were both derived from the longer native word, and both should have the native pronunciation of the last syllable.) (Author's note.) Baraga, Ibid, 300.

tightened up their inspections at ports of entry, but also intercepted Michilimackinac's ships and smaller craft.[22]

In another effort to evade the United States' taxes, a new device, which was a close parallel to some modern ones, was attempted, with the connivance of Astor. In 1808, Astor had organized his American Fur Company and had received a charter from the State of New York to operate for twenty-five years. With Astor as a partner, another new company came into existence in 1811. The other partners were the ones in the North West and Michilimackinac Companies. The new South West Company took over all of the Michilimackinac's properties and, with Astor to 'front' for it, as an American citizen, was able to retain the American posts and to escape the onerous taxes.[23]

The South West Company proved disappointing to Astor, for his connection with it was severed owing to the declaration of war between the United States and England in 1812. The situation was further disturbed by Tecumseh, the Shawnee chief, who initiated another Indian uprising. The American fort at Mackinac fell to the British a few weeks after war was declared, and all furs and trade goods could pass through that center without United States intervention. It also left La Pointe under the control of the English and the new South West Company. The 1812 and 1813 trade was excellent, but Astor failed to receive his share of the profits, and even later did not recover directly from the company.

The war ended in 1815, and Astor, to insure himself against the repetition of such an occurrence, persuaded the United States Congress to enact a law, reserving to American citizens only, the privilege of taking furs within its boundaries. This was the death knell of the North West Company and its dummy subsidiaries insofar as trading within the United States was concerned. Astor was then able to purchase the South West's holdings in the United States at a very low price, thus offsetting, to some extent, his previous losses in that company. He lost no time in moving in on the already established posts, and 1816 found him in possession of the one at La Pointe, with Michel Cadotte as its factor.

Until the advent of the American Fur Company, contemporary records had not revealed North West's location on Madeline Island. It has since been discovered that the new company occupied the same site as the older one.[24] In Lieutenant Henry Wolsey Bayfield's survey of 1823–25, the location of the American Fur Company is shown on his

---

[22] *Wisconsin Historical Collections*, 19:342.
[23] Kellogg, Ibid, 267.
[24] Thwaites, "The Story of Chequamegon Bay," Ibid, 13:416.

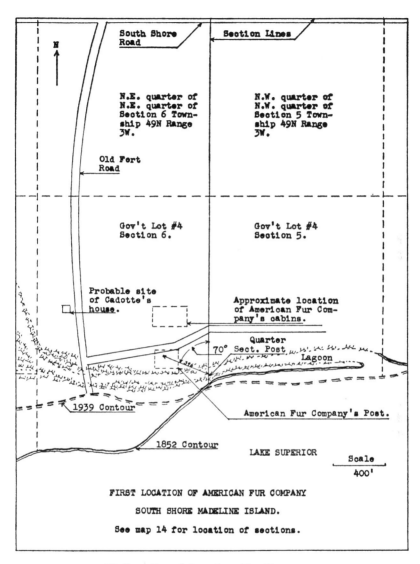

FIRST LOCATION OF AMERICAN FUR COMPANY

SOUTH SHORE MADELINE ISLAND.

See map 14 for location of sections.

20. Location of American Fur Company.

map. Also, by means of the United States Government survey of 1852, the exact location in respect to section lines is determined. Map 20.[25]

This change in ownership terminated Michel Cadotte's association with the North West Company and his former connection with the Alexander Henry-Jean Baptiste Cadotte partnership. But it is possible that another contact existed through Henry. The La Pointe Catholic Church baptismal records show that a Jean Baptiste Henry, Junior, was born to Jean Baptiste Henry and Theresa Kebeweke Henry on August 25, 1840. Did Alexander Henry leave behind some 'bois brules?'

[25] According to the field notes of Government surveyor Elisha Norris, dated September 10–12, 1852, the center of the American Fur Company's location was north, seventy degrees west, at a distance of six chains (396 feet) from the quarter section corner between sections five and six, Township 49 North, Range 3 West, in Government lot #4 of section six. A certified copy of these notes is on file in the City Engineer's Office, Ashland, Wisconsin. This would bring the site toward the northeast corner of the present (1957) Miss Arlene Richmond property. The same notes record that in 1852 there were eight or more cabins nearby, occupied by as many families.

There is no record to prove the exact location of Michel Cadotte's house. However, the Jean Baptiste Cadotte of the early 1900s said that it was located as shown on Plate 6, taken in 1897 by Dr. James S. Reeve of Appleton, Wisconsin. Since this Cadotte was born seven years before the death of his grandfather, Michel, his statement should be regarded as conclusive. The author personally knew this Jean Baptiste Cadotte who died in 1913 at the age of eighty-three years. (Author's note.)

CHAPTER FIVE

1817 I Go A-Fishing 1842

With the problems of the two wars apparently settled between the United States and England, there followed a long period in which the affairs at La Pointe closely followed those of the rapidly expanding country. The principal difference was that while the people of the eastern states had exploited the natural resources of that area, and then moved westward to others, the inhabitants of La Pointe remained to develop their local wealth before moving on to greener pastures.

In 1818, two New England brothers arrived to trade in the Lac du Flambeau and Lac Court Oreilles districts. They brought with them an heritage of education and patriotism which would have a considerable influence on the trade and culture of La Pointe. They were Truman Abraham Warren and Lyman Marcus Warren, descendants of a Mayflower ancestry, and relatives of Colonel Joseph Warren who had been killed at Bunker Hill. They came as independent traders and as competitors of the American Fur Company, selling their furs to the North West Company. With their Yankee background, they soon became successful in their ventures and won the respect of the Indians through their fairness and honesty.

In due course, they were recognized by the American Fur Company and hired as competent traders. As such, they moved to La Pointe where they became attracted to two of Michel Cadotte's daughters. In 1821, Truman married Charlotte, aged sixteen, while Lyman wed Marie who was twenty-one. The year of their marriages also marked the acquisition of the North West Company by the Hudson's Bay Company, leaving the older organization in full control of the Canadian fur trade.

The success which the Warren brothers had in their trade, in combination with the close family ties and the esteem which they had earned in the eyes of their father-in-law, enabled them, in 1823, to purchase Michel Cadotte's interest in the La Pointe post. Since Astor had continued with Cadotte the rather loose business arrangement instituted by the North West Company, it was natural for Astor to appoint the Warren brothers as his La Pointe agents. There is no confirmation as to which brother would be the chief factor, but that mantle seemed to have fallen on Lyman Warren, and he took charge in 1824. The little village was still at its location on the south side of the island, not yet having been moved to its present site.[1]

With the expanding business of the fur company, the facilities there were becoming inadequate. A sand bar, about one hundred yards off shore, prevented the larger vessels, then coming into use, from approaching the warehouses. Any pier built out to clear this bar would be exposed to northeast storms which at this point have a sweep of about three hundred miles across the lake. At such times no vessel could be docked.

The settlement, too was growing, necessitating larger stores for trading purposes. These factors increased the labor of lightering-in supplies from the off-shore vessels. The Warrens began to cast about for a better harbor, but even then the canny foresight of Astor was evident, in not desiring to add to his investment by such a move. He had begun to realize that the neighboring territory was being stripped of fur bearing animals, and that it would only be a matter of a few years before La Pointe would become a secondary post with little or no business. The factory, therefore, remained at the old site, even though the local partners had to labor under difficulties.

The Warrens, with growing families and a sense of some civic responsibility, realized the need of education for their own children

---

[1] The location of the post is shown on the map of Lieutenant Henry Wolsey Bayfield who made a complete survey of Lake Superior in the years 1823 to 1825. Bayfield was an officer in the British navy, and his survey was a monumental piece of work. This performance, no doubt, was a factor in his later promotion to Admiral. The present (1957) Canadian charts are still based on his work, and some of the United States maps, as late as 1907, acknowledged his fundamental labors. The United States did not complete its own survey until shortly before the Civil War, when it was done by General George Gordon Meade. Meade was reported to have said that Bayfield's survey was the greatest piece of work ever performed; it was done in the quickest time and his charts were the most correct ever made up to that time.

The author met a sportsman sailor in 1955 in the approaches to Nipigon Bay, who held a master's license for Lake Superior. This man, for many years, in his sailboat, had prowled the nearby islands where reefs, submerged rock pinnacles and tortuous channels were a navigator's nightmare. He took pride in his piloting prowess and stated that he had yet to discover an error in Bayfield's work.

The authority to survey United States' waters was given Bayfield by a special treaty between this country and England. (Author's note.)

and those in the enlarging village. Through correspondence with the American Board of Commissioners for Foreign Missions, in Boston, Lyman Warren convinced that body of the need for both teachers and missionaries at La Pointe.[2]

In consequence, the Reverend Mr. Jedediah D. Stevens of Peterboro, New York was dispatched to establish a school. He and his wife left their home on June 13, 1827, bound for their great adventure in the wild Northwest; a region reported to be filled with both savage Indians and wilder beasts. Upon their arrival at Mackinac, where a Presbyterian Mission had been established, the Reverend Mr. William Ferry persuaded them to remain as his assistants, on the ground that La Pointe was not yet ready for their services. They therefore did not reach La Pointe.[3]

At a later date, on one of his frequent trips to Mackinac, Warren became acquainted with Frederick Ayer, one of the lay teachers at the mission school, and persuaded him to come to La Pointe. At the same time, he renewed his appeals to the American Board for founding a real mission on Madeline Island.

In 1830, Ayer came to La Pointe to conduct the Warren's school.[4] During the following year, after the favorable decision of the Board, the Reverend Mr. Sherman Hall, a Presbyterian, arrived to start the mission and its allied school. With him came his wife and Mrs. John Campbell, who was to act as interpreter. Mrs. Campbell was a full-blooded Ojibway who had married a trader at the Sault. She left her husband and nine children and came with the Halls with an infant in arms.[5]

From Hall's journal, the church records which he kept, the letters which he wrote to his family in Vermont and his reports to the American Board, a fund of information can be drawn concerning La Pointe in his day. He and his party left Mackinac with five batteaux, in which seventy people took passage. At the Sault, they were joined by another

[2] "Relations to Ecclesiastical Bodies," *Memorial Volume of the First Fifty Years of the American Board of Commissioners for Foreign Missions*, Fourth Edition, (Boston, 1861), Published by the Board, Missionary House, Pemberton Square. 89. This organization was under the joint supervision of the denominations which the above describes as follows: "Of the present members, one hundred and five are Congregationalists, eighty-one are Presbyterians connected with the New School Church, seventeen are Presbyterians connected with the Old School Church, nine are members of the Protestant Reformed Dutch Church, and two belong to the Reformed German Church."

[3] Jedediah D. Stevens Papers, 1827–1876. Originals in Minnesota Historical Society. #A S844.

[4] Thwaites, "The Story of Chequamegon Bay," Ibid, 13:418.

[5] Sherman Hall Papers, 1833–1840. Copy in Minnesota Historical Society. #A H179.

convoy, so that the little fleet numbered fourteen batteaux. His description of this mode of transportation might make the modern traveler shiver. He recorded, ". . . upon articles of lading, with which each boat is filled, is the place for passengers, who have not other seats than they can form for themselves, out of traveling trunks, boxes, beds, etc." In this 'luxury,' rowed by six men, they started on their four-hundred-mile trip.

En route, Hall wrote to his father in Vermont under date of August 22, 1831, in part: "The persons employed by the traders as boatmen and laborers are mostly Canadian French. . . . They are generally Catholics, and have no fear of God before their eyes. They may be as wicked as they choose; the priest can pardon all their sins when they go to Mackinac next year. He will do it, if they pay him a few shillings. I have more fears that the Catholics will cause us difficulties, than the Indians will."

Again, concerning his arrival at La Pointe, he recorded: "August 30th. [1831] After sailing thirty leagues [ninety miles] in a day and a half, we arrived at La Pointe, the place of our destination, about noon today, all heartily glad to find a resting place and a shelter from the storm and cold. We were agreeably disappointed on finding the place so much more pleasant than we had anticipated. As we approached it, it appeared like a small village. There are several houses, stores, barns and outbuildings about the establishment, and forty or fifty acres of land under cultivation."

Upon their arrival, they were greeted warmly by Lyman Warren, who took them to his home, where they spent the winter of 1831–32. In fact, it appears that Warren did all in his power to make them comfortable and to ease their initiation into a new land. One of his first acts was to present them with a cow.

Hall wrote that the principal traders at the station were the ". . . two Warrens, Dingley, Oakes, Aitmunn [sic] [possibly either Aitken or Ashmunn], Holiday and Butterfield."[6] He lost little time in organizing a school, and by January 9, 1832 reported that he had an attendance of "15 or 20 under instruction."

On April 1, 1832, the Hall's daughter, Harriet Parker Hall, was born. She is believed to have been the first child of pure white parentage born on Lake Superior, west of the Sault. The Indians were much intrigued at seeing their first white baby, and the child was their general favorite. They called her their "Little Ojibwa."

On August 6, 1832, the Reverend Mr. William Thurston Boutwell,

[6] Besides the Warrens, these men were probably Daniel Dingley, Charles H. Oakes, Samuel Ashmunn or William Aitken, John Holiday and Charles Butterfield, all of whose names frequently appear in the records of the American Fur Company.

after his trip with Schoolcraft to the source of the Mississippi, arrived at La Pointe to join Ayer and Hall in their school and to plan with them the proposed new mission building.

Apparently Hall realized his limitations when it came to construction work, for, in addition to consulting with his Boston superiors in regard to the costs of his buildings, he took the tedious trip to Lac du Flambeau to inquire into the best methods of fabricating them.[7]

Until recent years it had been assumed that work on the mission building had commenced in 1832 and had been completed in 1833, consuming about seventeen months.[8] However, Hall letters indicated that the work did not start until 1834, and that he did not move into the nearly completed structure until January or February 1835.[9]

During this launching of the first missionary effort in the region since

The City of Aitkin, Minnesota (misspelled) was named after this trader. (Author's note)

[7] The Flambeau Trail, starting from Lake Superior at the Montreal River, was considered "one of the worst in Wisconsin." For the first twenty-five miles it was not possible to use a canoe. There were one hundred twenty-two "poses" between the lake and Portage Lake. (A pose was where the traveler deposited his pack and rested before going back for another load. The distances between poses varied with the character of the terrain.) The trail led up through the Penokee Range to a country of swamps, windfalls, black flies and mosquitoes. After arriving at the trading post on Lac du Flambeau, a distance of about forty-five miles from Lake Superior, Hall witnessed the old whipsaw method of making boards. In a letter to his brother, dated June 24, 1833, he wrote: "These boards are all made by hand. The log is cut and hewed on two opposite sides to the thickness of 9 inches or a foot. It is then raised to the height of 6 or 7 feet from the ground and rests upon timbers. Lines are then struck as near to each other as the thickness of the board requires, which the saw is made to follow. One man stands upon the sticks to be sawed, and manages one end of a saw 5 or six feet in length, while a second manages the other. — Two men will saw from a dozen to 20 boards per day, which are usually 10 or 12 feet in length."

Also, "The art of brick making has not yet got up so high as this [on Lake Superior]. There is clay here which I suppose might be wrought into bricks. The French, I believe, never built chimneys of stones. They are built in this country almost entirely of clay. The fireplace is made of clay and stones. The stones are generally small and round, something in shape and size of a man's head. They are mixed in with the clay which is wrought into mortar. In this way the chimney is formed as high as the mantletree."

". . . Four poles are [then] placed perpendicularly upon it, each one of which is to form a corner of the chimney. The poles are as long as the chimney is to be in height. Cross sticks are tied to the poles every 12 to 18 inches for a frame work. Straw and clay, mixed thoroughly together, are formed into pieces 4 or 5 inches in diameter and 2 feet long. These are placed upon the cross sticks, bending over them and hanging downward from one to the other. They are applied while soft and pliable, and wrought until they are completely formed into one mass. The sides of the chimney are of considerable thickness and when dried become almost as hard as brick. The hearth is also made of clay. The fireplace and hearth are troublesome always, getting out of repair." Sherman Hall Papers, Ibid.

[8] Thwaites, "The Story of Chequamegon Bay," Ibid, 13:419. John Nelson Davidson, "Missions on Chequamegon Bay." *Wisconsin Historical Collections*, 12:434–452.

[9] Letter from Hall and Boutwell to David Greene, the secretary of the American

the time of Father Marquette, a period of one hundred sixty years, affairs of moment were occurring in the American Fur Company. In 1833, Astor sold his holdings in the fur trade to Ramsay Crooks and a number of the latter's associates who had gained experience under his tutelage.[10]

The only partner in the La Pointe area was Lyman Warren who held ten of the company's one thousand shares, although Charles H. Oakes and Charles William Wulff Borup would acquire interests at a later date. The three men immediately initiated the move to the new site — the present location of the village. There seems to be no record of a definite date when the move was made. It was probably spread over a period of time, beginning in 1835.[11]

Board, in Boston. In part: February 7, 1833. "Missionaries are entirely dependent on Warren [Lyman] for living quarters and school room."
    Letters from Hall to Greene, in part:
    January 20, 1834. "Warren does not think they [the proposed mission buildings] can be built for less than one thousand dollars."
    October 17, 1834. "These buildings have been commenced."
    February 8, 1835. "Our house [the new mission building] was so far completed . . ., that my family had commenced to occupy it. . . . and our school is now removed to our new location."
Papers of the American Board. Copies in Minnesota Historical Society, Number BA 10 A 512.
    On account of having reecived Federal funds for the partial support of the mission and school, Hall was required to make yearly reports showing numbers of teachers, numbers of scholars, amount of disbursements and the value of property on hand. His report, in part, to Secretary of War Lewis Cass, dated October 1, 1834 read as follows:

"Property on hand."

"Neat Cattle	$200.00	
Tools	75.00	
Lumber and *Unfinished*		
Building	600.00	[A]
Total	$875.00"	

[A] Italics by Author.
National Archives. Microfilm copy with Bishop Baraga Association, Marquette, Michigan.
    Hall's letter to Henry R. Schoolcraft, U.S. Indian agent at Mackinac, dated February 3, 1835, in part:
    "We have built for the mission family during the past season, a house, which we now inhabit, though not yet entirely completed. It is situated not far from the ground on which the old French fort stood. [The fort founded by St. Pierre in 1718.] . . . We are about equally distant from the Old Fort [at the south end of the island] and the new [present La Pointe]."
National Archives. Microfilm Ibid.
    [10] It is generally considered that Astor sold his holdings in 1833 but only a general purchase agreement was effected in that year. Even though Crooks was in nominal charge during 1834, Astor still retained his stock until the end of the year. Thus, formal ownership by Crooks and associates did not begin until January 1, 1835.
    Grace Lee Nute, Collator and Editor, "Calendar of the American Fur Company's Papers," *Annual Report of the American Historical Association for the Year 1944*, (Washington, 1945. Government Printing Office), 2:521. 18, items 123 & 124.
    [11] *Calendar*, Ibid, 3:1574, Item 16,582. The map referred to in this Bundles

A dock was built at the new location, present La Pointe, which, either at that time or shortly thereafter, reached out into the bay for a distance of about four hundred feet, approximately one hundred fifty feet longer than the present one, and built in exactly the same place.[12] Some of the inhabitants remained at the Old Fort, but the majority of them moved to the new village. The total population of the Island now numbered about six hundred.[13]

An attempt was made by the local partners to call the new post Fort Ramsay, in honor of Crooks, but while Warren used the name for some time, the old calling persisted. Eventually the newer one was forgotten. The inhabitants referred to it as the New Fort.

Before becoming too deeply immersed in missions and fur companies, it might be well to touch upon the character and life of Ramsay Crooks, the new head of the re-organized American Fur Company. He had been born in Scotland in 1787. Coming to Canada, where he entered the employ of the North West Company, he spent the winter of 1806–1807 with James Aird on the Missouri River under the Michilimackinac Company. He then became associated with John Jacob Astor, probably through the North West-Astor combination of the South West Company. He took the terrible overland trip to Astoria, Oregon, arriving there on May 11, 1812. [14]

He later became Astor's agent in and around Mackinac and the Sault.

of Papers was one drawn by Lyman Warren, showing the location of La Pointe in 1834 at the Old Fort site. Photostat copy in possession of author. The 1835 date for the move is confirmed by the following letters:

February 18, 1835. Crooks to Warren. Discussed men and material in new building operations. 2:32, item 237.

May 6, 1835. Crooks to Warren. Discussed buildings built by Warren at La Pointe. 2:60, item 440.

Aug. 11, 1835. Crooks to Warren. Discussed new establishment at La Pointe. 2:95–96, Item 770.

[12] George Francis Thomas, Pen & Camera Sketches of Old La Pointe, (Milwaukee, 1898), 19. Although Thomas was not noted for his accuracy, we believe, in this instance, that he was correct as to the length of the dock. An old crib is still in existence about one hundred fifty feet beyond the end of the present pier. It is further confirmed by a letter from Borup to Crooks, dated February 24, 1840, in which he stated that by an addition of one hundred feet to the dock, his fish store was four hundred feet long. Calendar, Ibid, 2:776. Item 7734. (The author was acquainted with Thomas.)

[13] This number is an estimate. According to contemporary records, the population shrank to about two hundred during the winter, when the Indians and trappers were absent on their hunting expeditions. Upon the arrival of the first ship in the spring, this number would increase to nearly two thousand. When trading had been completed, there would be an exodus which would leave less than one thousand, but this, in turn, would not be permanent owing to extended fishing trips among the islands. (Author's note.)

[14] Gabriel Franchere, Voyage to the Northwest Coast of America, (Chicago, 1954), Lakeside Press Series, Milo M. Quaife, editor, 113. Also Washington Irving, Astoria, (New York, 1882), Home Library Edition. 2:130, 223, 280, 439.

Here he met and married the mixed-blood daughter of Bernard Pratte who would become a partner in the famous trading company, Pratte, Chouteau & Company of St. Louis.

Although in later years charges of conscienceless monopoly were hurled at him and his company, he was, at heart, a simple and kindly man who, perhaps, understood the Indians and mixed-bloods better than any person of his time. Around the posts of Lake Superior he was called Grandpa by the people who knew full well that both he and his wife had spent hours in New York shopping for toys for their children and books for themselves. One may appreciate, therefore, Warren's desire to name the new settlement Fort Ramsay.

The layout of the new village did not much resemble the present one, principally because the main street ran in a different direction than that of the modern one. It started at Pointe de Froid on the north, paralleled the shore and then joined the present Main Street in the village. Map 21. (Both this map and #22 may be slightly anachronistic. Like Rome, La Pointe was not built in a day.)

Across the street from the dock was an hotel, and to the west of the pier a large warehouse. A tram with light rails connected this with the one on the outer end of the wharf. Small stores and dwellings lined both sides of the street, mainly toward Pointe de Froid. Back of the buildings, on the north side of the highway, were orchards and garden plots which extended as far as the present Catholic Church. Map 22.

East of the pier, and on the north side of the street, was the La Pointe County Court House, built a little later than 1835, and known as Judge Bell's office. The remains of this were visible until about 1929. Between the hotel and the court house was the American Fur Company's office and store.[15] The road toward the Middle and Old Forts also had a number of cabins and small structures.

During the time that Hall was planning his new mission building, and while Warren was preparing to move the village to its new site, a meeting was held to organize the first Protestant Church in Wisconsin.[16] The minutes of that meeting have been preserved, and the original entry read as follows: [17]

[15] This was where Mrs. William ("Gram") Johnson's building now (1957) stands. (Author's note.)

[16] It is true that organization proceedings for the Protestant Church of Stockbridge, Wisconsin, were held at an earlier date, but the meeting took place in the East. (Author's note.)

[17] La Pointe Mission Church Records, 1833–1867. Photostat copy in Minnesota Historical Society. #BA3–2, L 315m.

In a meeting held August 24, 1834, a portion of the minutes read: ". . . A letter was received from the Presbyterian Church of Christ at Mackinaw, recommending to this Church Messrs. F. Ayer and wife, C. W. Borup and wife, L. M.

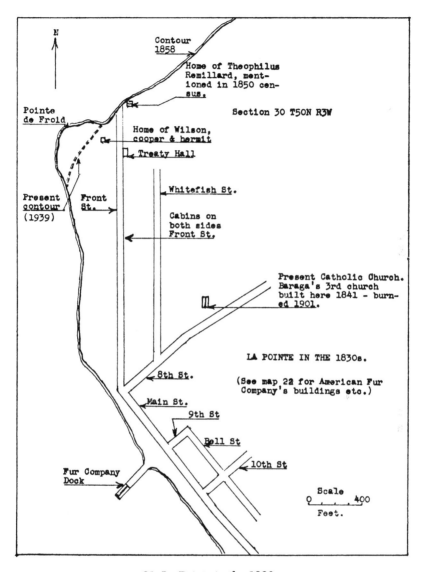

N

Contour
1858

Home of Theophilus
Remillard, ment-
ioned in 1850 cen-
sus.

Section 30 T50N R3W

Pointe
de Froid

Home of Wilson,
cooper & hermit

Treaty Hall

Whitefish St.

Present
contour
(1939)

Front
St.

Cabins on
both sides
Front St.

Present Catholic Church.
Baraga's 3rd church
built here 1841 - burn-
ed 1901.

LA POINTE IN THE 1830s.

(See map 22 for American Fur
Company's buildings etc.)

8th St.

Main St.

9th St

Bell St

10th St

Fur Company
Dock

Scale
0   400

Feet.

21. La Pointe in the 1830s.

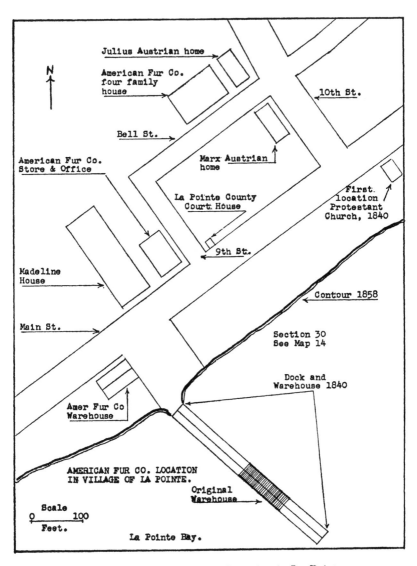

22. American Fur Company Location in La Pointe.

"La Pointe, Lake Superior.
August 20, 1833."

"The re-enforcement of the Chippewa Mission having arrived, and all members present, together with several other professors of religion, it was thought best that a church should be organized before those who are destined to other stations should leave this place; accordingly a meeting was held this evening for this purpose. After appropriate devotional exercises, a confession of faith, and Covenant was read by Mr. Boutwell and formally consented to by the members present. Mr. Lyman Warren was elected Clerk. It was thought inexpedient to elect other officers at this time."

"The individuals present who gave their consent to the confession of faith and Covenant, were Rev. W. T. Boutwell, Rev. S. Hall, Mrs. B. P. [Betsy Parker] Hall, Lyman M. Warren, Edmund F. Ely, C. W. Borup, Mr. John Campbell, Mrs. E. Campbell, Mr. F. Ayer, Misses Delia Cook and Sabrina Stevens."

Boutwell was one of ". . . those who were destined to other stations . . . ," and he left the next day, August 21, 1833, to take up his missionary work at Leech Lake, Minnesota, among the Pillager Indians. In 1834, he left his post long enough to travel to Fond du Lac where, on September 11, he married Hester Crooks, the mixed-blood daughter of Ramsay Crooks. Hall performed the marriage ceremony. Tea and doughnuts were served at the wedding feast. The couple then made its way to his station; the trip, over difficult portages, starting on the St. Louis River, required forty-three days.[18]

In 1834 work was started in earnest on the La Pointe mission building. The superstructure was made of logs, and was sheathed on the exterior with boards sawed out by whipsaw. It is probable that the system used was the same as Hall observed at Lac du Flambeau the year before. This was a variation of the standard manner in which the top sawyer stood on the logs to be sawed and the botton man was stationed in a pit below, but by either scheme he suffered the discomfort of getting sawdust in his eyes.

Warren, J. L. Seymour, Misses Sabrina Stevens, Delia Cook and Josette Pyant, . . ."
Ibid.

In a letter dated August 4, 1835, signed by Boutwell, Hall, Ayer and Ely, to Schoolcraft at Mackinac, the implication is that all four were Presbyterians at the time. *National Archives* —O1A. Microfilm at Bishop Baraga Association, Marquette, Michigan.

From the above, it will be seen that the majority of the church membership was Presbyterian.

[18] William Watts Folwell, *A History of Minnesota*, (St. Paul. 1921), 1:176, as to the doughnuts.

Edward D. Neill, *Macalester College Contributions*, 1892, 2nd Series, #1, 27, As to Hall.

No description of the foundations remains, but it is probable that the same method used in making fireplaces was adapted for the purpose: a mixture of moistened clay and stones, possibly tamped into crude wooden forms. A recent examination of the foundations tends to bear out this theory.

The interior was finished with a rough lattice work for lath, which supported a plaster of clay. Owing to the lack of lime, regular plaster was out of the question, but in later years, when lime was available, the clay was coated with whitewash. The building was fifty-six feet long, twenty-five feet five inches wide, and fifteen feet six inches from the foundations to the eaves. The west end was about sixty feet from the beach, and its gable end faced the lake. Diagram "A" shows the general plan of the first floor, but the arrangement of rooms on both this and the second floors has been altered to such an extent that it is almost impossible to show the original design. The only criticism which one might make of the missionaries' engineering abilities is that while the fireplaces were centrally located under the ridgepole, the chimneys were built at an angle before emerging from the roof.[19]

Hall wrote to his brother that neither lime for mortar nor nails for building were available.[20] Under these handicaps it is surprising that he accomplished what he did. It probably accounts for the appearance of the stern Vermont simplicity of the exterior, although his home environment no doubt had some influence in this respect. That these men built well is proven by the permanence of their handiwork. After twenty years of use, followed by nearly forty-five years of utter neglect, enough of the basic structure remained to warrant its being put into excellent repair. Plate 6A, taken circa 1895, shows the building before part of the roof over the kitchen end had collapsed.

The underlying plan of the whole missionary project was to make La Pointe the headquarters for the entire west end of the lake, with subsidiary stations at Fond du Lac, Leech Lake and other Minnesota points. It fulfilled this scheme for several years until changing conditions made other arrangements necessary.

[19] The measurements were taken in 1951 by the author who had gone through the building in 1897 before it had been rebuilt as a hotel. At the earlier time the building was being used as a cow stable. From memory, the location of the stairs to the second floor is correct, but, as noted on the diagram, the original arrangement of partitions on the first floor is speculative. The fireplace shown at the kitchen end of the dining room may have been in the kitchen, although the author believes that a stove was employed in the latter. The two doors, close together, opening into the dining room on the south side, present somewhat of a puzzle. Was there a partition between them? (Unless, in accordance with the old Yankee tradition, the large one was for the big cat, and the small one for the little.) Possibly the larger door was cut through in later years when the building was being used as a tenement, and a partition installed.

[20] Sherman Hall Papers, Ibid, Letter of June 24, 1833.

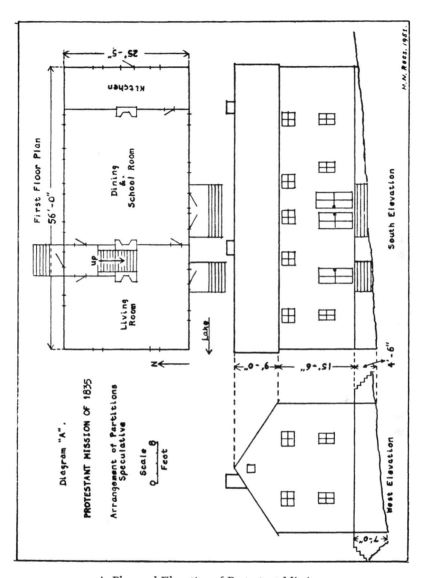

A. Plan and Elevation of Protestant Mission.

85

Under conditions existing at La Pointe, it would appear that the mission directed its efforts more toward school work among the children than at actual conversions among the adults. In 1832 there were one hundred eighty-five Ojibway of pure native stock on the island.[21] Of these, seventy-two were adults and one hundred thirteen were children. It is doubtful if there were more than fifteen whites there at the time. These comprised the missionaries, and the clerks, store keepers and executives of the American Fur Company. The remainder was made up of mixed-bloods, called bois brules, who, for the most part, bore French names, with a minor scattering of English and Scotch ones. In the main, those with the French background had drifted in from the Sault where their religious affiliations had been with the Roman Catholic Church.

The missionaries not only provided a school for the children, but also prepared some of the first books in the Ojibway language, the universal speech of the territory. Among these was the complete New Testament, written in large part by Hall. How many souls were saved by the labors and sacrifices of these men is a moot question. The church records, extending over thirty-four years, reveal only seven or eight mixed-bloods or Indians who joined the church by confession of faith.[22]

In many respects the Protestant missionaries were laboring under almost insurmountable odds. The large majority of the mixed-bloods were of Roman Catholic persuasion. The missionary board, in far-off Boston, had little conception of the problems confronting its representatives. The missionaries came with families, but with no adequate provision for helpers or servants to care for their kinfolk while the men were making the rounds of distant Indian villages. Illness of wives or children prevented the men from devoting their time to mission and school duties. The task of securing firewood alone for the comfort of their people required a tremendous amount of time, especially when one considers that fireplaces were the principal sources of heat.

As opposed to this, the later Catholic priests came to the region with no immediate family ties, which left them free to visit remote stations wihout worry or concern for anyone left behind. In comparing the results obtained by the respective missionaries, the Protestants suffer. This was due almost entirely to the above factors. However, in the matter of conversions, the comparison from a strictly numerical standpoint is not entirely fair. The Protestants required a lengthy prepara-

[21] Henry R. Schoolcraft, *Narrative of an Expedition Through the Upper Mississippi*, (New York, 1834), 220. On this trip, Schoolcraft had been requested by the Government to make a rough census of the Indian population at various centers.

[22] La Pointe Mission Church Records, Ibid.

tion with a final confession of faith. The Catholics of the time were admitted to the church on baptism with practically no preparation.

Moreover, in the case of La Pointe, the rather bleak faith, as revealed by the cold and austere Hall, probably did not appeal to the populace as much as the ritual and pageantry of Catholicism. There was considerable antagonism on the part of the Indians, who could not understand why the white man had so many different sects in the worship of a common Diety, nor why each one claimed the only true course to salvation. In addition, the legends of the natives had perpetuated the respect in which their ancestors had held the Jesuits. To them, any priest represented the ancient Mekatewikwanaie — Black Robes — and immediately commanded their attention and deference.

That some of the men on the ground appreciated this situation is evidenced by several joint letters written to the missionary board in Boston. The one quoted below, when Hall was laboring night and day to complete the translation of the New Testament into the Ojibway language, is typical. The letter, dated March 24, 1835, was signed by Frederick Ayer, Lyman Warren and Edmund F. Ely. Ely was visiting La Pointe from his station at Sandy Lake, Minnesota.

"The eyes of this region are turned toward La Pointe. We feel that the prosperity or adversity of the other stations are linked with its rise or fall — that a vigorous effort must be made to sustain it, and that beyond doubt, were Mr. Ayer to be sent here, under his management, its influence and prosperity would be increased." [23]

About all that can be said is that the Protestant missionaries labored long and mightily, and probably contributed much to the education of their charges. There can be no doubt of their sincerity. There are a number of references in the American Fur Company's papers to the wholesome effect which their work had upon the natives, although Father Otto Skolla, some years later, delivered a rather scathing diatribe against all of the Protestant efforts.[24]

Warren's interest in church and mission affairs did not distract him from the fur company's problems. Both he and the other partners in the company realized, as Astor had, that the territory was beginning to show signs of depletion in furs. Contrary to the old custom of the Indians, who always left a few beaver for propagation, the demands of the European and growing American markets caused the trappers to strip an area.

To offset this lack of income in the La Pointe area, the company made arrangements with the Hudson's Bay Company for the latter to

[23] Papers of the American Board, Ibid.
[24] "Father Skolla's Report on his Indian Mission," *Acta et Dicta*, Catholic Historical Society of St. Paul, Edited by Grace Lee Nute, (St. Paul, 1936), 7: #2, 262.

take fur in what is now the Minnesota Arrowhead country, that portion of the State which lies between the west end of Lake Superior and the Canadian border. At that time, this district was an Indian preserve, and no white settlers were allowed in it. However, the American Fur Company, under the original Astor franchise, was allowed to trade there. Since the company had no posts there and did not wish to go to the expense of establishing new ones, it made the rather extralegal agreement with Hudson's Bay in return for the latter paying a yearly honorarium plus the right for American Fur to fish in English waters.[25]

In 1835, Truman Warren died, a victim of pneumonia contracted from the hardships of a cold and rigorous voyage to the Sault. His family remained at La Pointe under the care and counsel of his brother, Lyman. In the treaty of 1826, the United States had agreed to cede certain sections of land to various Indians and mixed-bloods. In this treaty, sections were allotted to Truman Warren's children by his wife, Charlotte, as well as other sections, to his children by the Indian woman, Ugwadaushee.[26]

In the same year, the Roman Catholic Church, not to be outdone in missionary effort, decided to establish a permanent mission on Madeline Island, and sent Father Baraga there for that purpose. Irenaeus Frederic Baraga had been born in Austria, the son of wealthy and prominent parents of Slovene descent. (Later, Baraga dropped the first name and used only Frederic.) Desiring to enter the priesthood, he renounced the material advantages of his station, and after receiving education at the Royal Gymnasium and the University of Vienna, entered the seminary at Laibach.[27] He took his holy orders at this seminary. He came to the United States under the auspices of the Leopoldine Foundation, an Austrian missionary society. In fact, much of his later work was financed by that society.

He arrived in New York in December, 1830, and was assigned a mission at Arbre Croche (present Harbor Springs), Michigan, in May, 1831. Here he was initiated into the life of a missionary among the Indians, and labored diligently and devotedly, acquiring in the meantime, a remarkable mastery of the Ottawa language.

As early as 1832 Baraga, realizing that the mission at Arbre Croche

[25] Grace Lee Nute, "American Fur Company's Fishing Enterprises on Lake Superior," *Mississippi Valley Historical Review*, Milo M. Quaife, Editor, June 1925–March 1926. XII:488–489. The Hudson's Bay Company paid American Fur three hundred pounds, Sterling, under the agreement. *Calendar*, Ibid, 2:16, Item 109.

[26] Thomas L. McKenney, *Sketches of a Tour to the Lakes*, (Baltimore, 1827), 486.

[27] At this time in Austria, and particularly among the Slovenes, there was a revival of religion bordering on fanaticism. Many wealthy families supported such institutions as the Leopoldine Foundation in almost bounteous fashion. This accounts for the succession of Slovene priests who followed Baraga to this country, to spread the word among the pagans. (Author's note.)

was making excellent progress and that it would not be long before it could dispense with some of its teaching personnel, began to importune his superiors to transfer him to a mission on Lake Superior, preferably at La Pointe. His enthusiasm convinced the officers of the Leopoldine Foundation, and as the months passed by they were possibly somewhat critical of his continued stay at Arbre Croche.

In the meantime, he also was asking his bishop for the transfer. In a letter dated June 25, 1835 to Bishop Frederic Résé of Detroit, he wrote: "The Protestant ministers are so active in deluding the poor Indians of that place [La Pointe] into *damnable errors*; and we Catholics, we defer going to these good children of nature from one summer to the next to instruct them in the eternal truths?! . . . I beg you, Monsignor, to consider that seriously." [28]

It is evident from his letter of two days later (June 27, 1835), that he did not wait for his bishop's formal consent to go to La Pointe. However, there seems to be no record of any great displeasure which the latter may have felt for Baraga's action in setting out for Madeline Island. Baraga arrived there on July 27 of that year with but three dollars in his pocket with which to build a church and to care for his personal needs.

However, these conditions were not quite as severe as might seem. In a letter of Samuel Abbott, the fur company's agent at Mackinac, dated July 12, 1835, to Gabriel Franchere at the Sault, Abbott wrote as follows: "When Mr. Baraga left this place it was his intention to visit La Pointe, L'Ance and Fond du Lac in order to Baptise the Indians and their Children who had been prepared to receive the Sacrament and to return in the fall if Bishop Résé thought that he should do so. Should Mr. Baraga continue in his wishes please procure him a passage in some of the Company Boats and furnish him with 3 or 4 baskets lyed corn — 1 or 2 Barrells flour — 1 keg larde Some tea and Sugar and 1 keg Beef or Pork and charge same to my account. Have the goodness to say to Mr. Baraga that he better request the Bishop to send to the Sault the necessary provisions to enable him to pass the winter (Should the Bishop determine that he do so) and I have to request you my good friend Should they arrive at the Sault to forward them by Companys Schooner to such place as Mr. Baraga may be. I will be answerable for the freight. . . ." (Not at all apropos, the letter ended with a postscript which read: "Miss Catharine Dousman left her friends at 5 P M yesterday for the other world — they are much disturbed.") [28A]

From the deck of the schooner which had transported him, Baraga

---

[24] Baraga letters. Bishop Baraga Association, Marquette, Michigan.

[28A] American Fur Company letters in Public Library of Sault Ste. Marie, Michigan.

blessed the assembled mixed-bloods who had come to greet him; and then in the Ojibway language, blessed a number of Indians who had gathered in the background. Their stolidity prevented them from making any demonstration, but he was to discover in later days that this greeting, in their tongue, had had a profound effect upon them.[29]

That he was a man of ability and aggressiveness is illustrated by the immediate results he obtained. Inside of twelve days his prospective parishioners had built his new church, and he had baptized fifty of them. Perhaps with an eye toward the island's patriarch, his first baptism, on August 2, 1835, was Elizabeth, born November 15, 1834 to Benjamin and Carolina Cadotte.[30]

The new building was dedicated on August 9, 1835, under the name St. Joseph's Chapel. It was built of logs and of some abandoned material contributed by the fur company. It was fifty feet long by twenty feet wide by eighteen feet high. The work of building was in charge of Joseph Dufault, assisted by Theophilus Remillard, Louis Gaudin and other French-Ojibway whose names were well known in later La Pointe days.[31]

Immediately after the completion of the church, his new flock started to build a house for him, but as he later wrote to a brother priest in Detroit, ". . . they [the workers] grew *tired* of working for nothing and my presbytery has remained on the ground." When his house was finished later, a school room was incorporated in it for the instruction of the children. These buildings were located about one-quarter mile north of the Protestant Mission, between the sites of the old Middle

[29] James K. Jamison, *By Cross and Anchor*, (Paterson, N.J. 1948), 40. (Baraga had learned the Ottawa language at Arbre Croche, but the Ojibway tongue was similar enough so that, with a rehearsal, he could make himself understood. (Author's note.) Ibid, 39, states that Baraga arrived on the fur company's "John Jacob Astor." This is in error, since the "Astor" had not been launched at the Sault until August 3, 1835. *Gabriel Franchere's Letter Book, 1835–1837*, Sault Ste. Marie Public Library. Letter from Franchere to William Brewster at Detroit, dated August 4, 1835. Also Nute, Ibid, 494. It is reasonably certain that Ramsay Crooks arrived at La Pointe on the "Astor's" maiden trip, shortly before August 22, 1835. *Calendar*, Ibid, 2:83, 86, 90, 91, 95. The "Astor's" captain was Charles C. Stanard, and it is believed that on this trip he discovered the surprising shoal about twenty-seven miles southeast of Keweenaw Point and about thirty-two miles out in the lake from the south shore. Today it is known as Stannard Rock (modern spelling), and is marked with a lighthouse, the erection of which is a Great Lakes' saga. (Author's note.)

[30] Frederic Baraga, Otto Skolla & Angelus Van Paemel, *Liber Bantizatorum Missionis S. Joseph, in loco dicto: A la Pointe du Lac Superieur*, 1835–1854. Negative photostats at Wisconsin Historical Society, 1953.

[31] Dufault and Remillard were the paternal and maternal grandfathers of Mrs. Joseph Neveaux of 1957 Bayfield. The Gaudin name has since been changed to Gordon, families of whom reside at La Pointe and Red Cliff. The late Phillip Gordon, one of the few Ojibway ever to become an ordained Catholic priest, stemmed from the same family. (Author's note.)

Fort and the present Indian Cemetery. The church proper was about one hundred feet south of the graveyard.[32] Maps 23 and 24. Plate 7.

By October 1, 1835, Baraga had baptized one hundred forty-eight converts. His success in this direction was no doubt responsible for the drafting of a letter dated August 4, 1835 to Schoolcraft, the United States Indian agent at Mackinac, and signed by Boutwell, Hall, Ayer and Ely. In this they protested Baraga's presence, on the grounds that in the Protestant churches, at least, one denomination did not encroach on the missions of another. They hoped, therefore, that Schoolcraft would refuse a "license of residence" to the priest, and would advise him to ". . . locate & confine his labours to some of the fields not pre-occupied." Since Baraga remained on at La Pointe it is evident that Schoolcraft, whatever he may have replied to the Protestants, did not comply with their wishes.

Meanwhile Baraga saw that at the rate he was baptizing converts it would soon be necessary to enlarge his church and to procure assistants. He therefore determined to return to Austria in an effort to secure help and funds. At first thought it may seem strange that he would have to undertake this long and arduous trip, but at that time Catholicism, though nurtured and brought into this territory by the French, was struggling to secure a foothold in an otherwise preponderantly Protestant United States. The parishes of New York, Boston and Baltimore and the newer ones of Cincinnati and Milwaukee could not assume the additional burden of a mission in the wild Northwest. Therefore, in the following year, Baraga set out for his homeland to seek the necessary help.

During this missionary activity the American Fur Company was still carrying on. As a possible hedge against the eventual exhaustion of furs, the scarcity of which was troublesome in the La Pointe district, the new partners started in the fish business in a small and experimental way, even though two hundred eighty packs of furs had been shipped from there in 1835.[33] For many years, newcomers to the lake had been impressed not only by the size of the whitefish and trout but also with their palatability. It was hoped that a broad market might be developed for their sale.

The first trials were conducted that year on the north shore, at Grand Portage and Isle Royale, and at La Pointe. About two hundred barrels of fish were salted down and shipped. The ready market for the product so encouraged the partners that they decided to increase their facilities. By August 12, 1836, Warren reported that eleven hundred three barrels had

[32] Joseph Gregorich, Bishop Baraga Association, Ibid, Letter of June 18, 1852.
[33] Gabriel Franchere, Ibid, Letter of August 29, 1836 to Ramsay Crooks.

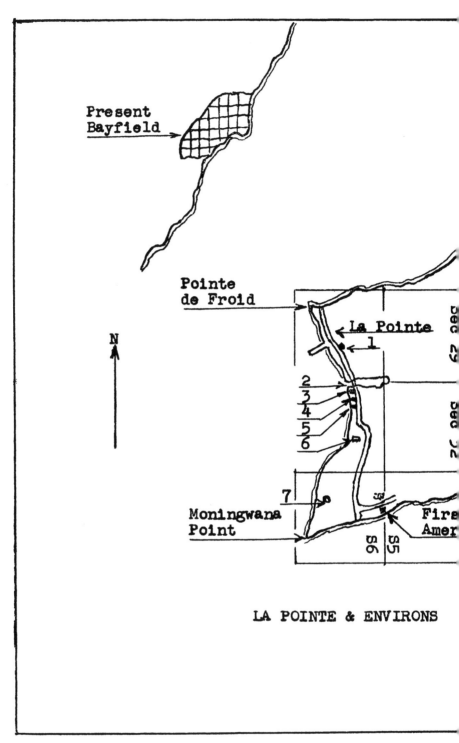

Present
Bayfield

Pointe
de Froid

La Pointe

N

Moningwana
Point

LA POINTE & ENVIRONS

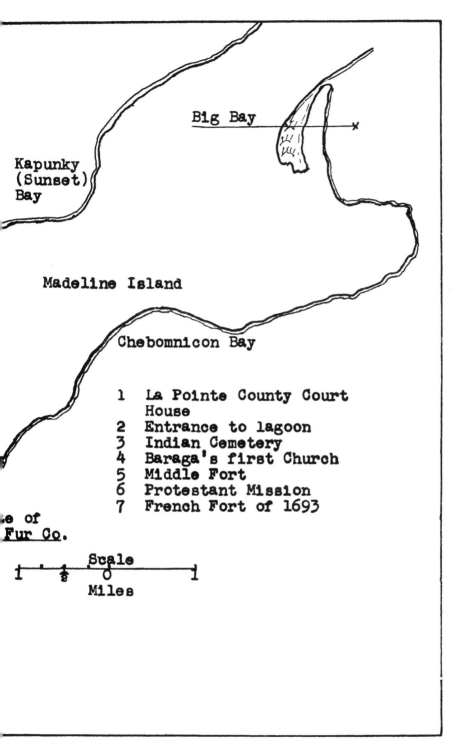

Big Bay

Kapunky
(Sunset)
Bay

Madeline Island

Chebomnicon Bay

1 La Pointe County Court
  House
2 Entrance to lagoon
3 Indian Cemetery
4 Baraga's first Church
5 Middle Fort
6 Protestant Mission
7 French Fort of 1693

.e of
Fur Co.

Scale

Miles

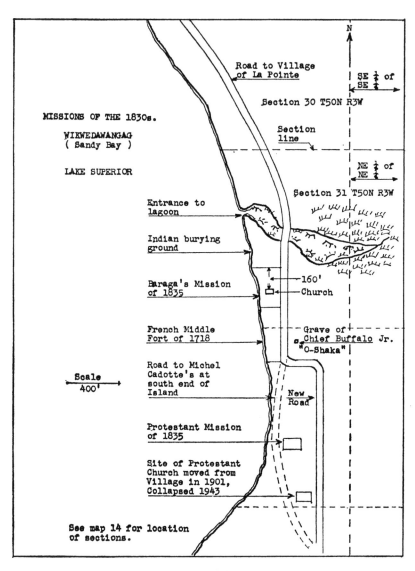

MISSIONS OF THE 1830s.

WIKWEDAWANGAG
(Sandy Bay)

LAKE SUPERIOR

Road to Village
of La Pointe

SE ¼ of
SE ¼

Section 30 T50N R3W

Section
line

NE ¼ of
NE ¼

Section 31 T50N R3W

Entrance to
lagoon

Indian burying
ground

Baraga's Mission
of 1835

160'
Church

French Middle
Fort of 1718

Grave of
Chief Buffalo Jr.
"O-Shaka"

N

Road to Michel
Cadotte's at
south end of
Island

New
Road

Scale
400'

Protestant Mission
of 1835

Site of Protestant
Church moved from
Village in 1901,
Collapsed 1943

See map 14 for location
of sections.

24. Missions of the 1830s.

been shipped from La Pointe alone.[34] In the same year Franchere notified Brewster, at Detroit, that he had received two hundred four packs
of furs from La Pointe.[34A]

Many of the fishermen and coopers on the north shore were moved,
with their equipment, to La Pointe in 1837. Also in that year William
Wilson, a cooper from Green Bay, was transferred to La Pointe. He
would later play a small part in the history of the village and would have
one of the Apostle Islands bear his name.[34B] The coopers were of great
importance, since in those days of slow transportation, the only way in
which fish could be shipped was to salt them down in barrels. The movement of the north shore men to La Pointe was made for two reasons.
First, La Pointe was the administrative center of the company's so-called
Northern Outfit; and second, the shelter offered by the many islands of
the Apostle Group made the taking of fish much easier than on the
unprotected north shore. However, small forces were left at Grand
Portage and Isle Royale. In this year about two thousand barrels of fish
were shipped to an apparently eager market.

Despite the shortage of fur in the La Pointe area, the company, as a
whole, was prospering. It paid a ten percent dividend in 1836, and fifteen
percent in 1837. This prosperity was reflected at La Pointe. Orders for
what might be termed luxury items were forwarded to New York by Dr.
Borup and Charles Oakes. In addition to these, Oakes, in 1836, built a
home of some pretention; one which more nearly followed eastern design and architecture than the crude shelters and log cabins of the territory. The house would be of considerable interest in later years, and
would assume the name of Treaty Hall. If no architect had been employed, Oakes or the builder, at least, possessed excellent taste in design.
It was a charming old home with interior halls in the form of a T traversing the first floor. At the junction of the T was a massive fireplace,
around which guests gathered in the building's later brief career as an
inn. Map 21, Plate 8.

The foundations were built of field stone, and the upper part was a
one story frame construction with white clapboards. It was placed on a
rise of ground overlooking the sandy beach of Pointe de Froid, the cape
nearest the mainland, and commanded a splendid view in three directions. A bronze tablet now marks the site.

The relations of Oakes and Borup were strengthened by their marriages to Julia and Elizabeth Beaulieu, respectively. These sisters were

[34] *Calendar*, Ibid, 2:216.
[34A] Franchere, Ibid, Letter of September 14, 1836, to William Brewster of Detroit.
[34B] Franchere, Ibid, Letters of October 11, 1837, to Eustache Roussain at Keweenaw and to Dr. Borup at La Pointe.

the daughters of Bazil Beaulieu who had been a trader at Lac du Flambeau in 1818, and who had later come to La Pointe.[35]

To these partners, as well as to the Warrens and other active traders, Michel Cadotte, in spite of his retirement, played the role of elder statesman. He was consulted on many matters of policy relating to the Indians. After he relinquished the La Pointe post he continued to live in his old home on the south shore of the island. Here, he could sit and gaze to the eastward at the play of shadows on the Penokee and Gogebic Ranges and the still more distant Porcupine Mountains; watch the ever-changing colors of the lake, and possibly dream of the days when he had roamed them all in the line of duty.

Here he died in 1837, at the age of seventy-three. He had made large profits in the fur trade, but he died a comparatively poor man owing to his generosity toward many indigent natives. He was buried in the old graveyard next to Father Baraga's first church.[36]

On October 8, 1837, Father Baraga returned from his journey to Austria where he had secured money for enlarging his mission. The assistants, whom he had sought, comprised Andrew Cesirek, who accompanied him in the capacity of a body servant. This poor man, frightened at the wilderness, and dismayed at Baraga's austere mode of life, left the next year. However, Baraga's sister, Antonia de Hoeffern, came with him to act as his housekeeper. She remained with him for two years, until failing health forced her to seek a less rugged life. She lived in the general neighborhood of New York and Philadelphia until 1846, when she returned to Austria.

The new church, with its attached quarters for Baraga, was finished in 1838. In spite of his happiness in the new building and the satisfaction of many new converts, he began to have some doubts concerning the adequacy of his new structure. With his usual zeal, he began to plan for larger accommodations.

Much has been written about the life and works of this devoted priest.

[35] Warren, Ibid, 5:382. Bazil Beaulieu had married Ogemaugeezhigoqua – Queen of the Skies – the daughter of Teegausha, Chief White Raven. She was generally called Mrs. Margaret Beaulieu. Bazil, two sons, Clement and Abraham, and daughter Eliza were buried in the cemetery of the present La Pointe Catholic Church. (See Chapter IX for Abraham's epitaph.) (Author's note.)

[36] Cadotte's tombstone, although fallen over, is still in reasonably good repair. His epitaph reads as follows:

SACRED TO THE MEMORY OF
MICHEL CADOTTE
WHO DEPARTED THIS LIFE
July 8, 1837.
Aged 72 Years
11 Months
16 Days.

The energy of this indefatigable and dedicated man was almost beyond belief. He not only labored among his local charges, but also made extensive trips by canoe, and by snowshoe during blizzards and bitter winter weather. It is little wonder that he was accepted in the lodges of the Indians as an honored and beloved guest.

On June 20, 1838, the Protestant staff of the La Pointe mission was increased by the arrivel of the Reverend Mr. and Mrs. Granville T. Sproat. Sproat, a Presbyterian, had come as an assistant in 1835. He had then gone East to marry Florantha Thompson of Middleborough, Massachusetts. The addition of this couple was most welcome. Sproat was of great help to Hall, and Mrs. Sproat relieved both men by taking over the mission school duties.

From the pen of Mrs. Sproat came one of the kinder and more humane Protestant references to Baraga. Upon the death of her infant daughter, born a year after her arrival at La Pointe, she wrote to her mother, with considerable feeling, that "Mr. Baraga" had joined the little funeral party.[37]

Another reference to Baraga was made by Hall. On August 16, 1838, he wrote to David Greene, the secretary of the American Board in Boston, as follows: "The Catholics generally are not prejudiced against the mission school. The Preist [sic] stationed here encourages their attendance." [38]

While Hall apparently never recorded the matter, Baraga wrote his bishop, Peter Paul Lefevere, in Detroit, on July 1, 1842: "They [the Presbyterians] teach them [the Indian children] to read and write in English and in Indian, but they do not speak a word to them about the religion, for I have warned them well that if they meddled with religion I would order all the Catholic children to leave their schools; and I am watching strictly this observance." [39]

In 1838 there was also a large expansion in the fish business of the fur company. The village was a hive of industry, with many coopers making barrels, and a comparable number of fishermen endeavoring to fill them. The partners seemed to have struck a bonanza in their choice of product, and that year shipped out four thousand barrels. The future prospects appeared so excellent that they began to make plans for greater growth. Coopers were kept busy all winter in anticipation of the following year's

[37] Florantha Sproat, "La Pointe Letters," *The Wisconsin Magazine of History*, (Evansville, Wis., 1932), September 16, #1, 90.

[38] Papers of the American Board, Ibid.

[39] Bishop Baraga Letters, Ibid, #314. In the same letter, Baraga inferred that the Protestant Mission was Presbyterian, for he wrote, "There are two regular schools here which the Presbyterians have established . . ." This is another implication that Hall and most of his assistants were of that denomination.

business. The company was in touch with its Montreal agents, urging them to engage more coopers in that area to be sent to La Pointe.[40]

The following list, compiled from the company's inter-departmental billings and invoices, shows, in round figures, the dollar value of the material and merchandise sent to La Pointe, and charged against that outfit.

1835	$30,000	1837	$29,000
1836	59,000	1838	46,000

The 1836 amount possibly reflected non-recurring charges due to heavy building operations. On the other hand, the low 1837 figure might show that the outfit had over-stocked in the previous year.

Another interesting figure, illustrating the current insignificance of the little beaver, is shown in the 1835 billings of skins and furs to the company's agent in London.[41] Out of total billings of $167,459, $121,223 represented deer hides. The balance covered all other furs; not broken down as to types, nor showing La Pointe's contribution to the total.

In 1838, Crooks found evidence of wasteful management at La Pointe on the part of Lyman Warren, and appointed Dr. Borup in Warren's place. Warren and his family moved to the Chippewa River, at the present small village of Brunet Falls. Here he worked as a farmer, blacksmith and sub-agent for an Ojibway reservation, and later erected a small sawmill at the same place.

Even in the American Fur Company, office politics were evident.

[40] *Calendar*, Ibid, 2:678 Item 6673, 681 Item 6707, 687 Items 6767, 6769 and 6771. A little known sidelight on the fur company's expansion program comes from the report which Gabriel Franchere made to Crooks in a letter from La Pointe dated September 4, 1839 in which he wrote: "Found the buildings in the same state they were in 1835, no additional buildings having been erected. Visited the intended place for the new establishment on the west side, and about 3 miles from the present factory, where a pier has been sunk in eight and one-half feet of water, and a number of small cribs to support a connecting bridge with the landing. The bridge is partly finished. The bay offers good anchorage, and perfectly sheltered from all winds. The land is wet for 80 or 100 yards, when its elevation is sufficient to afford a dry spot for buildings to be erected, and from thence at a distance of fifteen rods you come to a knoll of fine timber." Edward D. Neill, *Macalester College Contributions*, (St. Paul, 1892), Series 2, #1, 57–58.

(Inasmuch as the company by this time had become firmly established at present La Pointe, Franchere's new establishment, we judge, must have been located on present Sunset (Kepunky) Bay. In any event, Franchere's description perfectly fits that setting. The locally official name of Kapunky has an amusing origin. In the 1840s, Alexis Carpentier settled on this bay, and it became generally known as Carpentier's Bay. The Indians, struggling with the French pronunciation, arrived at Kapunky, by which name it has gone ever since, except for a brief time when the Vincent Roi family arrived there. It was then called Roi's Bay.) (Author's note.)

[41] In 1835, the company's agent in London was George Wildes & Company. The auction which determined the season's prices was held at Leipzig, the great fur center of Europe. (Author's note.)

After the appointment of Borup, one of the company's agents, James McKay, began to lay the groundwork for replacing Borup at La Pointe. After considerable correspondence with Crooks which ended in a personal interview, McKay was given the opportunity to resign, which he did. After the conference, Crooks wrote to Borup stating that the company had full faith in the latter's management of the post.

In 1839, the company shipped over five thousand barrels of fish. Because of the comparatively short navigation period in Lake Superior, the shipments had to be completed in early October to allow for transportation to the Sault, the portage past the rapids and the reloading on Lake Huron. This necessitated the procurement of warehouses in warmer climates so that distribution might be carried on the year around. The company made arrangements for these at Detroit, where one of its agents was located, and by the end of the year they were filled to capacity.

Like many another bonanza, forces were at work which would bring this one to an end. Some ingenious man in Europe had discovered a process for making hats without the fur of the beaver, at a great reduction in cost. At the same time, the silk hat was becoming the vogue. (The abandonment of beaver shakos by an English regiment caused even the mighty Hudson's Bay Company considerable apprehension.) These changes had immediate repercussions in the fur trade. In addition, the United States underwent one of its periodic and sudden panics, with attendant shortages of money. During this period the country was experiencing the ills of an unstable currency, largely due to Andrew Jackson's dissolution of the Bank of the United States with no compensatory substitute. Each state issued its own money which, very frequently, was not accepted by other states except at ruinous discounts. Philadelphia paper often was not acceptable in New York. The average mid-westerner would deal only in 'hard' money, and this was scarce, because of its natural flow toward the Atlantic seaboard. The comparatively rare slugs made their appearance at this time: crude gold coins, stamped, even more crudely, with the name of the issuing bank or individual. Lack, or slowness of, transportation also played its part. The fur company, in desperate need of funds in New York, experienced the plight of having agents at distant posts with kegs of specie which they were unable to forward.

Thus, by the end of 1839 the partners found their warehouses full of fish, with no buyers. They attempted to introduce their commodity in the eastern market, with small success. Their efforts to sell them in St. Louis and other southern communities succeeded no better. As a climax to these conditions, some of the fish began to spoil.

With the speculative instincts of many businessmen, the partners contracted for salt and seine twine, in the winter of 1839–40, for the 1840 season, on at least the same scale as the previous year. Crooks negotiated with Moses Burnett of Syracuse, New York, for two thousand six hundred barrels of salt to be shipped to the Northern Outfit upon the opening of navigation in the spring of 1840.[42]

In this alternate play of angling for fish and the souls of men, the Protestants, possibly viewing with some jealousy the successes of Father Baraga, decided to build a church in the Village of La Pointe in order to be nearer prospective converts. In 1839 they started work on this project, and completed it the next year.[43]

The building was located about two hundred yards southeast of the fur company's dock, between the road and the beach, and was on present Lot 1, Block 29 of the later Government and Town surveys. The site is the 1957 Binsfield property.

This was the first Protestant church building in the whole Northwest. It was constructed by the method so common at the time, with light logs or poles placed horizontally in slots provided by upright corner logs. The joints were chinked with moss and native clay, and the outside was sheathed with hand-sawed boards. Like the mission building, the inside was sealed with whitewashed clay plaster. The church was thirty-two feet long by twenty-five feet wide, and Hall wrote to David Greene of the American Board: ". . . It is a very decent and commodious building, sufficiently large to convene all who are disposed to attend a Protestant place of worship at this place. It is covered with clapboards on the outside, and finished within. It will seat from 150 to 200 persons. . . ."

Because Hall was a prolific writer on many subjects which are of great interest today, it seems rather strange that he did not set down in more detail matters which must have been close to his heart at the time. He did not chronicle when he started work on the mission building. He recorded no corner-stone-laying ceremony, if such were held. He made no mention of any dedication observance for either his mission or his later church building. The only way in which one may discover when his church was built was by a letter to the American Board, asking for a small bell for ". . . a small place of worship which is now building here."[44]

---

[42] *Calendar*, Ibid, 2:801. (The item of seine twine was one of no little expense. It was imported from France and England, and was made of both linen and cotton. The heavy grades were named maitre by the French, a calling which still persists, although the local fishermen speak of it as meter. The largest size is a three strand cotton line about three-sixteenths inch in diameter. Michel Cadotte's inventory, when he arrived at La Pointe in 1793, showed that he started with nine pounds of maitre which cost him nine shillings nine pence.) (Author's note.) The 1957 price was one dollar ten cents per pound.

[43] Papers of the American Board, Ibid. Hall's letter of March 16, 1840.

[44] Op. cit.

In his correspondence are many references to the inconveniences of the station, and at times definite notes of discouragement. But, aside from these, and his apparent austerity, one may conclude that he was a cordial host to his compatriots. One may imagine the sense of isolation created by his distance from his former home, and by the comparatively few white persons living on the island, the infrequency of visits by people who spoke his language, all overlaid with the knowledge that for hundreds of miles, in every direction, the country was populated with no one save crude trappers and unsympathetic Indians. It would be natural, therefore, for him to extend a warm greeting to the occasional traveler. During the years of his stewardship the mission was a gathering place, if not more or less of an hostel, for Crooks and his associates in the American Fur Company. Schoolcraft, on his trips of exploration and as an agent of the Government for Indian affairs, recorded the welcome he received.

The spirit of Puritanism still pervaded many of the Protestant clergy, and Hall was no exception. In February of 1841 he called a meeting of members, to 'church' Dr. Borup. Included in the list of accusations which the doctor was called upon to refute, if possible was: (a) he played cards and (b) he spoke in passion.[45] The doctor did not come before the meeting to defend himself, and was subsequently dropped from membership. That this excommunication was not too serious is evidenced by a letter from Hall to the American Board, dated October 12, 1842, in which he wrote, "I am happy to say that Doct Borup is now restored to our Christian fellowship."

The year 1840 was a troubled one for the fur company. From La Pointe, Dr. Borup reported to Crooks on June 9 that the "Northern Lake Company has arrived, bringing cargo of salt, provisions and few goods. Do not consider this rivalry of serious consequence."[46] Also the inventory of the Detroit warehouses was piling up with that season's catch of fish. At the same time the 1839 stock was moving very slowly. We find Crooks appealing to his various agents to assist in liquidating the holdings, and at the same time bewailing the fact that times were hard, and the fur business exceedingly slow.

Times were gloomy at La Pointe because of business conditions, and at the Protestant mission because of little progress. However, there was one bright circumstance appearing on the scene, in the arrival of the Reverend Mr. Leonard Hemenway Wheeler, accompanied by the Reverend Mr. and Mrs. Woodbridge L. James and Miss Abigail Spooner.

[45] Hall's entry in La Pointe Mission Church Records, Ibid.
[46] *Calendar*, Ibid, 2:863–864, Item 8704. (Crooks had previously warned Borup about this company, known as The Cleveland North Western Lake Company. Ibid, 744, Item 7378.)

One may assume that Hall was greatly heartened at this 're-enforcement' of five persons. He might have been more encouraged had he realized at the time the intelligence and sure grasp of affairs which Wheeler later displayed. Mr. and Mrs. James did not remain long, but Miss Spooner, a native of Athol, Massachusetts, proved to be a devoted worker who would spend many years in teaching among the Indians.

Wheeler had received his religious training at Andover Seminary, and was an ordained minister in the Congregational Church. He also had some grounding in medicine. Although Hall was a Presbyterian, the two evidently composed any religious differences, and worked harmoniously. Also, since the American Board was dominated by the two sects, missionary teaching had probably been more or less standardized so that there would be no conflict in the respective theologies. Wheeler always remained a Congregationalist and, in later years, Hall also become one.

After surveying the La Pointe field, Wheeler became convinced that the only way to bring a semblance of religion to the Indian was to raise his standard of living. His idea was to train him in the simpler arts and to give him a more scientific education in agriculture. Wheeler realized that Madeline Island did not fit the requirements of such a regime, and amidst his other duties he cast about on the neighboring mainland for a suitable place.

The only clue to the location of the new Cleveland North Western Lake Company is found in an early report of Wheeler to the American Board. From this it is probable that the company settled either on present Grant's Point or at the Old Fort site. In the same report he called the island Magdalen.

Mrs. Wheeler, fondly called Grandma by her later acquaintances, told many interesting tales of her experiences at La Pointe. One of them concerned the Indian cemetery near the mission. Over many of the graves were small structures, as there are today, which were calculated to protect the burial places from the elements. These small houses probably reflected the French influence, since they are fairly common in France. The Ojibway adopted the idea because of his desire for protecting his dead. The little building also served another purpose. Shortly after burial, the living relatives of the deceased would place food in it to nourish the departed on his long trip to his Gigig or Heaven.[47]

Among the supplies thus left was usually that Indian confection, made of cooked wild rice, mixed with maple sugar. This was a delicious com-

[47] Some of the local French-Ojibway maintain that the placing of food in the structures was always done at the request of the deceased as a generous gesture toward needy Indians. The latter could come at night to remove the offering without being observed by others, and thus suffer no embarrassment. (Author's note.)

pound, and was fairly common as late as 1900. The small Wheeler boys discovered the caches and at night would visit the cemetery and appropriate the rice-sugar mixture. Strangely enough, the Indians were very pleased at the disappearance of their offerings. They claimed that inasmuch as the ancestor had used their gifts, it was an indication of great pleasure on his part at the thoughtfulness of his descendants. They therefore replenished the supply, much to the delight of the young Wheelers.[48]

An incident which served to enhance Mrs. Wheeler's reputation among the Indians and which caused them to look upon her with considerable awe was brought about by the rather harrowing experience which her husband suffered. Upon one occasion, when at La Pointe, Wheeler had left the island on an extensive trip, in the company of two Indians in a birch bark canoe. They planned to return about September 20. When that time came, the party had not returned, and the equinoctial storms were in full blast.

The little community became concerned over their safety, and was wondering about what measures could be taken in the way of a searching party. After several days, Mrs. Wheeler related a dream which she had had, in which she had seen the party marooned on some island, with its canoe smashed.

Not much credence was given her dream, since the island in question was well off the course which the party would have followed. However, an Indian chief (there seemed to be as many Indian chiefs among the Ojibway as there were kings in Ireland) took the tale to heart, organized a searching party and returned with the travelers. They *had* smashed their canoe, and the rescuers arrived in time to save them from considerable hardship. From that time the Indians were convinced that Mrs. Wheeler was an oracle and always consulted her before undertaking any matter of importance.

The spirit of competition was not entirely confined to trading, on the island. Father Baraga, observing the new Protestant Church in the village, and the arrival of new missionaries, countered by building his contemplated larger church in the little settlement. Its site was the same as the present Catholic Church, and it was finished in 1841.

Father Otto Skolla, who later came as an assistant to Father Baraga, reported: "The church at La Pointe is fifty feet long and thirty feet wide. It has a beautiful altar, quite high, with an excellent picture of St. Joseph painted in 1834 by a skilled artist of Laibach named Lang. In the church are forty benches where the people knelt and prayed during the celebration of divine worship, and one bench near the altar was reserved for six chanters. There was also a chapel for celebrating Mass in the

[48] The author remembers Mrs. Wheeler telling this story in 1894 or 1895.

winter time, and joined to it was a room for the priest to live in." [49]
Plate 11.

The chapel referred to was a portion of the original church of 1835, enclosed by a part of the main structure, and containing many relics. A parochial school was built nearby. The church, as originally built, had two spires, but as Father Skolla later reported, "On account of its poor construction, whenever a storm raged, they shook and we were afraid the wind would destroy our church altogether, so we took both of them down and in their place built the one you now see in the drawing." [50] See front of jacket.

Father Skolla evidently was much impressed with the storms which Lake Superior could produce. He reported: "There are also underground winds at La Pointe which after a deep calm suddenly burst out of the earth, overturn everything in their path and hurl them aloft. The north winds, carrying rain and hail and terrific thunder and lightning, are so violent that they can hurl men and animals to the ground, overturn houses and shatter windows. Lake Superior too is often disturbed by fierce arctic tempests." [51]

During 1840 and 1841 there had been considerable correspondence between Baraga and the fur company's New York office regarding a bell which he had ordered for his new church. The company was acting as his agent in its purchase and transportation. Baraga's custom of emptying his purse in the advancement of his work caught him in an embarrassing situation in this instance. He had allowed other debts to accumulate on the company's books, and during the bell episode the company notified him that unless he settled his account, it would cease to extend further credit. Happily, his Leopoldine Society came to his rescue, and the bell was shipped. It weighed four hundred seventy-seven pounds and cost $178.00. [52]

The fame of Baraga's work among the Indians had spread to other European countries. A wine company named Loisson of Pierry, near Epernay, France, was much impressed. It sent a shipment of wine to the American Fur Company in New York with instructions to sell it and to apply the proceeds to the account of Baraga's mission. In time, further shipments followed. Not all of them were outright gifts, but in each case the profits were applied to Baraga's account. Baraga, in the meantime, was exhorting his parishioners to avoid the perils of strong drink.

[49] "Father Skolla's Report on his Indian Mission," *Acta et Dicta*, Catholic Historical Society of St. Paul. Edited by Grace Lee Nute, (St. Paul, 1936), 7: #2, 231.

[50] Antoine I. Rezek, *History of the Diocese of Sault Ste. Marie and Marquette*, (Houghton, Michigan, 1906), 1:366–367.

[51] "Father Skolla's Report," Ibid, 233.

[52] P. Chrysostum Verwyst, *Life of Bishop Baraga*, (Milwaukee, 1900), 203.

On September 10, 1842, the impending disaster fell upon the American Fur Company. Caught with large inventories of both furs and fish, and suffering from the general business stagnation, it suspended payment on its accounts and bills payable. George Ehninger, a member of the New York office, was appointed receiver. The company's debts amounted to about $300,000.

Under these conditions, fishing at La Pointe was virtually suspended, except for the needs of the local populace. In fact, as early as April 24, 1841, Crooks had advised Borup to stop all fishing at La Pointe and to concentrate on furs and skins.[53] This, of course, resulted in loss of employment to nearly all of the personnel. There is little or no information regarding the fate of the formerly prosperous village. It is possible that there was no general exodus because wherever they might go, conditions were the same. They could at least subsist at La Pointe, with fish, game, berries, wild rice and maple sugar for food, and the endless forests for fuel and housing.[54]

An indication of how the company's business had fallen off is reflected in the merchandise charged against the La Pointe post, as follows: (round figures)

1839	$46,000[55]	1842	$13,000
1840	45,000	1843	12,000
1841	20,000	1844	10,000

During the company's regime, the United States Government had established agencies throughout the northwest. These were designed to treat with the Indians concerning their problems, and to distribute the supplies and annuities which the Government had promised under various treaties. A sub-agency had been created at La Pointe which was in charge of the nearby territory. The Reverend Mr. Alfred Bronson had come in 1842 to take charge of this position. He had been a Methodist minister, but during his stay at La Pointe he conducted no mission work for the denomination. Discussion concerning the graft-ridden Bureau of

[53] *Calendar*, Ibid, 3:1047, Item 10,729.

[54] Maple sugar played an important part in the diet of La Pointe. Every year practically all of the villagers left for Odanah's nearby sugar bush, where they prepared thousands of pounds of the sweetening. (Author's note.)

[55] One of the few available records shows that one hundred twenty-nine packs of furs were shipped from La Pointe in 1839. Inasmuch as that year was considered a poor one for furs, it is evident that production had been greater in prior ones. *Calendar*, Ibid, 2:658, Item 6452, 689, Item 6795. (Not at all apropos, but in the inspection of the company's records, there is correspondence which might have been of interest to a modern United States Senate investigating committee. The company held Daniel Webster's notes in the amount of $3,000. At the same time it was lobbying in Washington for the payment of certain Indian annuities from which it hoped to profit. The correspondence revealed that Dan'l was decidedly poor pay.) (Author's note.)

Indian Affairs is not within the scope of this story, but as a commentary on its workings, Bronson's superiors found that he was too honest for the work, and so discovered excuses for letting him go.

The agencies posed puzzling problems for the partners of the fur company. If the supplies and monies were advanced in too great amounts, the Indians refused to go into the woods to hunt. On the other hand, if the monies came too late, the natives could not purchase goods at the posts, resulting in no profit to the company. This seeming paradox was due to the Government regulation that an Indian had to be on hand to receive the money personally.[56] If he was in the woods on an hunting expedition, when the money arrived, he could never claim it.

The timing of the arrival of the Government goods was an all important factor. If shipments could be delayed until the Indians believed they were not forthcoming, the hunters could be persuaded to go hunting. Then, if the goods came immediately upon their return, the company would profit, both from the furs collected and the monies given the Indians. There is considerable correspondence in the company's files protesting to the Government the delays of goods or their too early arrival.

Another matter of irritation was the ignorance of the Washington officials concerning the needs of the local Indians. On one occasion, the Bureau shipped fifty saddles for the Ojibway's use. In spite of the fact that Henry Dodge, the Superintendent of Indian Affairs, wrote a rather stiff letter to T. Hartley Crawford, the Commissioner of Indian Affairs, asking, under date of June 29, 1840, why saddles were shipped to the Ojibway, it took several months to convince the Washington clerks that the local Indians did not use horses.[57]

The local agency, in the meantime, did its best to dispose of the equipment. It persuaded several Indians to try horseback transportation, but, in riding through the woods, they suffered Absalom's experience, and gave up in disgust. There was a rumor that others were induced to mount saddles in their canoes, but lifelong habit was too strong. The shipment was eventually returned to Detroit where, after moldering for several years in some warehouse, it was sent on to the Sioux.[58]

Another factor which complicated matters was the American refusal or inability to understand the Indian psychology. Mrs. Sherman Hall wrote to her sister-in-law, describing the habit of the Indians in having

---

[56] *Calendar*, Ibid, 3:1568, Item 16,498.

[57] National Archives. Microfilm at Bishop Baraga Association, Marquette, Michigan.

[58] A possible modern parallel might be found in the twenty thousand tons of bird food for carrier pigeons which the United States Army left as surplus on Okinawa. (Author's note.)

a feast at the death of a relative. She was horrified to learn that the favorite comestible on such occasions was boiled dog. Mrs. Sproat was aghast at the shrieks and dancing upon the burial of one of their number. Another observer rather questioned the success of Christian missionary efforts by reporting that on a Sunday morning the Indians attended church in a most respectful and reverent manner, while in the afternoon they staged a great feast with decidedly pagan dances — somewhat at odds with their morning behavior.

CHAPTER SIX

1842 "The Forger—of Brass and Iron" 1877

As seemed usual in those days, the period of depression, while severe, did not last long. In 1842, after the report of geologist Douglass Houghton became known, public interest was drawn to the immense copper deposits of the Keweenaw Peninsula. Although it had been recognized for years that free copper had existed in uncertain amounts in the general area, it had not been realized that the metal was present in such enormous quantities, in well defined veins. By 1843, there was a concerted rush to the district. It is reasonable to presume that many left La Pointe to take advantage of this El Dorado.

These improved economic conditions were probably reflected at La Pointe through the increased business of the American Fur Company. In 1843 it was able to pay off twenty-five percent of its debts, with Crooks assuring its creditors that prospects appeared favorable for the discharge of the remainder in a reasonably short length of time. Either through these circumstances or the realization by the Government that La Pointe was of some importance, a post office was opened in October of that year, with Dr. Charles Borup as Postmaster.[1]

Because of the efficency of the La Pointe packers, or perhaps of the efficacy of the salt employed, the fish stored in the Detroit warehouses came through 1843 with little spoilage. It was, therefore, a source of great satisfaction when the New York office of the fur company received word from its Detroit agent, Anthony Dudgeon, that all fish had been sold. Dudgeon made his report with considerable jubilation, under date of November 29, 1843.[2]

This liquidation probably served to ease the financial stress of the company to a certain degree, but it was not enough to prevent bankruptcy proceedings being brought against it in the United States District

[1] *Calendar*, Ibid, 3:1344. Item 13,597.
[2] Calendar, Ibid, 3:1347, Item 14,002.

Court of Trenton, New Jersey, on May 8, 1844. It is possible that these were later dismissed, for there is no further reference to the matter.

True to its almost invariable record, Lake Superior that year unleashed its autumnal equinoctial storm. It is not known whether it was one of Father Skolla's underground winds, but at least on September 21, 1844 it was strong enough to cause the company's "John Jacob Astor" to drag her anchor at Copper Harbor, Michigan, and be cast upon the rocks. For some time thereafter hopes were entertained that she might be salvaged, but further storms upset the plans of her Captain, Benjamin Stanard, and she was finally pounded to pieces.[3]

Besides representing a severe loss to the company, the garrison at newly established Fort Wilkins, at Copper Harbor, near the tip of the Keweenaw Peninsula, was much perturbed because the "Astor" carried practically all of the fort's winter supply of provisions as well as many stores for the mining camps. Very fortunately these were replaced by a later vessel.

Because of the slowness of communications, the loss of the "Astor" was not known in New York before the disbursement of another twenty-five percent of the company's debt to its creditors on September 30. It is possible that the payment might have been postponed if the company had known of the vessel's loss.

From this time there was a gradual withering away of the company. In 1845, aside from a very few business communications with La Pointe, only two items appear which are of interest: Dr. Borup ordered a piano; and Crooks, after seeing Lyman Warren, wrote to one of the partners with the observation "Warren won't live long." From 1845 until 1850 the company continued to shrink in size and importance until its name and assets were finally purchased by Pierre Chouteau Jr. of St. Louis. The old name, however, persisted into the early 1860s. Thus passed one of the country's most colorful organizations: one which laid the foundations of fabulous real estate holdings in New York City, brought wealth and prominence to many more, and ruin to countless others: all based on the golden fleece of a little animal which rocked empires — and built La Pointe.

In nearly all the writings and books concerning Ramsay Crooks there is no reference to his son, Colonel William Crooks, who was stationed in St. Paul in the 1850s and who joined a group which was instrumental in promoting the first railroad in Minnesota, the St. Paul and St. Anthony line, now part of the Great Northern Railroad. Ramsay Crooks, after the

---

[3] Three Stanard brothers, Benjamin A., Charles G. and John J. captained various vessels of the fur company. Charles G. was in charge of the "Astor" on her maiden trip. Benjamin A. was unfortunate enough to have been in command at the time of her wreck. (Author's note.)

sale of the American Fur Company, moved to St. Paul where he engaged in independent trading for a number of years. During his business career with his fur company he had maintained close contact with Sir George Simpson, the head of the Hudson's Bay Company and generally known as The Little Emperor. This contact, no doubt, was responsible for his being appointed an agent of that company, and he was active in its behalf in the Red River Country in 1857 and 1858.[4] He died in 1859.

Dr. Borup also continued trading for a number of years on an independent basis at La Pointe, but he finally realized that this vocation in that locality had little future. He, too, removed to St. Paul where, after some years of further trading, he joined forces with Charles Oakes. The two partners organized a bank, and in later years became prominent in the financial circles of that city.

In 1844, iron ore was discovered on the Marquette Range. This discovery added to the furor of mining development on Michigan's Upper Peninsula. It also spurred on geologists and prospectors in the search for further mineral wealth, which resulted in finding iron ore in the Gogebic and Penokee Ranges. The latter brought a spark of hope to La Pointe until it was realized that no transportation was immediately available. More men left the village for the Keweenaw mines, and La Pointe appeared to have been caught in a temporary backwash.

It still retained its supremacy as the general receiving and assembly point for the commerce of the region, since the cities of Ashland, Superior and Duluth had not yet been founded. It remained the port of call for all vessels arriving at the western end of the lake. In fact, it was considered the harbor of refuge for all shipping. Boats, both great and small, ran for it when bad weather portended.[5]

During these parlous times the Madeline missionaries were hard at work. Father Baraga made frequent trips to the Keweenaw in answer to the fervent requests of incoming Catholic miners. These, in addition to a regular round of calls at Fond du Lac and the north shore as far up as Grand Portage, made severe demands on his physical strength. Fortunately, in 1845, the strain was somewhat eased by the arrival of Father Otto Skolla of underground-wind fame, who spent most of his time at La Pointe.

Wheeler of the Protestant mission had not remained idle. His search for a suitable place in which the Indians might be self-supporting was

[4] General James H. Baker, "History of Transportation in Minnesota," *Minnesota Historical Collections*, 9:19.

[5] David Dale Owen, *Geological Survey of Wisconsin, Iowa and Minnesota*, (Philadelphia, 1852), xxxiv. The harbor is still used for that purpose. The author has seen up to fifteen boats at one time anchored there awaiting calmer weather. These included both lumber hookers and large ore carriers.

rewarded in his choice of a site at the junction of the White and Bad Rivers, about nine miles east of present Ashland. Here was considerable level ground with apparently fertile soil. In fact, the Indians had cultivated it for many years. They had called it Tegoning — The Garden, also Gitigoning — Old Gardens. In addition, the locale had the advantage of proximity to a favorite sugar bush of the natives. Transportation problems were answered by the Bad River which flowed northward through the site to Lake Superior, and which was navigable for the boats of that time. The Kakagan River was within a few hundred yards of the location, giving access to the wild rice fields of the extensive Kakagan sloughs. Wheeler named his little town Odanah, after the Ojibway term Odena, meaning village, and in 1845 he erected a new mission house. He set about persuading the La Pointe Indians and mixed-bloods to move here. Map 11.

In addition to being well versed in religion and having some experience in medicine, Wheeler was equipped with a Yankee trait of inventiveness which found its outlet in numerous homemade devices. These were designed to make life easier, and were a never-ending source of interest to his pupils.[6] Among these mechanical contrivances was a windmill which was used to grind the Indians' corn.

During the same year, the Indians viewed with astonishment, and the white man greeted with enthusiasm, a new sight on Lake Superior. On November 1, the propeller "Independence," Captain Albert J. Averill, Jr. commanding, arrived at La Pointe.[7] The "Independence" was a ship of two hundred eighty tons, and could steam in fair weather at four miles per hour. She had been hauled over the Sault portage on wooden ways, and seven weeks had been required for the task.[8] One of her passengers was Vincent Roy, Jr. who had come from Rainy Lake, Minnesota, and had settled in La Pointe in 1838. In later years, his son, Vincent III, would play an important part in the founding of Superior, Wisconsin.[9]

The war in Mexico, in 1846, had no harmful effect upon La Pointe. In fact, either the demands of that war, or the copper craze, stimulated activity in the region. Three mining companies were at work on the

[6] What Wheeler did not realize, and what has not been appreciated until recent years, is the fact that the Ojibway Indian has had a decided bent for things mechanical.. Everyone overlooked his skill in the construction of a canoe — a real work of art. Very few can today match his accuracy with an axe. Instead of trying to develop these skills, he was relegated to agriculture and fishing, both of which were distasteful to him. (Author's note.)

[7] James Davie Butler, "Early Shipping on Lake Superior," *Wisconsin Historical Society Proceedings*, (Madison, 1895), 94.

[8] Records of the United States Corps of Engineers at Sault Ste. Marie, Michigan.

[9] Verwyst, Ibid, 472–476. Here, Verwyst calls Vincent III as Vincent, Jr., probably not realizing that there was an elder Vincent Roy on Rainy Lake who never saw La Pointe. Grace Lee Nute, *Rainy River Country*, (St. Paul, 1950), 30, 33–34. By

Montreal River: The Cypress River Mining Company, the New York & Michigan Mining Company and the Charter Oak Mining Company.[10] The Montreal River was about twenty-five miles distant from La Pointe, and possessed no suitable harbor for the large lake boats. It is probable, therefore, that supplies were unloaded at La Pointe and trans-shipped, in batteaux, to that river.

In the meantime, Ramsay Crooks' prophecy in regard to Lyman Warren proved correct. Warren returned to La Pointe in 1846, possibly with a premonition of his approaching end, and the wish to spend his last days where he had been most active and successful. In any event, he died on October 10, 1847, and was buried in the mission graveyard.[11] His wife had died on July 22, 1843, and had been buried at La Pointe. Because she had been of the Roman Catholic faith, she had probably been buried in the Indian cemetery, but today no grave marker exists to indicate the place. Neither is there any tombstone nor evidence to show where Warren was interred.

The discovery of iron ore on the Marquette Range had spurred the Government geologists in the hunt for still other deposits of that mineral. In 1848, the year in which Wisconsin achieved statehood, iron was discovered on the Gogebic and Penokee Ranges. Until the respective states had become state conscious, the Gogebic, which lies in Michigan, and the Penokee, in Wisconsin, had gone under the Penokee name, inasmuch as the two, actually, belong to the same chain of hills.[12] These were not immediately worked because of lack of transportation. While considerable interest was aroused, it was overshadowed by the discovery of a huge, five hundred ton nugget of free copper in the Ontonagon district. (A twelve foot cube of the metal would weight nearly this much.)

means of Baraga's baptismal records and the La Pointe census reports, it is possible to trace both Vincent Jr. and Vincent III.

[10] Owen, Ibid, 437.

[11] J. Fletcher Williams, "Memoirs of William W. Warren," Ibid, 5:12.

[12] The name Gogebic was supposed to have originated from the Indian name Gogibic which they applied to the lake of the same name. Gogi or kogi meant he dives down, and bic refers to a body of water. Verwyst, *Wisconsin Historical Collections*, 12:391. The Reverend Fr. William Gagnieur confirms the above translation, but does not associate the lake with the name. "Indian Place Names," *Michigan History Magazine*, 2:545.

In re Penokee:

Colonel Charles Whittlesey surveyed the range in 1860. At that time he named it Pewabik, thinking that he was using the Ojibway term for iron. The actual Indian word is Biwabic but the Ojibway pronunciation can easily be mistaken. When the Colonel's notes were transcribed, a compositor either could not read the Colonel's writing, or else made a mistake. In any event, the word appeared as Penokee and has never been changed. Colonel Charles A. Whittlesey, "Penokee Mineral Range," *Geology of Wisconsin*, Ibid, 3:216. (However, to the average American, the name sounds like a good Ojibway one — or a brown sugar fudge.) (Author's note.)

The prospectors of the Minesota [sic] Mining Company investigated an old and partially filled-in shaft which had evidently been sunk by the Indians. At the bottom they found this extraordinary block of copper. From the collection of prehistoric hatchets, axes and sledge hammers found in the shaft, it was deduced that the original weight must have been considerably greater. Also, out of the shaft was growing an old hemlock tree which, when cut, displayed rings indicating an age of three hundred ninety-five years. This was almost incontrovertible evidence that the shaft had been worked prior to 1435.

During this prospecting activity of 1848, the Ontonagon Boulder, reduced in weight from the time of Alexander Henry to about three thousand pounds, was removed and placed in the Smithsonian Institution of Washington. If this had been a true cube of copper, without its surrounding matrix of stone, it would have measured about twenty-one inches on a side. Schoolcraft, on his trip of 1820, had inspected the rock and had written a very exact and scientific report concerning it.[13]

With improved economic conditions throughout the country, and the demand for food in the new mining camps, the fishing industry was revived at La Pointe. Unlike the previous venture, where the business had been dominated by the American Fur Company, the catching and packing of the product was undertaken by a number of different individuals. Thus the cooperage shops enjoyed some measure of prosperity, there was activity in the warehouses because of increased shipping, and a few newcomers arrived on trips of inspection for possible investments. The La Pointe output of fish in 1848 amounted to one thousand barrels.[14]

A few men may have become infected with the fever of the '49 gold rush, and departed for California, yet the population remained fairly stable at around 500. Father Baraga continued as a tireless worker, with Father Skolla relieving him of many duties. Baraga had established subsidiary missions at Fond du Lac, Minnesota, and L'Anse, Michigan. The latter became so important as a center out of which to work in the adjacent mining territory that in 1850 he was transferred to that place, where he was to remain for several years.

Upon reviewing the 1850 census of La Pointe, one is impressed with the number of French names appearing therein. One is also struck with the struggles which an American census taker had in spelling many of the French pronunciations. Thus the name Neveaux was correctly transposed to Nephew, but Newago became Na Wagon. A substantial number of the older men, listed as voyageurs, gave their birth places as Montreal or Quebec.

[13] Henry R. Schoolcraft, *Narrative Journal of Travels in the Year 1820*. (Michigan State College Press, 1953), 121–122.
[14] Owen, Ibid, 437.

That Michel Cadotte and his descendants did not believe in race suicide is evidenced by the fact that in this census, out of a total population of four hundred eighty-five, forty were Cadottes.[15] The census, written in a beautiful copperplate hand, shows that there were eighty-two families living in seventy-one dwellings. The same record gives five hundred ninety-five as the total population of La Pointe County which, at that time, embraced all of present Ashland and Bayfield Counties as well as parts of Douglas and Iron Counties.[16] The Odanah enumeration showed the Wheeler family with five children.[17]

In 1825 a son had been born to Lyman and Marie Cadotte Warren. With the mother's Ojibway blood-tie, and with the respect in which his father was held by the Indians, young William Whipple Warren was a favorite visitor in the cabins of the mixed-bloods and Indians. His companions, for the most part, were children of the same people. He spent many evenings around the camp fires of the Ojibway, listening to their tales and legends. He mastered their language so thoroughly that the natives claimed he understood it better than they, and he often served as an interpreter.

His father sent him to school in the East where he acquitted himself most creditably. Upon his return from school in 1841, he became the official interpreter of the post. On August 10, 1843 he married Matilda Aitken, a daughter of William Aitken, the trader.[18] Sherman Hall performed the wedding ceremony. In 1845, Warren and his wife moved to Crow Wing, Minnesota. A short time later he went to Two Rivers from which district he was elected to the Minnesota Territorial Legislature in 1850.

Because of his Indian background and his knowledge of Indian affairs, his friends urged him to record his experiences, and to set down some of the lore and legends of his tribe. In failing health, he wrote his "History of the Ojibways," which he completed in 1852, one year before his death. Since that time his work has become a classic, and is generally regarded as an authority on matters pertaining to that tribe. In his book he recorded his method of determining when the Ojibway came to Madeline Island, when they left and when they saw a white man for the first time.

1852 and its succeeding five years were ones of significance to La

[15] An official census taken in 1840, showed a population of four hundred fifty-eight. However, it has not been considered complete, since many men may have been absent on hunting and fishing trips for the American Fur Company. (Author's note.)
[16] There is some doubt concerning the accuracy of this total also.
[17] One child, born March 22, 1842, dead upon birth, had been buried in the mission graveyard at La Pointe. See Florantha Sproat, Ibid, December, 1932, 16, #2, 192. No marker is in evidence today.
[18] La Pointe Mission Church Records, Ibid.

Pointe and its surrounding territory. Even though the little village was beginning to lose some of its former prominence, the Government recognized the importance of the general area and in 1852 erected the first lighthouse toward the west end of the lake. This was located on present Long Island, about twenty-eight hundred feet west of the more modern principal light.[19] Possibly someone in the Lighthouse Service took the trouble to investigate the history of the region, for he named the station The La Pointe Light, which is still its official calling. The foundations of the former keepers' quarters are still in evidence. One of the early keepers was Captain John Daniel Angus, several of whose descendants are still (1957) living on Madeline Island.[20]

The first signs of approaching inroads on the village's supremacy as a port made their appearances in 1853 when the City of Superior, Wisconsin, was founded, to be followed the next year by its rival, Duluth, Minnesota, then called Oneota. These two were to become the principal roadsteads at the head of the lakes. As a matter of fact, it would be several years before these twin ports would diminish the shipping of La Pointe and later Bayfield, since Duluth had no direct entrance from the lake into St. Louis Bay, and the Superior entry was partially blocked by sand bars which the captains of larger boats refused to negotiate.[21] This resulted in the lake vassels breaking bulk at La Pointe, with smaller ships and bateaux taking the cargo the rest of the way.

Another major loss in La Pointe's population then occurred: the third, including the hegira of the Ojibway in 1610, and the exodus to the copper country in 1843. The village would retain some of its leadership for a few more years, but other forces would gradually gnaw at its former position of consequence.

The first and innocent actors in this play of transition were Mr. and Mrs. Asaph Whittlesey and infant daughter, who arrived in La Pointe in June of 1854. Whittlesey's decision to come to the region had been prompted by the enthusiasm of his brother, Colonel Charles Whittlesey. The Colonel had traveled on foot over a large part of the Gogebic and Penokee Ranges, engaged in an United States geological survey.

After spending a few days at La Pointe, the family set out in a row boat, with all its worldly possessions, with the present site of Ashland as its destination. It was accompanied by George Kilbourn on this trip

[19] In the alternate changes from peninsula to island, old records are vague as to its status in 1852. It was an island in 1857. (Author's note.)

[20] James Peet Diaries, 1857–1859. Copies in Wisconsin Historical Society. Entry of May 20, 1859.

[21] Duluth's entry was not cut through until 1871. Lieutenant Bayfield's map of 1823 showed eight feet of water over the Superior entry bar. A later chart showed but three feet of water over the same bar. John Warren Hunt, *Wisconsin Gazeteer*, (Madison, 1853), Chart opposite page 25.

of about twenty miles. The little group landed toward the west end of the present city, about one and one-half miles east of where Radisson and Groseilliers had built their cabin nearly two hundred years before.[22] Here, on July 5, 1854, Whittlesey started the construction of his home.

Later in the year he was joined by Martin Roehm and family who took up a claim nearby. During the autumn, new comers arrived, but decided to venture further south. Junius T. Welton, who had previously spent some time at La Pointe, traveled southward to locate on a water power of the White River, where he erected a small sawmill. Another, Thomas P. Sibley, went still further and chose a place on the Marengo River, the Maringouin (Mosquito) of earlier French calling. Colonel Whittlesey, in his survey of 1860, showed these two claims on his map. Map 9.[23]

A rival settlement was also set up the same year in what is now the east end of Ashland, some little distance from Whittlesey. The prime movers in this village were George Stuntz, David Lusk, Frederick Prentice and John Daniel Angus.[24] These settlers called their little community Bay City.[25] The following year, with new families arriving, the Whittlesey location was named after its founder. Later, both villages combined under the name of Ashland, although there was some discussion over the name Equadon, which its proponents claimed meant "At the head of the bay."[26] Plate 12.

The immediate cause, however, for the loss of one-third of La Pointe's population was the treaty of 1854 between the Government and the Ojibway. The treaty dealt with the affairs of the tribe over a large region, but those portions affecting the natives of Madeline Island touched upon the establishment of reservations at Odanah and Red Cliff. The latter is

[22] Guy Burnham, Ibid, 211. A plaque now marks the spot.

[23] Welton's name was listed in the La Pointe census of 1850, State Historical Library, Madison, Wisconsin. (A daughter of Sibley later married George Frederick Wheeler, the sixth child of Leonard Wheeler.) (Author's note.)

[24] George Stuntz was a Government surveyor who had conducted portions of the original survey near Ashland and Superior. Not much is known about Lusk, except that he joined the other three in setting up a small trading establishment. Frederick Prentice would later be known as the founder of the brownstone quarry industry in the region. Angus had captained various boats for the American Fur Company, among them the schooner "Madelaine" of about twenty tons. He was the father of the late Captain Daniel Russell Angus of later days at La Pointe. (Author's note.)

[25] Some of the old records called this Bayport. The author chose the Bay City name because of a creek running through the location which is still called Bay City Creek.

[26] Guy Burnham, Ibid, 247. Equadon was probably confused with the Ojibway name for Ashland, i.e. Wikwedong, meaning In a Bay. (Author's note.) The name of Ashland was adopted at the suggestion of Martin Beaser, one of the city's early settlers. He was an admirer of Henry Clay whose home at Lexington, Kentucky, bore this name. *History of Northern Wisconsin*, Western Historical Company, A. T. Andreas, Proprietor. (Chicago, 1881), 67.

about four miles north of present Bayfield. Nearly two thousand Indians gathered at La Pointe, and after several weeks of debate with the Government Commissioners, Henry C. Gilbert and David B. Herriman, the final draft was signed. Many knotty problems were solved, with apparent good feeling on both sides. The treaty was executed on the lawn, in front of the former Oakes home, which accounted for the later name of Treaty Hall.[27] Map 21.

Under the treaty, the Indians of Catholic persuasion were to move to Red Cliff, and the others to Odanah. At the same time, one hundred acres of land were reserved for them on the northeast point of Madeline Island.[28] This reserve, still in existence, was to serve as a base from which they might fish in their favorite waters toward Michigan Island.

It might appear that the Catholic and Protestant missionaries had entered into some sort of arrangement whereby the former would have a free hand at Red Cliff and the latter at Odanah, but the division had a slightly more practical aspect. At that time, the Government was making a financial grant to only one missionary at any given reservation. Since Wheeler was already at Odanah, and was the recipient of this help, any Catholic mission there would not share in any Federal aid.[29]

A few Indians remained at La Pointe, which they were allowed to do under the treaty. In the event they left, they were supposed to go to the reservation assigned them. This understanding was effected because

[27] Benjamin Armstrong, *Early Life Among the Indians*, (Ashland, 1890), 45. In the early 1850s, Oakes sold his home to the Indian agent, Henry C. Gilbert. The latter, in turn, sold it in 1855 to Frederick Prentice for six thousand dollars. The later Judge Bell bought it in 1867, and lived there until his death. George F. Thomas, *Pen & Camera Sketches of Old La Pointe*, (Milwaukee, 1899), 23. (Thomas was Bell's son-in-law and still later inherited it.) (Author's note.)

[28] This preserve has the only stand of virgin timber on Madeline Island. Logging operations are wistfully looking at it.

[29] The matter of Federal aid was a sore point with Father Baraga. Shortly after his arrival at La Pointe he noted that the Protestant mission was receiving one thousand dollars per year from the Government, and that he should be entitled to some of it. In the treaty of 1842, two thousand dollars per year was allotted for schools. In a letter dated October 5, 1842 to Bishop Lefevere of Detroit, Baraga implied that the Protestants were to receive the entire sum, but that he would like to have at least three hundred dollars of it. He then asked Robert Stuart, acting Indian agent then at La Pointe, to intercede for the Catholics for that amount. Stuart replied that he would have to take it up with the Secretary of War. After a year's delay Baraga was successful in receiving the three hundred dollars.

Another sidelight on the bitterness between Protestant and Catholic was the later action of Father John Chebul who baptized Wheeler's eldest daughter, Julia, in the Catholic faith. Naturally, this precipitated a family rift which endured for years, and also made Wheeler an avowed enemy of Chebul. After that event, Chebul appeared in Odanah to start a Catholic mission. Wheeler and a Federal agent who was there found Chebul hiding in a second story room, mauled him considerably and then forced him to leave the settlement. Letter to author from Sarah Wheeler Bunge (Mrs. George), a granddaughter of Leonard Wheeler, dated June 7, 1952.

certain Indians found steady employment in the warehouses of the village.

Having foreseen the effects of this treaty, Hall, the founder of the Protestant mission, had moved away in 1835 to a mission at Sauk Rapids, Minnesota. He left on the island the grave of his second son, Elias, and the marks of over twenty years of labor.[30] Upon the adoption of the treaty, the usefulness of the missions on the island came to an end, and Hall's building was left to decay.

On the surface it might appear that Hall's years of work, as well as those of his assistants and co-workers, were of little or no use in the mission field; yet it must be realized that La Pointe fulfilled the basic concept of the original missionary project. It was the central station. It was here that the idea of education, instead of entire emphasis on religion, was started; also it was here that the first translation of the New Testament into the Ojibway language was made. Even Baraga, who at first decried the educational work being done by Hall as opposed to straight religious efforts, finally adopted this translation at his mission in L'Anse, Michigan.

From La Pointe, Wheeler went to Odanah, and his work there was probably instrumental in the founding of Protestant churches in Ashland and nearby towns. James, Boutwell, Hall, Ayer and Ely went to Minnesota points where they founded lasting missions and performed the necessary spade work for later permanent churches. The La Pointe mission was caught in a backwater of economic evolution and there atrophied and died, whereas the Minnesota stations thrived through being in the path of that peculiar westward urge which so thoroughly permeated the eastern United States.

Therefore it is probable that the imponderable assets of the La Pointe mission far outweighed its tangible liabilities.

The same treaty opened territory in Minnesota's Arrowhead country which had previously been set aside for the Indians. It also ended the arrangement which the Hudson's Bay Company had with the old American Fur Company, under which the former was taking fur in the region. This marked the final operation of any foreign fur company in the United States.

An event in the year 1855 which was to have a tremendous influence on the entire lake, and still later to the whole country, was the opening

[30] In a letter dated January 22, 1852, Hall wrote to his sister Lydia: "Elias was taken sick with a fever December 18, 1851, seemed to rally at times but died at 1:00 a.m. January 15." The epitaph on the son's grave in Old Mission graveyard reads as follows:

ELIAS CORNELIUS HALL
DIED JAN. 15, 1852.
AGED 17 YEARS.

on May 24 of the first practical locks at Sault Ste. Marie.[31] For the first time in history a ship from the lower lakes could carry its cargo to Lake Superior without breaking bulk at the Sault. The first craft to use the locks was the sidewheeler "Illinois," upbound on June 18, 1855. The new locks were arranged in tandem, each three hundred fifty feet long, seventy feet wide, with eleven and one-half feet of water over the sills, and a lift of nine feet. These comparatively small locks were the predecessors of the larger locks of today which, in their seven months of service per year, handle more tonnage than the annual traffic of all the ship canals of the world combined.

Not quite as spectacular was another event of the year 1855 which would affect future Bayfield and, to a lesser extent, La Pointe. This was the arrival of Elisha Pike, his wife Elizabeth, their daughter, Nancy Adeline, son Robinson Derling and Pike's widowed mother, Mrs. Sallie Pike, aged seventy-five years.

On an earlier trip of inspection, Pike had been asked by Julius Austrian, the Government agent in the area, to repair a small sawmill which had evidently been built by the American Fur Company, and which Austrian then owned. The mill was located on a small water power about one mile up present Pike's Creek, on the mainland, at the junction of the West and North branches of that stream. Pike was so impressed with the site and the immediate region that he bought the mill and the southwest quarter of section twenty-one of Township 50 North, Range 4 West, about three miles south of the present Bayfield. His later holdings included the remainder of the section and the site of the modern State Fish Hatchery.[32]

Since there was no settlement on the mainland, Pike landed at La Pointe where he remained for some days owing to the illness of his wife. Upon her recovery, the family moved to the site of the mill where he built their living quarters. Although he had come seeking investment, his principal reason for having left his old home in Toledo, Ohio, was to escape the malaria which had reached endemic proportions in that city.

At about this time Madeline Island was achieving its first publicity as a summer resort. It even received notice in the *New York Daily Tribune* of June 26, 1854, whose traveling correspondent reported, "This [La Pointe] is certainly the most delightful situation on Lake Superior."

[31] Records of the United States Corps of Engineers at Sault Ste. Marie, Michigan. The May date was when the locks were certified complete. The same records show that rather embryonic locks had been built by the North West Company in 1797–98 on the Canadian side of the rapids. The one set was thirty-eight feet long, eight feet nine inches wide, with a lift of nine feet. A tow path, on which oxen were used, served to haul batteaux and canoes through the upper rapids.

[32] In later years the son would donate this site to the State of Wisconsin. (Author's note.)

The Madeline House, built by the American Fur Company, located across the street from the village dock, was an hotel of three stories with accommodations for seventy-five guests. During the summer months it enjoyed a measure of prosperity, induced by the opening of the Sault locks and the potential wealth of the copper and iron mines, all of which brought men of means, seeking investment. Among these was Henry Mower Rice of St. Paul.

Rice, a native of Vermont, came to St. Paul in 1839 and became a trader for the American Fur Company. He conceived the idea of supplying the company's posts on the upper Mississippi by way of St. Paul instead of by the St. Louis River portage route. He built warehouses in St. Paul, supplied by boat from St. Louis, Missouri, and developed trade above St. Anthony's Falls by horse-drawn boats.

This relationship with the fur company acquainted him with the La Pointe region where he saw possibilities of investment in timber and mining lands, especially in the general neighborhood of Bayfield. His business and political activities brought him into contact with such nationally-known figures as John C. Breckinridge, William Aiken, General William S. Harney, Stephen A. Douglas and William Corcoran, as well as with lesser lights from the South and from along the Atlantic Seaboard.[33] All of these men came for first-hand inspection and information.

Breckinridge invested in some real estate near Bayfield, according to tax records of 1857.[34] Old abstracts covering Madeline Island property disclose that Harney purchased tracts of land there the same year.[35] The names of all of the above appeared on the register of the Madeline House.[36] A contemporary traveler warned an acquaintance of the thin walls of the House and the reverberations from the heavy slumbers of fellow guests.[37]

In 1856 the City of Bayfield was founded, named after the young British lieutenant who had so efficiently discharged his orders in the

[33] Breckinridge, a Kentuckian, was the Vice President of the United States from 1857 to 1861 under the James Buchanan administration. Upon the outbreak of the Civil War he joined the Confederacy and became a Brigadier General in that army. He was appointed Secretary of War for the Confederacy in January, 1865. Aikin was the Governor of South Carolina, 1844–1847. Harney was a General in the United States Army, and in the 1850s he was engaged in protecting white settlers and their wagon trains in and about Fort Laramie, Wyoming. Upon the advent of the Civil War he joined the Confederate forces. He came from Mobile, Alabama. Douglas was an Illinois Senator and Corcoran a Washington banker. (Author's note.)

[34] James Chapman, *Journal*, 2. Bayfield Public Library.

[35] Abstract covering author's own property.

[36] George F. Thomas, *Picturesque Wisconsin*, (Milwaukee, 1899), 19. Grace Lee Nute, *Lake Superior*, Ibid, 276.

[37] Guy Burnham, Ibid, 223.

survey of the lake.[38] Credit for the actual founding should probably go to Rice because he bought up the land and platted the town. Local stories associate Benjamin S. Bicksler with Rice in this honor, but his name does not appear in any of the contemporary records, although it does at a later date. There is a memorandum of the building of a log shack, the first habitation in Bayfield, by nine men, started on March 24, 1856 and completed March 26. Bicksler might have been one of the nine.

On March 28, John M. Freer arrived from Superior with a team of horses, bringing with him "Mr. McAboy" who commenced the survey of the town.[39] The first family, that of John Hanley, came from Superior on May 8 aboard the schooner "Algonquin," the first vessel to land at the new town dock. On October 5 a census was taken which showed one hundred twelve persons, of which seventeen were women and twenty-two were children.[40]

The first steam sawmill (as differentiated from one driven by water) was started by John T. Cahoe. The mill had been completed some time in advance of the arrival of the propeller "Mineral Rock" which brought the mill engine on July 27, 1856. (The mill was burned January 12, 1857.) At a later date another steam mill was built by Samuel S. Vaughn. The old records are a bit vague as to when this mill was discontinued, but it was probably closed shortly after Vaughn moved to Ashland in the early 1870s.

There does not seem to be any record of the possible mixed feelings which the La Pointers may have had in seeing the rapid growth of a new rival, directly across the channel. Nevertheless, Bayfield remained dependent for many things on its elder sister. Bayfielders went to La Pointe to have their property deeds recorded, their shoes resoled and their watches repaired by the redoubtable Judge Bell. (In many instances the watches had to be sent elsewhere after the Judge's ministrations.)

Even though La Pointe had experienced considerable loss in her population because of the Indian treaty, enough people remained to cause Father Baraga to assign a lay teacher to the village for instructing her children. Church services had also been maintained under Father

[38] Bayfield was a personal friend of Rice, and the latter named the town in Bayfield's honor. (Author's note.)

[39] McAboy's first name was William but contemporary records, for the most part, omitted it. One record called him Major. He was vice-president of the Bayfield Lyceum, organized in 1857, and was Bayfield's first superintendent of schools. For a time he was the mail carrier between Bayfield and St. Paul. (Author's note.)

[40] Andrew Tate, "Census of Bayfield," Letter March 4, 1858. Letter privately held in Bayfield, but photostat copy in State Historical Library, Madison, Wisconsin. This and other information in the letter thoroughly agree with that in the James Peet diaries. (Author's note.)

Otto Skolla, but he frequently had to leave on other assignments. On July 23, 1857, Baraga brought Dillon O'Brien to La Pointe to take up the duties of a lay teacher. O'Brien was one of the first Irishmen to come since the short stay of John Johnston. He was accompanied by his wife and four children, and remained at La Pointe for a number of years until further decreases in population no longer warranted his services. He was transferred first to Red Cliff, and then to St. Paul.

The founding of Bayfield, and its attendant growth, attracted both the Presbyterian and Methodist Churches. In 1857, ministers of these faiths arrived to establish their churches. Very fortunately, the diaries of James Peet, the Methodist, have been preserved. In addition to re-flecting his feelings of optimism and pessimism, they give many homely sidelights on the customs of the time. After reading them, one may grasp the increasing importance of the little town as a lake port, and its influence on the fading prominence of La Pointe.

The census of 1860, as well as the minutes of meetings of the La Pointe Town Board, give much information concerning the village. Ashland had assumed enough importance and attracted enough people to organize as an incorporated town. It had also taken over as County Seat for the newly formed Ashland County, thereby robbing La Pointe of that distinction. The census of La Pointe showed a population of three hundred seven – with seventy-three vacant houses. The old French names still predominated, but there were English and Scotch ones such as Armstrong and MacArthur, and an infiltration of Germans with names of Stene, Austrian, Mandelbaum and Smitz. There was an absence of the occupation of voyageur which was so common in the 1850 enumeration. Dillon O'Brien's pursuit was listed as "Gentlemen." The Angus family had moved from Ashland and Long Island to Bayfield Township in La Pointe County, where it was listed with its five children, ranging from one month to twelve years. (Captain Daniel Russel Angus was then two years old.) John W. Bell attested the accuracy of the census as notary and register of deeds.

The minutes of the Town Board also indicate the growing promi-nence of John Bell. For many years he would be known as King John, Squire, Judge, Old Whackum or Old Whackery. He had been born in New York State in 1805, and then emigrated to Montreal. After working for a number of years as a cooper for the Hudson's Bay Company, he arrived in La Pointe in 1835 to pursue his trade under the American Fur Company.[41] His first wife was named Angelica Gamindedons. She was probably an Indian or of mixed-blood. Two children were born of this marriage. It is assumed that this wife died, because his remaining seven

[41] Thomas, *Pen and Camera Sketches*, Ibid 37.

Fish Creek, a voyageur's highway in the early days.

Houghton Point near Washburn, circa 1900.

Lower falls of the Black River, from a lithograph drawing, circa 1878.

Grant's Point, 1897, looking northeastward toward the probable location (near a clump of bushes at right) of Le Sueur's fort of 1693.

Soldier's Rock, circa 1905.

Probably site of Cadotte's house, 1897, from a photo by
Dr. James S. Reeve of Appleton.

Protestant mission, circa 1895. Village school at end of point; Father Baraga's 1841 Catholic church at right center.

Indian cemetery, 1897.

Treaty Hall, circa 1910. (George F. Thomas at left;
Edward F. Hansen, right.)

View of La Pointe, circa 1847, from David Dale Owen's *Geological
Survey of Wisconsin, Iowa and Minnesota* (1852). Protestant
church at right center, near shore.

Protestant church, circa 1878. Part of the D. R. Angus house is visible in the background.

Father Baraga's Catholic church of 1841, pictured about 1895. Cemetery is at the right.

Dr. Edwin Ellis.

Indian payment at La Pointe, 1869. Seated at the table, left to right:
Asaph Whittlesey, Agent Henry C. Gilbert, William S. Warren
(the son of Truman Warren), and John W. Bell.

A Wisconsin Central railroad bridge over the Bad River, circa 1878.

An old cooperage shop, circa 1890, on the site of R. D. Pike's shingle mill. Left to right: John Armbruester, Nelson Cadrant, Sr., and Thomas Stahl.

Wisconsin Central bridge over the White River, 1885.

When logging was in flower, circa 1894: a sledge laden with
34,500 board feet of white pine logs.

Island View Hotel, Bayfield, circa 1895.

Lake Shore and Western Railroad ore dock nearing completion, 1885.

Charcoal blast furnace, Ashland, circa 1890. It was built in
1888 and discontinued in 1924.

Launching a whaleback at the shipyards of Capt. McDougall,
Superior, circa 1890. Photo courtesy of St. Louis
County Historical Society.

Whalebacks in Duluth harbor, circa 1894. Note funicular railway in background. Photo courtesy of St. Louis County Historical Society.

"Pig boat," circa 1894. Photo courtesy of St. Louis County Historical Society.

A "pig boat" grows a wintry beard, circa 1898. Photo courtesy of St. Louis County Historical Society.

North Wisconsin Academy, Ashland, circa 1895.
(Now a part of Northland College.)

Cedar Bark Lodge,
Hermit Island,
circa 1900.

Dog-drawn "Traino" ready to depart Madeline Island
with the U.S. Mail, circa 1930.

Protestant mission, 1898.

Nebraska Row, circa 1910. The owners in 1910, left to right, were: George Sheldon, Frank M. Spaulding, Col. Frederick M. Woods, Archibald L. Haecker, Mark Woods, and William Dorgan. The owners in 1957: William H. Sweney, Woods estate (house moved back), Thomas C. Woods, Woods estate, Mrs. Archibald (Helen Woods) Haecker, Mr. and Mrs. Lee Metcalfe, Mrs. George Woods, and Arthur Raymond.

Nebraska Row in winter, 1948.

Col. and Mrs. Frederick M. Woods (center) arrive on the the steamer "Plow Boy," circa 1901. Thomas Stahl stands at the left.

A mackinaw boat, 1907. The square stern is not true to type, but the sails are typical.

Interior of Father Baraga's 1841 church. The painting over the altar depicts the Holy Family in St. Joseph's carpenter shop. It was brought from Austria by Father Baraga in 1837.

Protestant church on the site of the Old Mission.

The "Lizzie W." of Capt. D. R. Angus, circa 1907.

Docking a ferry boat in December 1948.

Icebreaking in spring: freeing the La Pointe dock, 1949.

A modern "wind sled," 1954.

View of La Pointe, 1953.

children were born to him and Margaret Brabant between 1843 and 1856. In 1860, or possibly a little later, he had acquired influence with the Federal Bureau of Indian Affairs. Whether his standing in this respect was self-appointed or not, is unknown. Plate 13.

At the foot of the slope on which Treaty Hall was situated, and slightly to the right, or north of it, was an old cooperage shop originally built by the American Fur Company.[42] A man by the name of William Wilson occupied it at the time of this tale, and for some reason he and Bell were none too congenial. This lack of friendliness developed into frequent and caustic encounters, and at last was brought to a head, according to the old story, by Wilson threatening to kick Bell's dog. Although the song "They Gotta Quit Kickin' my Dog Aroun'" of circa 1910 had not yet been composed, Bell expressed its sentiments in a voluble manner. The result was that the two agreed to engage in a fisticuffs match, the loser to quit forever the shores of Madeline Island.

After some debate, it was decided to stage the affair on the streets of Bayfield, and the date was set. The opponents were evenly matched, both of powerful physique, and the tide of battle ebbed and flowed for the greater part of one day.[43] Tradition does not specify whether there were periods of King's X in which they refreshed themselves, but ultimately Wilson was defeated. True to the agreement, he left La Pointe. He settled as a hermit on the small island which today is still called Wilson's Island, although the official title is Hermit.[44] There death overtook him in 1861. He was buried in an unmarked grave, at his own request, in the mission cemetery on Madeline Island. To that extent he violated the agreement. For some years thereafter, rumors of Spanish doubloons and pieces of eight took treasure seekers to his Hermit Island home, but, so far as is known, no one found any of the trove.

By 1857 Ashland had at least fifty houses, and bade fair to be much larger owing to the boom hysteria which permeated the northern country. This was induced not only by the iron discoveries on the Gogebic Range, but also by the promotional talk of a rail line from the Gogebic to Ashland. It was also hoped that copper mines, rivaling those of Michigan, might be developed in the Bois Brule area.

However, in that year the bubble burst, through another nation-wide panic, with tragic results for this new and apparently prosperous town. Between the panic and the advent of the Civil War, Ashland gradually

[42] Parts of this building have since been incorporated in the modern summer home of Mrs. Christopher D. O'Brien, Jr.

[43] John B. Chapple, *The Wisconsin Islands*, (Ashland Daily Press, Ashland, Wisconsin, 1945), 1.

[44] There are a number of different versions to this tale. The author has chosen the one which most appealed to him.

lost its population. By the end of 1863 only one family remained. Thus, for a period of six years, Martin Roehm and family of five, held the fort and allowed the city to boast a continuous existence from the year 1854.

Through this loss of population, the County Seat was moved back to La Pointe, where Judge Bell apparently assumed several offices in the county administration. Although other men were elected to various county duties, they seemed happy to have Bell to do all the work. Bayfield, too, gained through its neighbor's loss. Asaph Whittlesey moved to the newer town, which managed a degree of prosperity through its sawmill and fishing industry.

The region contributed its share of man power to the Civil War. Many of its youth joined the famous Iron Brigade which achieved lasting fame thoroughly in keeping with its name. Others joined the 8th Wisconsin Infantry Regiment which had "Old Abe" as its celebrated mascot. This eagle was said to have flown over its contingent in battle, screaming for victory.

Elisha Pike's son, Robinson Derling Pike, enlisted as a private in the 27th Michigan Infantry, but at the end of the war was a Captain in the First Regiment of Michigan Cavalry, General George Custer's Regiment.[45] William Henry Wheeler, the second son of the Odanah missionary, also enlisted, and ended his army career as a Captain. William Neveaux, of Ojibway descent, journeyed from La Pointe to join Company K of the First Michigan Sharp Shooters, where he won signal recognition, and emerged as a corporal.[46]

In October 1866, Wheeler retired from his missionary work at Odanah, because of ill health. The Indians turned out in force to wish him Godspeed, and displayed great emotion at his leaving. He had won their friendship and confidence through many deeds of kindness. At one time he had gone overland, on foot, in the dead of winter, via Eau Claire, Wisconsin, to Madison where he had entrained for Washington. Here, his forceful presentation of facts in their behalf had secured the revocation of an order which would have moved them from their homeland to points further west. Again, in an argument between the settlers of Ashland and his Indian charges over a boundary line, he had interceded to effect an harmonious understanding.[47]

After his retirement and removal to Beloit, Wisconsin, where he died

[45] Historical Records, Bayfield Public Library.
[46] His tombstone in the La Pointe Indian Cemetery bears the following simple epitaph:

CORP. WILLIAM NEVEAUX
CO. K. 1ST MICH. S. S.

[47] Guy Burnham, Ibid, 31. This was a published letter of William H. Wheeler, the second son.

in 1872, the windmill which he had invented at Odanah, and which was the first of the solid wheel type, became the chief product of the Eclipse Wind Engine Company of that city. This company, founded by his sons, was the forerunner of the present Fairbanks, Morse & Company of Beloit.[48]

Upon his removal to Beloit, Wheeler took with him the church records of the La Pointe-Odanah Protestant Church. On April 24, 1867 he made the last entry in these records, and listed the membership as of October 1866.

The entry read:

"Members of the Church.

Names	Number
L. H. Wheeler & Wife	2
Rhoda W. Wheeler [49]	1
Mary Green	1
Dr. Ellis[50]	1
Sarah	1
Yellore Henderson & Wife	2
Hannah	1
Mrs. La Pointe	1
Mrs. Leihy	1
Mrs. Benjamin Morrin	1
Henry Blatchford & Wife	2
Babomigorhigehwa	1
Total	15" [51]

After Wheeler's departure from Odanah, his station was taken over by the Presbyterian Church. The Reverend Mr. Isaac Baird, a minister of that church, came to Odanah on March 15, 1873, and remained until 1884, when he went to Crystal Falls, Michigan.[52]

Either through lack of support by the Presbyterians or through the indifference of the populace, the missionaries left. They were followed by a Catholic organization which today maintains a sizeable school,

[48] Until well into the 1900s, after the Fairbanks Company had operated for some years, an employee would state that he worked at the *E' –clipse*. (Author's note.)

[49] The wife of Leonard H. Wheeler, Jr. (Author's note.)

[50] Dr. Edwin Ellis came to Ashland in 1856, and stayed there until Ashland lost its population during the Civil War. He later returned to Ashland where he practiced medicine for many years, and was one of the city's prominent men.

[51] La Pointe Mission Church Records, Ibid. The originals were left with Wheeler's son, the Reverend Mr. Edward Payson Wheeler, who later gave them to the Chicago Historical Society.

[52] Chrysostum Verwyst, "Reminiscences of a Pioneer Missionary," *Wisconsin Historical Society Proceedings*, "Separate" #173.

while practically all of the inhabitants are now communicants of that church. A small and struggling Methodist Church, which leads a precarious existence, is the only present-day indication of the earlier Protestant efforts.

The end of the Civil War brought its many problems to the whole country. It was the era of licking wounds until conditions, both economic and moral, might be restored. It was a period of readjustment during which few people came to La Pointe or the northern territory. The soldiers returned to a region which was more or less marking time, waiting for something to happen.

In 1868, Father Baraga, who first became Bishop of Amazonia and later the Bishop of Sault Ste. Marie and Marquette, died at his headquarters in the latter city.[53] In his later years he found much happiness in visiting the missions which he had founded. He had remarked that he would much rather have been missionary among the Indians than to have become a bishop. Toward the end of his life, in reviewing his labors among them, he said, "I make pretty good Christians of some of them, but men? No: It is impossible." [54]

In 1866, upon his return from the Civil War, Captain Robinson D. Pike built a shingle mill in La Pointe. It was east of, and adjacent to, the village dock. Plate 14. After a short period of operation it met with a rather tragic end due to a boiler explosion which killed Gabriel Stahl and caused a number of other casualties.[55] It also set fire to a large part of the village, destroying the warehouses of the old fur company, the Madeline House, and many of the houses, stores and cabins between the pier and Pointe de Froid. Fortunately many of the houses were unoccupied. This accident occurred on May 17, 1869. The town records of the time reveal that Judge Bell was a versatile man, since he officiated at the amputation of a leg of a man who had been injured – for which he collected a fee from the village.[56]

Either shortly before this accident or immediately afterward, Captain Pike built another sawmill in Bayfield, for by October 20, 1870 his Bayfield mill had produced in that year 300,000 feet of lumber and 1,000,000 shingles.[57]

[53] During 1954, beatification was bestowed on Baraga as a step toward his eventual sanctification. (Author's note.)

[54] John N. Davidson, *In Unnamed Wisconsin*, (Milwaukee, 1895), 173.

[55] Gabriel Stahl was a brother of Thomas Stahl who had come to La Pointe in 1861, and who became a prominent citizen of the village. He lived there for over sixty years. (Author's note.)

[56] Minutes of the La Pointe Town Board, 1857 et seq.

[57] *Bayfield County Press*, October 20, 1870. The same issue gave the production of Elisha Pike's mill, at its original site, as 150,000 feet of lumber and Samuel Vaughn's mill as 800,000 feet of lumber and 600,000 shingles.

In 1868, Frederick Prentice returned from Toledo, Ohio, whence he had moved as a result of the Ashland depression of 1857. He came back, enthusiastic over the possibilities of Lake Superior sandstone as a building material. After a short time of investigation in the nearby area, he found what he desired on the southern end of Basswood Island, and there opened the first commercial quarry in the region.[58]

Also, in the same year, the whole Lake Superior territory was much interested in the tour of Mrs. Abraham Lincoln to the head of the lakes. There are entries in an hotel register in Sault Ste. Marie recording her arrival and that of her son, Robert Todd Lincoln. The daughter of Asaph Whittlesey records meeting Mrs. Lincoln at Ontonagon, Michigan, and advising her not to stay at a certain hotel at La Pointe: "— it's full of knot holes and the men snore something awful." [59]

It is doubtful whether Mrs. Lincoln stayed over night at La Pointe, but she did visit Father Baraga's church there. Bayfield was all agog at her stay in Smith's hotel in that town. From there Mrs. Lincoln went on to Superior and Duluth.

By 1869 newcomers began to filter into the territory. More families re-occupied Ashland. The old feeling of potential prosperity, fostered by the new mines, attracted them, and this time there was a more substantial development of the town.

That La Pointe was gradually losing its importance is shown by the census of 1870, when two hundred five inhabitants were listed. The same enumeration showed nineteen persons employed at the quarry on Basswood Island, twelve of whom had been born in Ireland. Besides seeing a penchant for quarrying, one observes the migration of that nationality into the Lake Superior region.

Another indication was the choice of base for the first steamers on Chequamegon Bay. The "Eva Wadsworth," owned by Samuel S. Vaughn, made her home port in Ashland, and engaged in free lance trade in the general district — just two hundred years after the arrival of Father Marquette. She was available for charter for virtually all purposes: from conveying passengers to carrying live stock and hay. In 1871, the "Frank C. Fero" maintained a ferry service between Ashland and Bayfield, the same year that the City of Chicago was destroyed by fire. The principal business of the "Fero" was freighting material to and from Ashland to make connections with the lake boats at Bayfield. At that time the lake captains did not care to risk their vessels in the shoals of Chequamegon Bay. Also, at about that time, the lake boats no longer

[58] Guy Burnham, Ibid, 258, 341 as to Prentice.
    Roland D. Irving, *Geology of Wisconsin*, Ibid, 3:210 as to date.
[59] Guy Burnham, Ibid, 204, 222–223.

stopped at La Pointe. Any freight destined for that port was unloaded at Bayfield, for trans-shipment, by local craft, to the village. To add insult to injury, Ashland had again assumed her position as County Seat in 1872, probably to the discomfiture of both La Pointe and Judge Bell.

At last, in 1871, the long dreamed-of hope on the part of Ashland appeared to be on its way to fulfillment when the Wisconsin Central Railroad started its survey from Milwaukee to Ashland. This news brought in many more people, not only to work on the new project, but also to take advantage of any unearned increment in real estate investments. Actual work started on the Ashland end of the line in 1872. The contract for this portion of the road covered about thirty miles of track from Ashland to Penokee Gap, a few miles south of the present City of Mellen, Wisconsin.[60] Map 9.

After traversing what geogologists term The Lake Superior Lowlands for a distance of about twenty miles, the railroad was to follow the course of the Bad River to and through the gap. This valley was of considerable importance to the builders, since it offered the only convenient water-level route through the rough and high Penokee Range. In 1872 six miles of the line were finished, and the remainder was built in 1873.

However, towards the end of 1872 it appeared that further construction might be brought to an halt through the inability of some of the subcontractors to complete their work. The Phillips-Colby Construction Company, which held the general contract, assumed the smaller contracts, but it too ran into financial difficulties, and was compelled to suspend all operations. This forced approximately one thousand men out of work, and precipitated what was locally called the Ashland War.

Since Ashland was the headquarters of the construction crew, it bore the brunt of the men's dissatisfaction because there was no place for them to go. Superior, the nearest city of any importance, was eighty miles away, over rough and uninhabited roads. The embryonic stage service, running only when the roads were snow covered, had not yet started operations. Chequamegon Bay was frozen over, thus forestalling boat transportation. The company paymaster was late, and when he did come, the men demanded pay up to the time of his arrival. The paymaster refused their claims with the result that the men were in an ugly mood, threatening to rob him. Local law enforcement agencies

[60] Penokee Gap has been of immense interest to geologists, because the Bad River has cut through the various vertical strata of rocks, revealing their extreme age and proving the existence of the ancient mountains, of which the Gogebic and Penokee Ranges are the puny remnants. The river, in encountering the different resistances of the respective strata, has assumed a whole series of right-angled turns. (Author's note.)

were helpless, and an emergency appeal was made to Bayfield for help. On New Year's Day of 1873 this was answered by Sheriff Nelson Boutin who enlisted Captain Pike with his company of Bayfield Rifles. Order was restored, and the men gradually left town, mostly on foot.[61]

It may seem strange that Ashland, with its prospects of a railroad, and with its larger population, should find it necessary to appeal to Bayfield for help in weathering its civic troubles. Yet the smaller city, in many respects, appeared to have a more stable type of citizen and a steadier economy; the latter no doubt due to the town's deep water port which made it more attractive to lake shipping than Ashland's.

The last twenty-four miles of construction work was commenced in the spring of 1873. The ten miles toward Penokee Gap were probably the most difficult of any on the Wisconsin Central Railroad. They involved the building of at least sixty bridges, the blasting of considerable rock along the tortuous path of the Bad River, as well as maintaining reasonably easy grades in the seven-hundred-foot climb from the lowlands. Plate 15.

Much of the right-of-way in this distance resembled mountain type construction, with its many curves, the bridges crossing and re-crossing the tumbling and roaring waters of the river, and the high hills towering on each side. Adding to the strangeness of the scene was the peculiarity of the stream itself. Its waters were a chocolate brown, with a frosting of pure white at the falls and rapids. The discoloration was due to the swampy sources of the stream.

Among the sixty odd bridges were two which taxed the engineering abilities of the builders. One of these spanned the White River, about ten miles south of Ashland. The other crossed Silver Creek toward the foot of the highlands. The White River bridge was sixteen hundred feet long, one hundred seven feet high and cost one hundred forty thousand dollars. Plate 16. The one over Silver Creek was eight hundred sixty feet long, eighty-seven feet high and cost sixty thousand dollars.[62]

[61] Guy Burnham, Ibid, 257.
[62] Guy Burnham, Ibid, 253. Another source gives the bridge lengths as fifteen hundred sixty and six hundred fifty, respectively. *History of Northern Wisconsin*, The Western Historical Company, A. T. Andreas, proprietor (Chicago, 1881), 65–66.

The contractors for the bridges were Messrs. Stoughton Brothers. Both bridges were of rather novel design. Heavy girders were not available for long spans, nor was the proper steel or iron for a double cantilever structure. They were built up by means of four decks; the bottom one supported by fabricated columns resting on masonry piers, and tied together with lighter built-up beams and a series of truss rods. All spans between the piers, except the central one over the river, were about thirty feet, and the vertical columns were about the same. Each deck was supported in the same manner by the one below. The spans of the top deck, which carried the ties and rails, were of inverted king post design.

It is doubtful if steel was available at the time, even though the Bessemer con-

As long as these bridges were in service, all trains slowed down as they crossed. With a little imagination, one was certain that the White River bridge, in particular, swayed anywhere from a few inches to several feet, as the train crept along.[63] In the early 1900s the bridges were removed, much to the relief of the traveling public, and their places taken by great earthen fills with apparently tiny culverts at the bottom. The red sandstone abutments and piers of the original bridges are still visible.

With the completion of the final mileage, and with rumors of a further contract to extend the line, hopes ran high in Ashland, with attendant speculation in city lots. The news of another nation-wide panic dashed these expectations, and brought despair to the town. The repercussions of this depression were especially severe in the over-extended building of railroads, and the year 1873 will long be remembered in rail circles as the one in which Jay Cooke and his Northern Pacific Railroad went bankrupt.

Again Ashland was in the doldrums, with a steady decrease in its population. One saving factor was the small employment offered by the Ashland Lumber Company which had started a sawmill that year. The mill was owned and operated by W. R. Sutherland and C. A. Sheffield. It had a capacity of about 50,000 board feet of lumber per day.

An old warehouse record book of Samuel Stewart Vaughn, recently brought to light, points out the importance of Bayfield in a conclusive manner.[64] It, also, had been kept in that meticulous copper plate hand of the era's expert bookkeeper. The entries showed the names of all arriving and departing vessels, their respective captains, the cargo discharged or loaded, its origin or destination, the accrued charges and the weights.

This old book disclosed that in July of 1873 thirty-eight vessels docked at Bayfield to deliver merchandise and to accept shipments of fish and lumber. The first receipts in the spring comprised much fresh meat along with several barrels of whisky, the latter, no doubt, to replenish supplies exhausted during the winter. Also, the last receipts in the fall were composed of substantial tonnages of coal, received in barrels, and also kegs of whisky for certain of the local gentry. The saloons, too, laid in barrels for their winter supply.

Hardware was discharged for the Ashland firm of Leihy and Garnich, predecessors of the 1957 Emil Garnich & Sons Company. There were

verter was coming into production. Tonnages of steel were very limited. It is probable, therefore, that these bridges were built of wrought iron. (Author's note.)

[63] The author, when a little boy, was quite sure that the sway was several feet.

[64] Samual S. Vaughn Warehouse Records of 1873. Wisconsin Historical Library, Madison, Wisconsin .

supplies for the Brown Stone Company, of Basswood Island, and the R. D. Pike Lumber Company of Bayfield. Many barrels of crackers were consigned to each of the latter.[65] Surprisingly, too, there are records of canned oysters being received.[66]

The Philadelphia Centennial Exposition of 1876 sounded the tocsin for the end of the depression. Both the United States and Ashland rebounded with great vigor. The first telegraph line was completed into the latter in April of 1876. The demand for lumber increased, which spurred on the completion of the southern portion of the Wisconsin Central Railroad. This connected with the finished Ashland line at Penokee Gap, where Asaph Whittlesey, on June 2, 1877 drove the last spike. Thus for the first time, the city and the Chequamegon Region were brought into rail communication with the more developed areas of the United States. All Ashland was present on June 16, when the first train arrived from Milwaukee.

On August first of that year, the famous hostelry, built by the railroad company, opened its doors. Very fittingly, it was called the Hotel Chequamegon. It would be popular for many years, a Mecca for hay fever sufferers, and an inn to serve a new and booming territory. It was located on the site of the present Ashland County Court House. It was built in the shape of an L, with one hundred twenty feet frontage and eighty feet depth, was three stories high, and had sixty guest rooms. A contemporary report stated: ". . . is fitted with electric bells, and furnished nicely throughout; . . ."

According to local enthusiasts, the hotel was the deviser of the Lake Superior planked whitefish. However that may be, the comestible was a *specialite de la maison*, and acquired wide appreciation. A boast of the house was that it used only white pine planks in the preparation of the viand, and it further claimed that no plank was used more than four times. Its argument was that to obtain the authentic Chequamegon flavor, it was necessary for the sap or pitch of the pine to permeate slightly the adjacent skin of the fish. It is true that a new white pine plank does impart a savor to a whitefish which can never be achieved by the charred, grease-soaked and ofttimes rancid oaken planks which so frequently greet guests in hotels and restaurants that seek to feature the dish.

[65] The Brown Stone Company, due to its isolation, ran its own boarding house. The Pike company operated several in its logging camps.

[66] There are other records extant, some as early as 1845, which refer to this tinned product. (Author's note.)

CHAPTER SEVEN

1878 Behold the Fire and the Wood 1888

The period of the late 1870s was the beginning of the booming lumber industry on Lake Superior. It was also an era when La Pointe reached its more modern low from the standpoint of animation. People continued to move away, not content with the stagnation which appeared to have set in. Any new arrivals were viewed with suspicion. The general attitude of the older inhabitants was: "Why had these outlanders came to this out-of-the-way place, unless to escape something in their former lives?" The few who could withstand this distrust found that it was necessary to remain several years before being accepted as true Islanders. The little community remained as a torpid slough, surrounded by the swirl of nearby feverish excitement.

In neighboring Ashland, sawmills were built on the waterfront until the shore was filled for a distance of four miles with their installations. In 1879, with the founding of Washburn, immediately across Chequamegon Bay from Ashland, two more mills were added.[1] There was the Old Pike Lumber Company of Bayfield, and the Red Cliff Lumber Company further north. Following around the Bayfield Peninsula, additional mills were located at Cornucopia, Herbster and Port Wing.

The mills ran night and day. The shrieks of their saws could be heard for miles on a quiet night. Each mill was equipped with a refuse burner which disposed of the edgings, sawdust and waste slabs.[2] The burners were immense affairs, sometimes up to twenty feet in diameter and one hundred feet in height. They were lined with fire brick, and the refuse

[1] The town was named after former State governor Cadwallader Colden Washburn. Before the more formal founding of the town, there had been a small community which was called McClellan. (Author's note.)

[2] At first, the refuse was dumped into the lake, but this became such a nuisance and killed so many fish, particularly in Chequamegon Bay, that legislation forced the mills to adopt the burners. (Author's note.)

was fed into them by endless chain conveyors. They were in truth, pillars of cloud by day, and pillars of fire by night.[3]

As usual in these booming frontier towns, everything was wide open. The main streets of Ashland, Washburn and Bayfield had their full quotas of saloons and dives.[4] In the spring, when the lumberjacks came in from the woods, after their long winter of hard work and isolation, the bordellos let out extra links for their entertainment. It was nothing unusual to find a jack dead broke the day after his arrival in town, the victim of too much liquor and the old trick of rolling — robbing him while he was unconscious. The jacks were rather philosophical about the experience, adopting the attitude of easy come, easy go. Fights were frequent, and extra police were deputized to handle the spring rush.

To feed the maws of the sawmills, logging trains, with their extremely adaptable but most ludicrous appearing Shay locomotives, brought their logs from the hinterland. Immense booms of logs were towed in from the lake's surrounding territory by powerful tugs. The occasional rafts which one sees today, with their gathers of match wood for the paper mills, are mere pygmies compared with the giant rafts of that era, containing their big saw logs. To be fair to the modern rafts, however, it must be admitted that they are towed across the open lake from the north shore at about one mile per hour, while the earlier ones were largely sheltered by the islands. Plate 17.

To add to the ferment of the times, considerable excitement developed over the discovery of copper, in unknown quantities, in the neighborhood of the Bois Brule River, on the so-called Copper Range. This range is the geological phenomenon connected with the great Lake Superior fault, where the copper bearing rocks of the Keweenawan Series lies very close to the surface.

There had been considerable indiscriminate prospecting in that area for more than fifty years, with inconclusive results. Lumps of float copper had been picked up from time to time, but never enough to cause a concerted rush. However, with the opening of the Percival Mine, near the Bois Brule River, in 1873, which disclosed a promising vein, a minor scramble resulted, with numerous test holes sunk by inexperienced persons. As might be expected, these holes yielded nothing but disillusionment for the amateur miners.

A tract of land comprising five thousand seven hundred acres, bought

---

[3] The modern mills on the Pacific Coast chip up the wood which is not suitable for lumber and sell it to the paper mills. The remainder they run through a 'hog' and use it under their own boilers, selling the excess to other plants requiring steam power. (Author's note.)

[4] The La Pointe Town Board at first charged fifty dollars per year per liquor license. In successive meetings, after listening to the objections of the saloon keepers, the licenses were reduced to ten dollars each. (Author's note.)

from the Government by various individuals during the years ranging from 1855 to 1863, was sold to the Consolidated Land & Mining Company of Lake Superior in 1865 for a consideration of one hundred thousand dollars. In 1873, this company sold ten hundred forty acres to the owners of the Percival Mine for three thousand forty dollars, a price which might have indicated some disappointment on the part of the company in its original investment.[5] The Percival Mine, after a reassuring start, discovered that its veins were pinching out, and the venture failed. However, as late as 1900, various companies and individuals tried to operate the mine, but without success. Map 12, p. 38.

One geologist observed that with the exception of the Percival mine, these ventures had been initiated by men with little or no experience, and without the guidance of competent geologists. He was fairly optimistic in his belief that the area might later produce substantial tonnages of high-grade ore, after it had been surveyed and prospected by men with scientific and practical knowledge.[6] Thus far, at least, there have been no startling discoveries of copper ore.

This flurry of mining was followed by an interesting social experiment in the same region. It was started and partially carried through on the Bois Brule River by Samuel Budgett of Bristol, England. He purchased thirty-three hundred acres of land in 1873, part of which included the Percival mine site. The remainder lay along the shore of Lake Superior, having a frontage of about three miles, of which about one-half mile was on the west side of the mouth of the Brule, and the remainder to the east. Map 12 shows the location of his little settlement which he named Clevedon.

His idea was to reward old and faithful employees of his provision trade with a start in a new and apparently promising country. A sawmill was built and orchards set out, with the thought of founding an independent and self-supporting community. The records of the time indicate that a number of families, comprising about thirty persons in all, took advantage of this opportunity. By 1884, a gradual exodus began, and the colony was soon deserted. No doubt the Lake Superior winters played their part in discouraging men accustomed to the milder English ones.[7]

Another project of the 1880s, affecting the Bois Brule, was the proposed Lake Superior-Mississippi Canal, one of the many plans suggested for the connecting the Great Lakes with that river. The Bois Brule-St.

[5] Leigh P. Jerrard, "The Brule River of Wisconsin," *The Westerners Brand Book*, (Chicago, March, 1950), 5.
[6] E. T. Sweet, *Geology of Wisconsin*, Ibid, 3:339.
[7] Leigh P. Jerrard, Ibid.

Croix route was surveyed by Government engineers. Their estimates totaled about eight million dollars.[8]

The mining activities and Budgett's settlement project were conducted chieifly from Superior, Wisconsin. To reach the Bois Brule area after navigation closed, it was necessary to resort to land communications. An old highway which played an important part in the transportation facilities of the time was the Bayfield Road which ran from Superior to the smaller town. The original trail was undoubtedly of Indian origin, and its exact route is not known, except that it followed the lake shore for some distance out of Superior as far as the Flag River.[9] From the lake it probably led up that river to its headwaters in or near the barrens. It was then about fourteen miles to the source of the Sioux River, and the latter was followed to its mouth. Map 11.

Alex Butterfield, in his ninety-second year, a grandson of the American Fur Company trader, Charles Butterfield, and a life-long resident of Bayfield County, stated that the original road not only followed the Sioux River, but also, from its mouth, headed northward along the lake shore to Bayfield.

According to Butterfield, this route was later shortened by a road built along Pike's Creek, and joining the older one at Moose Lake which is about five miles west of the Sioux headwaters. Map 25. Although Butterfield had been born after the construction of both of these roads, the original route had been impressed upon his mind by the tales of his father, Stephen Butterfield. The latter, with John Dunomie, drove fifteen head of cattle from Eau Claire, Wisconsin, to Bayfield in the late 1850s, and en route experienced many adventures from the subborn waywardness of the half-wild beasts.

Since the trail out of Superior was no doubt rudimentary, one further inland was later developed. It is shown on map 25 and named the Old

[8] According to one survey, the canal was to start from Superior harbor, run eastward and intercept the Bois Brule River near the present Village of Brule. This route, despite its length and the bridging of numerous intermediate streams, would be cheaper, in the opinion of the engineers, than constructing a lake harbor off the mouth of the Bois Brule, where cargoes would have to be transferred to canal barges. An harbor here would involve much expensive dredging and the building of long and massive breakwaters. (Author's note.)

[9] Verwyst, *Life of Bishop Baraga*, Ibid, 237–238. Also Armstrong, Ibid, 49.
Verwyst related that Baraga and a guide left Fond du Lac, following the south shore of the lake and camped the first night at Ga-Pakweiagak. No translation of this Ojibway word was given nor does it appear in Baraga's dictionary. However, by breaking down the word into its components, it doubtless meant the region of the Flag River. This stream flows into the lake at the present Village of Port Wing, Wisconsin.
A friend of the author very much doubts Baraga's ability to have traveled this distance of about forty miles in one day, in the winter. However, Armstrong, op. cit. claimed to have covered the same route in one day on January 20, 1855 with four

Bayfield Road. Unfortunately for the trail-curious, the only record thus far available shows the road ending at the east boundary of Township 48 North, Range 12 West, about eleven miles east of Superior. Its further eastern course is a matter of conjecture.

The diary of the Methodist minister, James Peet, tells of his trip from St. Paul to Superior in 1857 over a rather embryonic road. On one occasion the conveyance in which his wife was riding became jammed between two trees, and considerable time was spent in extricating it.[10]

This road ran southward from Superior to the St. Croix River where it was joined by the St. Croix Trail from Chequamegon Bay. When the trails had developed to the stage where horse-drawn sleighs might be used, the quickest route from Superior to Bayfield in the winter was south from Superior to the St. Croix, thence on the St. Croix Trail for about seventeen miles, and then on the Gordon Trail to Bayfield. The latter route was named after Antoine Gaudin, an early mail carrier and a member of an old La Pointe family.

The St. Croix Trail left Chequamegon near Whittlesey Creek and headed southwestward to Gordon, Wisconsin. There is a record of its existence in 1858.[11] Colonel Charles Whittlesey also showed it, in part, on his map of 1860. Map 9.

By 1872 the Bayfield Road used the Superior-St. Croix highway to the south boundary of Township 48 North, Range 13 West, about eight miles south of Superior. It then struck out almost due east for about fourteen miles and then swung slightly to the north of east, directly past the Percival Mine and on to Moose Lake. Map 25. At the latter point it connected with the Pike's Creek cut-off from Bayfield. Map 26 shows a number of these old roads.

In 1872, the Ashland, Bayfield and Superior Stage Company was brave enough to advertise a tri-weekly stage service, in the winter only, with a schedule of two to three days en route, the time depending on the weather and the condition of the roads. It built four stations between the terminals for the accommodation of over-night travelers. These were located at Moose Lake, Pine Lake, Poplar River and Bois Brule River. An early stopping place, used mostly by Bayfield to Ashland traffic and not operated by the stage company, was the Silvernail home, at the junction of the Sioux and Little Sioux Rivers.

men and two dog trains, the sledges of which were loaded with furs. He said, "We all went on together and camped that night at a place well known as Flag River." En route, the men took turns in breaking a path for the dog teams. Possibly both Baraga and Armstrong possessed Bunyanesque qualities. (Author's note.)

[10] James Peet Diaries, 1857–1859. Wisconsin Historical Library, Manuscript division.

[11] Albert Stuntz Diaries, 1858–1864. (April 3–19, 1858), Wisconsin Historical Library, Manuscript division. (Wis, Mss., N.Z.)

Stage service was discontinued in 1884 upon the completion of the Northern Pacific Railroad between Ashland and Superior. The Bayfield Bridge of the old highway, which crossed the Bois Brule about nine miles south of Lake Superior, and which was not far from the Percival Mine, was a landmark for the later devotees of that stream. It has been claimed that the ruts of the old road are still visible near the site of the former bridge.

Thomas Stahl, who came to La Pointe in 1861, and became one of its leading citizens, was perhaps the only person to experience practically all methods of transportation between Bayfield and St. Paul. He recounted how he had walked over the trail in its early days, stopping at many of the places which Albert Stuntz mentioned in his diaries. His next trip was by means of an ox team, followed very shortly by one with a team of horses. At a later date he traveled by railroad, and still later by automobile. His son, living in St. Paul, had arranged for him to take the trip by airplane, but this was prevented by his death in 1922.

In 1883, another railroad, attracted by the lumbering and mining industries, was built into Ashland, Washburn and Bayfield. The Chicago, St. Paul, Minneapolis and Omaha, commonly called the Omaha, was completed into Bayfield in that year. Amidst tooting of whistles of the sawmill and of loading lumber hookers, and the cheers of spectators, the first train pulled into the Bayfield station at 4:04 p.m. on Friday, October 12, 1883.[12]

Bayfield, at the time, was the main terminus, with a branch into Ashland from Ashland Junction (which Ashland viewed with jaundiced eye). The decision to give Bayfield this honor was due to two factors; the first was that Ashland Harbor was still beset by many shoals, and the second to the influence of Henry M. Rice. Between the time when Rice had founded Bayfield in 1856 and the arrival of the railroad, he had accumulated large tracts of timberland in the surrounding neighborhood. In addition, he had achieved financial stature in the City of St. Paul. In the 1880s, he was serving in the United States Senate. These factors were no doubt of considerable influence in the making of the decision. One of his tracts of land lay on present Rocky Island. For many years this was called Rice's Island, and many of the local inhabitants still call it that.

The Omaha entered the region from the southwest, coming from St. Paul, and connecting with the main line between Chicago and Duluth at Spooner, Wisconsin. Noting the success of the Wisconsin Central's Hotel Chequamegon in Ashland, the Omaha immediately opened a rival inn at Bayfield. Its Island View Hotel won as much fame as its Ashland counterpart.

[12] *The Bayfield County Press*, October, 1883. Files of Press at Bayfield.

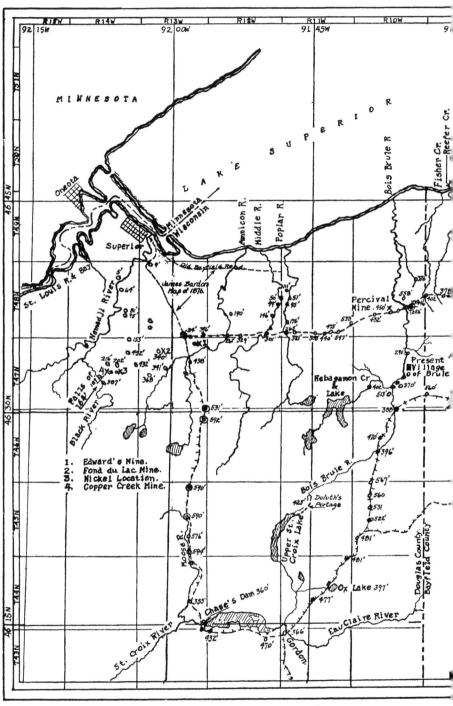

138   25. Old Trails and Roads, Bayfield Peninsula.

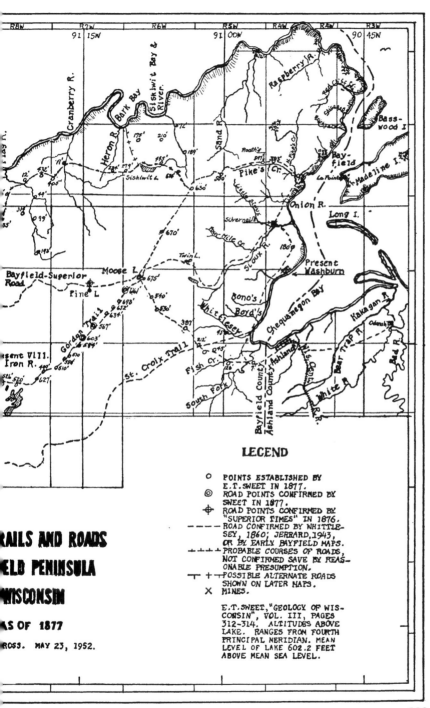

R8W R7W R6W R5W R4W R4W R3W

91 15W 91 00W 90 45W

Cranberry R.
Siskiwit Bay & River
Bark Bay
Heron R.
Sand R.
Raspberry R.
Bass-wood I.
Red Cliffs
Bay-field
Roath's
Pike's Cr.
La Point
Madeline I.
Onion R.
Long I.
Silverneil
Four-Mile Cr.
Sioux R.
Present Washburn
Twin L.
Moose L.
Bayfield-Superior Road
Pine L.
Gordon Trail
Bono's
Boyd's
Whittlesey
Chequamegon Bay
Kakagan R.
Present Vill. Iron R.
St. Croix Trail
Fish Cr.
South Fork
Bayfield County / Ashland County
Ashland
White R.
Bear Trap R.
Bad R.

LEGEND

○   POINTS ESTABLISHED BY
    E.T. SWEET IN 1877.
◉   ROAD POINTS CONFIRMED BY
    SWEET IN 1877.
⊕   ROAD POINTS CONFIRMED BY
    "SUPERIOR TIMES" IN 1876.
---- ROAD CONFIRMED BY WHITTLE-
    SEY, 1860; JERRARD, 1943,
    OR BY EARLY BAYFIELD MAPS.
+-+-+ PROBABLE COURSES OF ROADS,
    NOT CONFIRMED SAVE BY REAS-
    ONABLE PRESUMPTION.
⊤ + ⊤ POSSIBLE ALTERNATE ROADS
    SHOWN ON LATER MAPS.
✕   MINES.

E.T. SWEET, "GEOLOGY OF WIS-
CONSIN", VOL. III, PAGES
312-314. ALTITUDES ABOVE
LAKE. RANGES FROM FOURTH
PRINCIPAL MERIDIAN. MEAN
LEVEL OF LAKE 602.2 FEET
ABOVE MEAN SEA LEVEL.

TRAILS AND ROADS
BAYFIELD PENINSULA
WISCONSIN

AS OF 1877

ROSS. MAY 23, 1952.

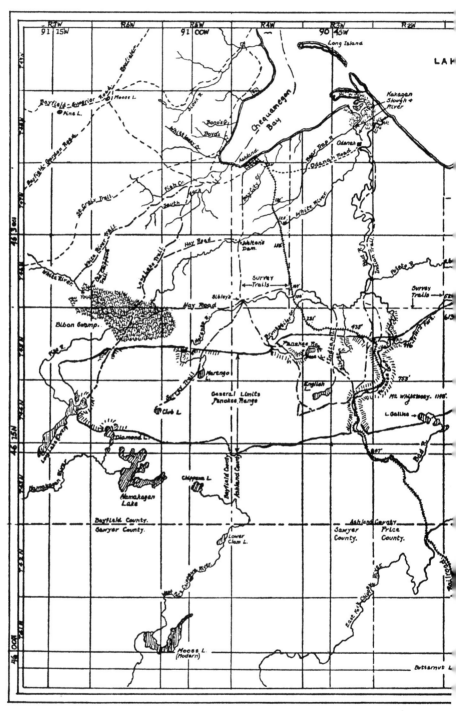

140   26. Old Trails and Roads, Near Ashland.

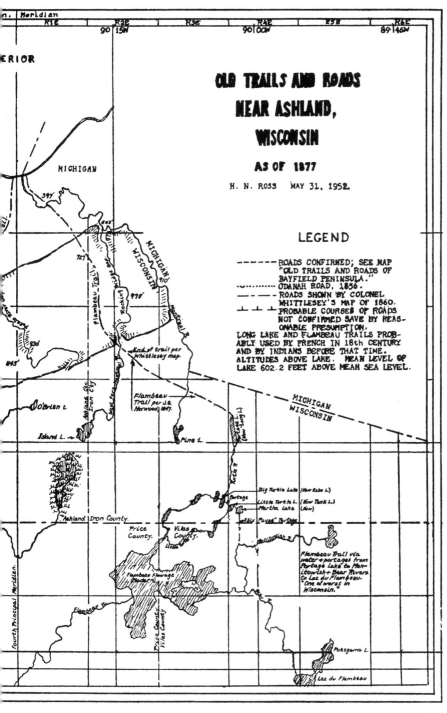

OLD TRAILS AND ROADS
NEAR ASHLAND,
WISCONSIN

AS OF 1877

H. N. ROSS   MAY 31, 1952.

LEGEND

```
------  ROADS CONFIRMED; SEE MAP
        "OLD TRAILS AND ROADS OF
        BAYFIELD PENINSULA."
.......  ODANAH ROAD, 1856.
-- --   ROADS SHOWN BY COLONEL
        WHITTLESEY'S MAP OF 1860.
+ + +   PROBABLE COURSES OF ROADS
        NOT CONFIRMED SAVE BY REAS-
        ONABLE PRESUMPTION.
```
LONG LAKE AND FLAMBEAU TRAILS PROB-
ABLY USED BY FRENCH IN 18th CENTURY
AND BY INDIANS BEFORE THAT TIME.
ALTITUDES ABOVE LAKE. MEAN LEVEL OF
LAKE 602.2 FEET ABOVE MEAN SEA LEVEL.

141

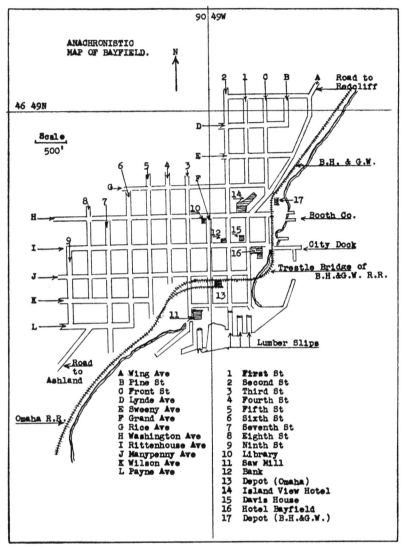

27. Anachronistic Map of Bayfield.

It was built on a side hill, a short distance from the lake, and one block north of the present (1957) Hotel Bayfield. Plate 18. Map 27. It commanded a remarkable view of Madeline, Basswood and Long Islands with their intervening channels. The nearby streams abounded in brook trout and the woods were full of game. The lake offered excellent rock fishing for the larger speckled trout. Consequently, the hotel was an haven for anglers and hunters, and was even more popular than the Chequamegon Hotel to hay fever sufferers. It enjoyed substantial custom from the railroad and from a line of lake steamers which made Bayfield a port of call. The original manager of the hotel was the same one who opened the Chequamegon. Charles N. Willey was a popular boniface, with a very wide following.

In 1885, the Milwaukee, Lake Shore & Western Railroad, now part of the Chicago & Northwestern Railway, completed its line into Ashland from Ironwood, Michigan, thus connecting the newer Michigan iron ranges with a nearby Lake Superior port. In spite of the fact that iron had been discovered on the Gogebic Range in 1848, mining had been slow in developing. The first ore was not shipped until 1884, and even then it traveled eastward by rail to Marquette, Michigan. No ore came to Ashland until 1886, when the Lake Shore had finished its first ore dock. Plates 18A and 18B. The maiden shipment from Ashland occurred on July 29, 1886 — thirteen hundred tons in the barge "Cormorant." [13]

In 1887, the Wisconsin Central built its first ore dock after it had constructed a line from Ironwood into Mellen, Wisconsin, where it connected with the main line from Milwaukee to Ashland. Its right-of-way followed the valley between the so-called Copper and Iron Ridges of the Penokee Range.

Also, in 1887, the Duluth, South Shore & Atlantic Railroad opened service between Duluth and the Sault. Its route appeared to avoid studiously all towns of importance. It looped southward from Superior, Wisconsin, in a strange series of right-angled curves and other bends. It touched at Winneboujou (a corruption of the Ojibway Nanabazhoo) on the Bois Brule River. Still avoiding the direct approach, it curved northward to the Village of Iron River and gingerly picked its way through the lakes and swamps to the southwest, to skirt the northern edge of the Bibon Swamp. It crossed the Omaha at Bibon Junction, and continued in a northeasterly direction to cross the Lake Shore near Saxon.[14] It gave

[13] Guy Burnham, Ibid, 259.

[14] The Bibon marsh comprises part of the Lake Superior Lowland, and drains into the White River. Map 9, p. 22. Bibon Junction is about twelve miles south and west of Ashland. The name stems from a French trader who, so rumor claims, conducted a still in the secret depths of the swamp. (Author's note.)

the Cities of Hurley and Ironwood an unsocial avoidance of five miles by passing north of them. Thus, on to the Sault!

During all this bustle, La Pointe dozed on. It was partially aroused in 1887 by a group of optimists who formed the "Madaline [sic] Island Resort Company." The latter was incorporated on November 10 of that year, with a capital of thirty-two thousand five hundred dollars. Its principal office was in Milwaukee.[15] Its 'brochure' claimed the authorship of "Mr. George Francis," whom everyone knew was George Francis Thomas, and it offered shares in the company at ten dollars each. It also extolled the advantages of investing in an island which had unlimited future possibilities. The booklet contained a map showing the restricted building area of Sainte Magdalaine, centered around Sunset (Kapunky) Bay. This was platted, giving fanciful names to the different streets, all approached by "Marquette Avenue." There was a proposed State Park of five thousand acres which included nearly all of the northeast end of the island.

There was an historical resumé of the island, with the statement that Father Marquette had personally brought the *original* Ruben's Descent From the Cross, and had hung it in Baraga's 1841 church.

Another incident of local importance on Madeline Island was the death, on December 30, 1887, of the winner of the epic struggle with the cooper, Wilson. Judge Bell had taken an active part in the administration of village and county affairs. In these, too, he had injected himself into official capacities in the earlier days, without formal election. He apparently had assumed control of all county functions, to the relief of all concerned. He had had the reputation of extreme honesty and efficiency, but according to the minutes of the Town Board, of which he seemed to be the perennial chairman, Old Whackum appeared to have received more remuneration, on some score or other, than the other members.[16]

During the periods when La Pointe had been the County Seat, he had dispensed his brand of border justice which gratified all, save culprits. He had relinquished his power by the time Ashland had again assumed the reins of county government in 1872.

Bell had had great influence with the Indians and mixed-bloods, due, in part, to the fact that he had married two of them. He had also shown great political sagacity by always making sure that at least one of the Indians or bloods was elected to the Town Board. When the father of his current wife died (local legend again averred that the father had

---

[15] *Madeline Island Resort Company*, (Milwaukee, 1887), Wisconsin Historical Library, F 902 M13 MA

[16] *Minutes of the La Pointe Town Board*, 1857 et seq. Originals in La Pointe Town Hall. Copy in Historical Library, Madison, Wisconsin.

been a chief), Mrs. Bell inherited a tract of land which ran from the village northward for approximately a mile. Upon the death of Mrs. Bell, their daughter, Sarah, succeeded in ownership. The daughter married George Francis Thomas, and after her death in 1884, without issue, the land fell to Thomas. In later years, he sub-divided it and sold various lots to incoming summer residents.[17]

With this brief flurry in its life, La Pointe again subsided into its lazy economy of agriculture, fishing and just plain sitting. It had the appearance of being awed and confused at the briskness of the neighboring lumbering industry.[18] Some of its youth departed to ride the lumber hookers, the vessels for transporting the finished product down the lakes. At first, these craft were all sailboats, for the most part schooner rigged. The "Maple Leaf" of the R. D. Pike Lumber company was one of these. Each fall a pool was made up in Bayfield with wagers as to the ability of her Captain Larsen to bring her back from her last trip before the ice formed. He always did, although there was one occasion when his ship was partially frozen in between Basswood Island and Bayfield. Helpful citizens chopped her free and brought her in.

As the tempo of the industry increased, these ships proved to be too slow, and steam barges were introduced. Since it seemed wasteful to scrap the sailboats, the steam barges were used to tow several of the hookers. It was nothing unusual to see a barge with four of the older boats in tow, reminding one of a mother partridge with trailing progeny. Whenever there was a fair wind, the hookers raised their sails to help the mamma barge gain speed. It was an impressive sight to see the procession pass.[19]

Between the briskness of the lumber trade and the increase in ore handling, the lake fairly swarmed with shipping. A count was made in 1903 from the vantage point of the Devil's Island lighthouse, and one hundred twenty vessels were in sight at one time. The lighthouse keeper said that this number was not unusual. Even then, the lumbering industry had commenced to fade.

[17] The tombstone of Sarah Bell Thomas is in the Indian cemetery. Her epitaph reads:

"SARAH
WIFE OF G. F. THOMAS.
Born June 25, 1856.
Died July 26, 1884.
Infant babe buried with mother."

[18] The reaction of many later summer residents. (Author's note.)
[19] In lake parlance, the term hooker was applied to both steam and sailing vessels which carried lumber. The differentiation made above is for the purpose of simplification. (Author's note.)

The lumber was shipped to all cities of importance on the lower lakes, but the outstanding receiving port was Tonawanda, New York. Here, large facilities were built to handle the incoming cargoes for distribution by rail to the east coast cities.

A contemporary addition to Ashland's boom was the erection of a blast furnace in 1888. It was built by James York to produce some of Lake Superior's famous charcoal iron. It was a logical move, the location having some of the world's finest ore at hand, and an apparently inexhaustible supply of potential charcoal at its back door. The popularity of Superior's charcoal iron was due not only to its high grade ores, but also to the fact that the irons produced by the coal and coke methods still lacked chemical control. There are more or less high percentages of sulphur in these fuels, and in the refining process of the blast furnace, iron has a great affinity for sulphur. Consequently, if a furnace should use a coal or coke with a high sulphur content, the resultant iron would be of poor grade. Charcoal, on the other hand, contains no sulphur, and this made the Superior product one of uniformly high quality.

There were a number of these furnaces near the lake, principally on Michigan's Upper Peninsula, all of which enjoyed a highly profitable trade for about thirty-five years. Each furnace had a brand name for its product, and customers usually ordered a specific brand from their iron agents. The Ashland pig iron was called Hinkle, and it had an excellent reputation in foundry circles. Plate 19.

With the production of the iron went the manufacture of charcoal. At first, this was carried on near the source of the hard wood, which might have been at some distance from the furnace. The charcoal was made in ovens similar to the beehive affairs used in the production of coke. The ovens were built of brick or stone, round affairs from eighteen to twenty feet in diameter, and about the same measurements in height. They were frequently arranged in a battery of three or more, with an elevated runway, so that wagons, delivering the wood, could drive up on it and discharge their loads into the top openings of the ovens.

One of the spectacular sights of the time was the night effect of burning gases issuing from the tops of the ovens. Later, the ovens were moved to the blast furnaces where, by distillation methods, many by-products were recovered — but without the splendor of the flames.

CHAPTER EIGHT

1889   *There go the Ships*   *1900*

At the height of the lumbering business, the ore carrying trade began to assume enormous proportions. The old wooden sailing and steam ships were found to be inadequate for the purpose. In 1899, Captain Alexander McDougall, a man of long experience on the lakes, introduced his first steel whaleback. He built this in his own yards at Superior, Wisconsin. As a matter of fact, he was forced to construct his boat because no so-called reputable builder would undertake the fabrication of such a radical design.[1] Plate 20.

The practicality of this new type of craft immediately met with the approval of the ore carrying business. The whaleback had a rather flat bottom to accommodate large tonnages, and to navigate in comparatively shoal water. At the water line, when loaded, the sides curved inward to a rounded top deck, the general appearance of which was not unlike that of a whale. The bow was of truncated and modified conical design which plowed through the water like the uptilted end of an immense cigar. The pilot house was placed well forward, and the engine room at the extreme stern. This arrangement left plenty of cargo space in between. Plates 21 and 22..

Adopting the hooker scheme of transportation, a number of these ships were built without motive power, to be towed by their engined sisters. Since the slanting, rounded bow was dubbed off like a pig's snout, with the anchor hawse pipes resembling nostrils, both types were called Pigs or Pig Boats. Plate 22A.

The design met with great success. The vessels hauled immense tonnages of ore, but there were certain drawbacks which eventually eliminated them. They rode very low in the water, and even in moderate

[1] Nute, *Lake Superior*, Ibid, 128.
    Dr. Arthur T. Holbrook, *From the Log of a Trout Fisherman*, (Plimpton Press, Norwood, Mass., 1949. Privately printed.) 77.

seas the waves would wash over the amidships section. This was not especially detrimental, even if the forward personnel could not, at times, make its way aft to the galley. The principal trouble was encountered when large seas would batter at the pilot house or engine room, and unless the captain could ease his ship, either by steering tactics or by seeking some lee, one of these houses would be breached or carried away, exposing the then vulnerable hull to a flood of water. The Government charts of 1905 showed the locations of a number of these foundered vessels. The whaleback was superseded by a smaller version of the ore boat as it is known today.[2]

During the late 1880s, the brownstone quarries were developing. Reference has been made to the one opened on Basswood Island in 1868 by Frederick Prentice. Two more were begun on the mainland, one about four miles south of Bayfield, on present (1957) Wisconsin highway No. 13, owned by Robinson D. Pike, the other at Houghton Point. The latter was the largest in the region. (This point is the Charybdis to Chequamegon Point's Scylla, at the entrance to Chequamegon Bay.) Map 28.[3]

The largest known monolith was quarried here in 1892, intended for the Chicago World's Fair, the following year. It was meant not only to advertise the pre-eminence of the quarry but also to surpass Cleopatra's Needle in height. It was ten feet square at the base, four feet square at the top before narrowing to the apex, one hundred fifteen feet long (to the Needle's seventy feet), and weighed over four hundred eight tons.[4] However, its weight precluded its shipment by the freight cars of the time, and prevented it from being carried as a deck load on any existing lake vessel. It was too long to be maneuvered through any ship's hatch, and it was eventually cut up into building blocks, leaving the Needle supreme. Thus the fate of the Wisconsin Monolith.[5]

Other quarries were opened on Hermit and Stockton Islands. All, save Pike's, were owned and operated by Prentice. The Milwaukee County Court House was built with the sandstone from Basswood Island, and many of New York's Fifth Avenue 'brownstone fronts' originated in the La Pointe district. These ventures were fairly prosperous

[2] To salt water men, the term boat is a misnomer for vessels of this size. However, it is universally used on the Great Lakes. (Author's note.)

[3] The Charybdis characteristic can be proved by cruising near the point in even a moderate northeast breeze. The resulting chop can be most uncomfortable to the occupant of any boat up to thirty feet in length. (Author's note.)

[4] Lura J. & J. M. Turner, *Geography Hand Book and Gazeteer of Wisconsin*, (Burlington, Wis., 1898), 35.

[5] The Cleopatra's Needle referred to is located in New York City. There are three others: one in London, another in Paris, and the third in Rome. Of the four, the latter is the tallest, measuring one hundred five feet in height. (Author's note.)

for a period of fifteen years owing to the wide use and popularity of the product. However, the same Chicago World's Fair which proved to be the bête noire of the Needle's rival, heralded the advent of the steel frame building. Due to the new design, with the beams of each floor supporting their own loads of facing stone, the rather cumbersome and heavy sandstone was superseded by lighter materials. Thus technical progress rendered the quarries useless, and they were gradually abandoned.[6]

Following the erection of the Knight Hotel in 1890, with its brownstone façade, Ashland momentarily turned away from its material progress, with the founding of its North Wisconsin Academy in 1892. The Academy was able to secure a small private-endowment, some assistance toward a building fund from the American or State Board of Missions, and a few local donations. Architect's fees were eliminated by the gift of plans by Beloit College, which had just completed its own Academy building. The school's success was largely due to the selfless labors of the Reverend Messrs. Thomas G. Grassie, George W. Nelson and Edward P. Wheeler. Wheeler was the son of the La Pointe and Odanah missionary, Leonard Wheeler, and was the pastor of the local Congregational Church. The other two men lived in Ashland, engaged in home missionary work for the same denomination.[7] The dedication ceremonies were held on July 14, 1892, with Professor James J. Blaisdell, of Beloit College, delivering the principal speech. Plate 23.

The purpose of the school was to provide Christian educational advantages to a territory largely devoid of high schools. After about fifteen years, the need for this type of school was satisfied, and the Academy was converted into a college, to be known as Northland College. This institution has performed yeoman service in a large area, and its expansion has been steady and progressive. The labors and sacrifices of the early founders were no doubt responsible for the deaths of Grassie and Nelson in their prime of life.

In the early 1890s, the old Village of La Pointe was leading a sleepy

---

[6] There were three other quarries located on the Bayfield Peninsula. They were smaller and not as important, although one operated from time to time as late as 1912. These quarries were located as follows:
  1. At Siskiwit Point, between Siskiwit and Bark Bays.
  2. On the point about one and one-half miles west and north of Port Wing.
  3. On the Iron River, about fourteen miles north of the village of the same name, Map 25.
The third one was served by a railroad spur built from the Village of Iron River. All three produced the so-called Orienta Sandstone which was lighter in color and of a different chemical content than the Chequamegon. See Fredrik T. Thwaites, *Sandstones of the Wisconsin Coast of Lake Superior*, (Madison, 1912), 43.

[7] John Nelson Davidson, *In Unnamed Wisconsin*, (Milwaukee, 1895), 256.

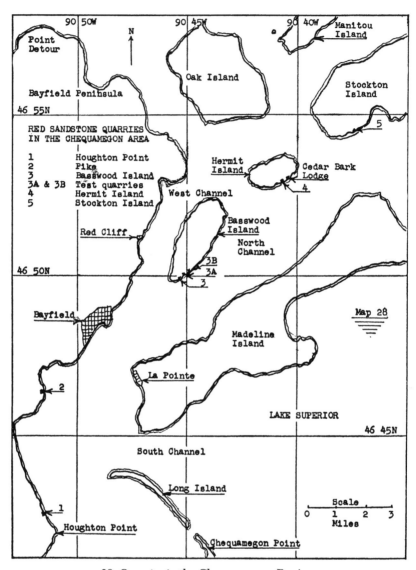

28. Quarries in the Chequamegon Region.

150

existence, with a population of scarcely seventy-five. A boat builder named Henry Rowe followed his trade in a desultory fashion on the site of the old Middle Fort. There was a slight effort made in the field of agriculture. A small sawmill was running on the east side of the island, on the opposite shore from La Pointe. A few Norwegians and Swedes had come, to turn their old country hands to fishing.

It was rumored that at least two of the populace had entered into some sort of incipient piracy.[8] It was whispered that they might have stolen up the Bad River in their boats, to raid a standing boxcar at Odanah. Or they might have glided into an empty lumber slip at Ashland or Bayfield, of a moonless night, crept up to the railroad yards and garnered their loot from those sources. And it was common knowledge that the raiders were like modern Robinhoods, generous after their forays, distributing their gains very widely in the village — in the dead of night. Some of the villagers still recall the sacks of flour left at the back door of a certain kindly woman, famed for her baking.

The old Protestant mission building, after serving as a dormitory to assorted itinerants, had fallen into a sad state of disrepair. Part of the roof had collapsed; the floors were in poor condition, with grass growing in the cracks of the boards, and portions of the building were being used as a cow stable.[9]

Its companion church in the village was much weather beaten, although an attempt had been made in the early 1890s to repair and revive it as a Presbyterian mission church, through the efforts of the Reverend Mr. Alfred Terry. It had seen service as a hay barn and as a loft for the women of the village to cut and sew sails for the boats of their men.

A peculiar situation had existed in regard to the title of the land on which the church had been erected. The American Fur Company, through an arrangement with Governmental authorities, had the right to parcel out pieces of property for its own use, and for that of its employees, pending an official survey by the Government. It is assumed that the company gave its consent for the building of the church on its original site. When the official survey was made in 1852, the procedure was for the Government agent, Julius Austrian, to give title to the occupant of the property, upon the payment of a very nominal amount. Through some oversight, the title to the church property passed to Austrian, either originally or at the time when he bought up considerable other property in and near the village at one dollar and twenty-

[8] The names of the two are known to the author and some of the older inhabitants. For obvious reasons they are not given here.
[9] This was the condition when the author first saw it in 1897.

five cents per acre.[10] Before the matter could be adjusted, the Protestant mission had been discontinued, and the whole matter forgotten save by the later individuals who held title to the church property.[11]

In 1892, the Reverend Mr. Edward P. Wheeler obtained title to the property from George F. Thomas and Julia Cadrant (Mrs. Nelson Cadrant, Sr.); the land seemed to have been divided into two parcels by that time. Wheeler, with some ceremony, passed it to Eugene Arthur Shores as Trustee for the Lake Superior Congregational Church. Shores was a prominent lumberman of Ashland, much interested in civic and church affairs. The ceremony had had considerable advance publicity given it in church circles, and was well attended by men of high standing in Wisconsin Congregationalism.

The services were held in the old church, and the overflow audience was accommodated in a tent which the Reverend Mr. George W. Nelson used in his evangelical work. The ninetieth Psalm was read by the Reverend Mr. Thomas Grassie; an address was made by the Reverend Mr. Judson Titsworth of the Pilgrim Congregational Church of Milwaukee, and the memorial prayer by James J. Blaisdell of Beloit College. The exercises were held on July 13, 1892, the day before the dedication of North Wisconsin Academy.[12]

The local populace, including a number of the old French-Ojibway, was much interested and moved, by the appearance at the service of Mrs. Leonard H. Wheeler. In fact, whenever a member of the Wheeler family came to La Pointe he was greeted most affectionately. A local legend avers that upon the occasional appearance of William H. Wheeler, he would announce his presence with an Ojibway war whoop which caused the cabin doors to fly open and the occupants to spill out. There would then be much back-slapping and a gutteral exchange of greetings in the Ojibway language.

In spite of its dormant condition, the Village of La Pointe had retained one element of its former importance. When its County Seat had been removed to Ashland (it was part of Ashland County), it had kept the right to collect real estate taxes from La Pointe Township, an extra large one comprising nearly all of the Apostle Islands. As the lumbering industry prospered, the value of the timberlands increased. This resulted in money pouring into La Pointe, far beyond its needs and almost beyond its hopes. Of course, it was simple to remedy this state of affairs.

[10] *New York Daily Tribune*, June 26, 1854. Reported from La Pointe June 12, 1854.

[11] There is a complete record of transfers, commencing in 1879, in the Recorder's office of Ashland County Court House. However, these records would not show the later sale of the building only, and its move to the mission property. (Author's note.)

[12] Davidson, Ibid, 255–256.

The village spent it!! Franklin D. Roosevelt had been born forty years too late.

Village offices were rotated so that all might have a chance at the 'kitty.' A local form of WPA was devised, whereby the inhabitants could find work in building roads.[13] And many roads were built. Thus, in a somewhat Utopian atmosphere, the village dozed, arousing from time to time to watch the hookers and whalebacks pass, on their missions of supply to a more active economy. There was so little communication with other parts of the country that its old postoffice was discontinued, forcing the inhabitants to travel to Bayfield for their mail.[14] This was done, in the lake's open season, by row boat or sailboat, and in the winter by a dog-drawn traino over the ice.[15] Plate 24.

In 1894, the populace was somewhat shocked out of its lethargy by something new in its experience — the arrival of summer residents. The Reverend Mr. Thomas Gordon Grassie and family came, to occupy two small shacks near the present Town Hall and to examine the facets of island life and scenery. Among the former was the amusing purchase of bread from Mrs. Alvin Bentley, whose prices might have startled even the OPA.[15A] She sold her product for, "Seven cents a loaf or three for a quarter." It has never been divulged whether three members of a family came in separately, each with his seven cents. One might also buy milk from one of the inhabitants at a price of "five cents per quart from the milk cow, or at six cents per quart from the cream cow," that is, if one were patient enough to wait for the cows to come in from the woods.

A fascinating evening might be spent by inveigling an old man of mixed French and Ojibway descent to tell of the legends and customs of his forefathers, and to explain the machinery of the village "sideboard." His indiscriminate use of personal pronouns would, at times, make his tales a bit confusing, but they added to the local color.[16]

Altogether, this trial of the island's potentialities convinced the Grassie

[13] The Works Progress Administration was one of the so-called Alphabetical Agencies of the Government during the depression years of the 1930s. Basically sound but scandalously administered by various politicans. (Author's note.)

[14] The post office had been discontinued on June 14, 1887, per National Archives and Records Service, letter of Dec. 13, 1956.

[15] The word traino was in common use well into the 1890s. It evolved from the French traineau, meaning sledge or sleigh. (Author's note.)

[15A] Office of Price Administration. Designed to ration food and to control prices during World War II. Another poorly managed and politically influenced Government agency. (Author's note.)

[16] The term sideboard seemed to be a La Pointe colloquialism. In local parlance, the Town Board comprised a Chairman and a Side Board. An example of the use of personal pronouns was: "My wife, he went to Odanah last week, an' if she don't come back pretty soon, I go down after him and beat her up." (Author's note.)

family that it should have a shelter of its own in this historic place. It whiled away the succeeding winter months by drawing plans for a cottage and making arrangements with George F. Thomas for procuring a site.

In 1895, the family was somewhat dismayed to learn that John O'Brien of St. Paul had arrived on Madeline Island and had built a summer cottage. O'Brien was a son of the 1857 lay teacher, Dillon O'Brien. The Grassie cottage was finished somewhat later in the year, and the two families became well acquainted, with the question of who came first a matter of friendly banter.[17] An article of furniture which the Grassie family never discussed in public was a very large and sturdy walnut diningroom table, the gift of an Ashland saloon keeper.

In the same year, a house was built on Hermit Island, near the site of the stone quarry. It engendered a story of frustrated romance which was enlarged upon through the succeeding years. Frederick Prentice, the owner of the quarry, built the home for his bride. It was a pretentious structure, considering the times and the location, and must have represented a considerable investment. The building was a three-story affair with all of the wooden gingerbread of the era tacked on. There were Romeo and Juliet balconies leading out of rooms of the second and third floors. These commanded breath-taking vistas of the nearby islands and the open lake beyond. The exterior was covered with cedar shingles, and wherever possible the trim was of cedar on which the bark had been left. From this feature, the house received its name – Cedar Bark Lodge. Plate 25.

The interior was equally impressive, with well-laid oak floors, but with the inevitable wooden trimmings and grills. The house boasted four large fireplaces, at least two of which were brownstone monoliths with the openings cut out of the solid stone. Each had carvings over the openings; one, on the first floor, having that of a lion's head, with snarling mouth.[18]

The accuracy of the generally accepted story that the bride arrived, took one look and then demanded her return to Ashland, cannot be vouched for, but it is considered substantially correct. In 1898 the lodge was unoccupied but in excellent repair. The elements and vandals grad-

[17] The clear white pine lumber for the cottage was delivered to the building site by an Ashland sawmill for eight dollars per thousand!

[18] In 1957, the author learned that one of the fireplaces had been preserved, and was in the home of Carl E. Carlson of Salmo, Wisconsin, near the State Fish Hatchery. The face and upper part were in two pieces, each about four feet wide, making the fireplace about eight feet in width. These were covered with carvings of oak branches with intertwined ivy. The front edge of the mantle was carved as an oaken branch.

ually brought it to ruin, and the last vestiges were torn down in the early 1930s to prevent possible injury to sightseers.[19]

The early 1890s was a period when the railroad building craze had thoroughly innoculated the Chequamegon region. Five more roads, whose names have fallen into virtual oblivion, were conceived and partially built. Their promoters, now that we may look back with superior complacency, appeared to have had some very nebulous ideas as to where the rails would run and what they would carry. The first of these was the Bayfield Harbor & Great Western Railroad, with its subsidiaries, the Bayfield Transfer Railway, and the Bayfield, Superior and Minneapolis Railroad. This combination was the brain child of William F. Dalrymple, and was later to be dubbed Dalrymple's Dream.

The venture started by the incorporation of the Transfer on July 26, 1883, followed by that of the Great Western on August 24, 1885. The Bayfield, Superior and Minneapolis, whose incorporation papers, if any, were never filed, owned part of the right-of-way of this combine.[20] The Great Western achieved the status of an holding company, if you please. To make matters more complicated, the Transfer was the operating company for all three. The Transfer, as a corporate entity, owned and operated the line from Bayfield to Red Cliff on 3.86 miles of track. At Roy's Point, immediately south of Red Cliff, the Great Western branched off from the Transfer to run six miles to Raspberry River. From here, the Bayfield, Superior & Minneapolis took over, to run six miles to Rachet Creek, a tributary of the Sand River.

There is some confusion in the available records as to when trains began to run. The Wisconsin Public Service Commission's records indicate that the date was in 1898, but it qualifies the statement with the remark that the record only shows scheduled operation of the first train, and that it is possible that earlier unscheduled runs may have been made. Local 'Old Timers' are reasonably sure that the date was 1892.[21]

This assemblage of companies was designed to break the "strangle holds of Jim Hill's and Wall Street's octopus railroads." The plans were not insignificant. From the Sand River it was proposed to follow the south shore of the lake to the City of Superior. Minneapolis might have been its published destination, but it was secretly hoped that a Pacific terminal might be achieved. At least, the rails did reach Red Cliff, and a scoot made one round trip per day for a number of years. Frustrated

[19] The author, when a child, visited the lodge in 1898, and was a bit nervous about the lion.

[20] Records of the Public Service Commission, Madison, Wisconsin.

[21] The author saw the Transfer in operation in 1897. A La Pointe woman claims 1892, that date being fixed in her mind because she came to Madeline Island that year to be married.

in its dream of empire, the road gradually shed its more imposing names, and ran under the single one of the Bayfield Transfer.

In 1914, the line was purchased by the Wachsmuth Lumber Company of Bayfield for use as a logging road, serving that company until 1924 when it was abandoned and the tracks removed. The old right-of-way between Bayfield and Red Cliff may still be seen along the lake shore.[22]

Two more railroads were added in 1895. One of these was the Minneapolis, St. Paul & Ashland Railway, and the other the Washburn, Bayfield and Iron River Railroad. They were financed, in part, by Ashland and Bayfield Counties, respectively, to be nicknamed the Peerless and Battleaxe roads.[23]

[22] Dalrymple owned extensive wheat lands in western Minnesota and Dakota, and the new railroad was to transport his product to large Bayfield elevators for trans-shipment to eastern and European ports. He was not alone in his idea of a rail line from the wheat fields to Bayfield. As early as 1872, or before, the Northern Pacific Railroad had completed plans for a road from St. Cloud, Minnesota on an almost straight line to Bayfield. The plans no doubt fell through owing to the panic of 1873. See frontispiece map in Edward D. Neill's *History of Minnesota*, (Minneapolis, 1873).

[23] The promoters of the Peerless very cannily risked little of their own capital in the venture. They succeeded in selling their idea, as well as some of their stock, to the voters of Ashland County, with the result that by a popular vote, the County was authorized to issue sixty-five thousand dollars of bonds, the proceeds of which were to be used in financing the road. Guy Burnham, Ibid, 325–326.

The Ashland terminal was located close to Chequamegon Bay, slightly west of the present Lake Superior District Power Company's power house. From here it headed westward, parallel to the causeway of highways U.S. 2 and Wisconsin 13. This area was very swampy, and the rails were supported on a piling trestle at least one and one-half miles long. Its piles were driven into the lake bottom, a short distance from shore.

After leaving the trestle and reaching firm ground, it passed the site of Radisson's cabin, and aimed for the town of Moquah, which is about nine miles west of Ashland. From here, it paralled the tracks of the Northern Pacific for about seven miles to the west, where it swung sharply to the south, connecting with the Duluth, South Shore & Atlantic at Chequamegon Junction. The junction boasted the mechanism of a switch only. This leg was about thirteen miles long. The junction was in Section 23, Township 46 North, Range 7 West.

Here, the money ran out, and all construction work stopped, although contemporary maps showed the proposed right-of-way continuing southward to the south boundary of Bayfield County, no doubt on its way to the advertised destination of the Twin Cities. The line never carried a revenue passenger, and its freight returns were almost nil. Some years later, with probably no legal formality, it was taken over by a logging company, without recompense to the county. Even in this capacity its life was short, and the rails were torn up in 1906. The long trestle was converted to highway purposes, and in spite of the clatter of loose boards, it served in that capacity for about ten years. Some of the old piling was still visible in 1957. The county paid off the last of the bonds in 1918.

Not to be outdone by her sister, Bayfield County authorized the issuance of two hundred twenty-five thousand dollars of bonds in 1895 for the construction of her railroad. From the size of the bond issue, it was apparent that her Battleaxe was to

At La Pointe, the leaven of the O'Brien and Grassie cottages began to ferment. In 1896, William M. Tomkins and Russell W. French of Ashland, arrived to build two more. The same year, a fifth was added,

be bigger and better than her rival's Peerless. While the western terminus of the Washburn, Bayfield & Iron River Railroad was nominally Iron River, Wisconsin, much greater things were expected in the way of an ultimate western goal. The Washburn end was located at the present Omaha depot in Washburn, thus giving that town the prestige of an Union Station.

From Washburn, the road paralleled the Omaha for about two miles and then turned westward for about six more. From here, it described a large arc to the northwest, to its station of Lenawee, a short distance south of the lake of the same name. After making a few hesitant turns, it headed directly southwest into Iron River.

From a somewhat mythical town of Headquarters, a branch line was planned to run northeastward to Bayfield, possibly following the route of the old Bayfield Road. Somewhere along this proposed line, another branch was to run northward to intercept the Bayfield, Superior & Minneapolis at imaginary Bayfield Junction, in the Sand River district. These two branches were never built.

In its palmiest days, Headquarters consisted of scarcely more than one house, and its most useful function was to serve as a whistle stop for blueberry pickers. The road handled some coal from the Washburn docks, and also served as a logging road for that city's sawmills. It went into the hands of the receivers who sold it to the Northern Pacififlc in 1900, and it was finally abandoned in 1916.

Unlike its contemporary sisters, the Battleaxe could muster the names of a number of stations along its line. Starting at Washburn, there were Engoe, Grand Junction, Enderline (was pun intended?), Headquarters, Lenawee, Coda, Slow Bridge, Bena and Iron River. Near the southern limits of Washburn the old right-of-way was in sight in 1957. The tax payers continued to pay for their dead horse until 1922, when the last of the bonds was retired.

It is not known what the origin of the nicknames was. A few persons are inclined to think that they were terms of derision, originating from the then popular smoking and smokeless tobacco, Peerless, and the plug tobacco, Battleaxe.

In addition to the above more prominent lines of the era, there were a number of logging roads, some of which bore impressive names, but none of which enjoyed long enough life to achieve a sobriquet. Among these was the narrow gauge Washburn & Northwestern Railway which paralleled the Battleaxe out of Washburn for several miles, and then ended its fourteen-mile length in the nowhere of Section 18, Township 48 North, Range 6 West. This road was the property of A. A. Bigelow & Company which operated a sawmill in Washburn.

A second road, known as the Ashland, Siskowit & Iron River, started at Shores' Landing, a short distance north of Whittlesey Creek, and angled its rather tortuous way up to Siskiwit Lake, crossing the Battleaxe at Grand Junction. It apparently never made any pretense of even aiming at Iron River. This line was owned by the E. A. Shores Lumber Company, of Ashland.

A third one was the Ashland, Odanah & Marengo, a logging road of the John Schroeder Lumber Company, which ran south from Odanah for about ten miles. A fourth one, belonging to the same company, branched off from the Northwestern Railway near Cedar, Wisconsin, and angled to the northeast toward the mouth of the Montreal River.

A fifth, somewhat out of the immediate Chequamegon region, was the Lake Superior & South Eastern Railway. This connected with the Omaha at Grand View and proceeded in an easterly direction to join the Wisconsin Central (Soo) at Foster Junction, a short distance west of Mellen, Wisconsin.

a joint venture of William F. Shea and Clarence A. Lamoreaux, of the same city.[24]

In 1897, the old Protestant mission property was purchased by Edward P. Salmon of Beloit, Wisconsin. His holdings comprised all of the lake shore frontage from 18th Street to the South Shore Road, a distance of about three-quarters of a mile. In some places his acreage ran back from the lake for about one mile. A substantial amount of this land was purchased from the heirs of Julius Austrian, one of Crooks' partners in the last days of the American Fur Company, and the Government land agent for the area.[25]

After rather hurried and sketchy repairs, in which Salmon was assisted by a later Jean Baptiste Cadotte, of La Pointe, the old building was opened in 1898 under the name of The Old Mission.[26] Since Salmon was a retired minister, he conceived the idea of serving, primarily, other members of the cloth. The first year of hotel life saw many ministers and their families as guests. The atmosphere was no doubt responsible for the rules posted in each guest room. One of them was to the effect that all lights should be extinguished at ten p.m. Plate 26.

During the same year, Salmon built a cottage on the mission property for Colonel Frederick M. Woods of Lincoln, Nebraska. The Colonel had become familiar with the region through his acquaintanceship with General Allen C. Fuller of Belvidere, Illinois. The General had come to Bayfield to escape hay fever, and there had built a comfortable and roomy house.[27] The Colonel also suffered from the same affliction, and spent several summers in the same town.[28]

The Colonel, an energetic gentleman, was not satisfied with the rather circumscribed facilities for entertainment at the Old Mission. He saw the possibilities of the island as a summer resort and hay fever haven. He wished to build a bowling alley on the mission grounds for moments of relaxation. This did not fit into the somewhat Victorian standards of Salmon, with the result that there was a friendly parting of the ways. The Colonel then built a summer home in 1899, northwest of the Village of La Pointe.

[24] All five of these cabins are still in existence; the O'Brien and Grassie owned by their descendants, the Tomkins by Mrs. Charles Bennett, the French by Miss Mae Mielenz and the Shea-Lamoreaux by Mr. and Mrs. George E. Michael.

[25] 18th Street lies at right angles to the lake shore near the site of the Middle Fort and Chief Buffalo's grave, Map 24.

[26] This Cadotte was a grandson of Michel Cadotte, and a great grandson of Jean Baptiste Cadotte, the Henry partner. (Author's note.)

[27] This house still stands in Bayfield, at the northwest corner of Rittenhouse Avenue and Third Street. (Author's note.)

[28] Frederick M. Woods, *Memoirs of Colonel F. M. Woods*, (Privately printed, 1926), 21.

The local Rocking Chair Brigade could not understand the Colonel's choice of location. The site was totally devoid of trees, although it commanded a beautiful view of the channel and mainland. He set to work planting trees. His sons and friends built neighboring cottages. He satisfied his longing for a bowling alley. In short, his Nebraska Row hummed with activity, and before his death, in 1928, he saw trees and flowers on the former fallow pastures. Plates 27 & 28.

It may be rightfully claimed that Colonel Woods was one of the most important individuals in the development of Madeline Island as a summer retreat. In due course he acquired the first power boat to be owned at La Pointe. The "Nebraska" was his pride and joy. With great enthusiasm he would don his Captain's cap, shout orders to his sons and passengers, twirl the steering wheel with great gusto, and jangle the signal bell to his engineer. The latter, who had had considerable boating experience, rather disregarded the Colonel's frantic signals, and used his own judgment.

In a sense, the "Nebraska" was a competitor of the local ferry boats. Every morning, except Sunday, at 9:00 a.m. sharp, she left the La Pointe dock for Bayfield in order that the Colonel might do the family shopping. Any and all persons who *happened* to be on the dock were issued cordial invitations for the trip. Needless to say, many accepted.[29] With his big 'turnip' in hand, the Colonel stood on the pier, closely inspecting the minute hand of his watch and chafing at its slowness. Promptly on the hour, he would step aboard the boat and signal the engineer, even though members of his family might be madly racing to make connections. At such times, the Colonel leaned out of his pilot house, shouted some remark about promptness — but never turned back.

The Colonel was probably the most outstanding livestock auctioneer in the country. He entered this vocation through his great interest in pure bred animals. He saw that the only way to provide for the increasing demands for meat in a rapidly expanding country was to introduce blooded sires. He not only followed this theory on his own farms in Nebraska, but also was a pioneer in encouraging neighboring farmers to follow suit. It was often remarked that at an auction the Colonel could secure higher prices for his clients than any other auctioneer.

This career provided him with a fund of experiences and homely stories. When a local benefit was planned at La Pointe, it was not considered successful without his leadership. In addition, many local families knew his kindness and generosity in times of stress. All in all, the Colonel was a most respected and revered gentleman. Plate 29.

[29] The author was a steady customer.

Another man who was responsible for developing the island and bringing in a surpisingly congenial group of persons was Edward P. Salmon. In selling building sites from his mission acreage, he used great discrimination. He, too, was greatly interested in the welfare of the local inhabitants, and was the quiet distributer of much assistance. One of his kindly acts was to see that every island family with children was the recipient of the then popular and instructive *Youth's Companion.*

Salmon's Old Mission possessed an hidden asset, the potentialities of which were not realized until after its purchase. This was the long-forgotten cherry orchard, planted by the early missionaries. How this survived its many years of neglect has surprised many prominent horti-culturists. By an apt coincidence, Mrs. Edward P. Wheeler, a daughter-in-law of the missionary, was the first manager of the new inn, and the fame of her cherry pies was widespread.

Thus, the summer resort business was launched on Madeline Island —two hundred years after Le Sueur's command at the same place, and nearly three hundred years after the visit of the first white man.

With more people coming into the region and with the renascence of the fishing industry, the demand for faster transportation increased. This was answered by the newly developed internal combustion engine which at first was none too reliable, but which was rapidly brought to a high degree of perfection. In the Chequamgon region the first gaso-line-powered boat made its appearance in 1898. It was owned by Nelson Bachland and Herbert Hale of Bayfield.[30] The experimental stage of the engine was exemplified in this boat. Fortunately the craft was equipped with sails, and it must be admitted that her mileage was much greater by this means than by her engine.[31]

She was somewhat a parallel to Mark Twain's Mississippi steamboat whose engines stopped when she blew her whistle. In this case, the engine produced more noise than power. When the crew managed to start it, the popping could be heard for miles. The records do not reveal her baptismal name, but she came down in local history as the "Cracker-jack," a name adapted from her noise and from the then new confection of the same calling.

A matter of interest and of some concern to the early summer visitors on Madeline Island was the number of dogs. For the most part they were of nondescript breeds, but all were of good size. They were used as sled dogs in the winter when they were grudgingly fed a diet of fish heads, put up in barrels in the fall and allowed to freeze. In the summer

[30] Guy Burnham, Ibid, 287.
[31] The author rode on this boat in 1898.

time, however, their owners apparently declined any responsibility for them, with the result that they roamed the island in search of food.[32] Some of them became very adept in raiding unsuspecting visitors' caches of food. In some instances they were known to have manipulated ice box door catches to clean out the contents of the refrigerator.

In the fall of 1898, sundry and mysterious men began to appear on the island, all seeking the more healthy and powerful dogs. Some of the animals were virtually given away until it was discovered that there was an active demand for them in the Klondike. They then became very valuable, and many were sold at exorbitant prices. The result was that there were very few of the canine population remaining, and thenceforth the only cause for complaint was the jangle of cow bells under one's bedroom windows in the dead of night.

[32] Many of the older inhabitants claim that there were scarcely any deer on the island at that time in comparison with the present hundreds. Between the hungry dogs and the wolves, the deer population was kept down to a very low number. (Author's note.)

CHAPTER NINE

1901 Old Things are Passed Away 1957

The beginning of the new century appeared to mark another period of transition in the region. Old faces and industries began to fade out, with fewer new ones to replace them. There were doleful shakings of heads at the passing of the good old days. A new generation, oblivious of former times and events, had its eyes on the future. Ancient and crumbling Spain had been rocked off her decaying pedestal of world power, shouldered away by a young and vigorous republic which had not yet paused to assess its strength.

The heydey of the lumbering industry was departing, to the confusion of those who were unwilling to realize it. The Ashland mills, fewer in number, were apparently busy and prosperous, but their owners appreciated that their logging roads were becoming too long for the economical harvesting of isolated and distant timber. Their tugs now had longer hauls in towing the rafts. A few were even crossing the lake to procure logs from the Minnesota shore.

Young men were seeking their fortunes elsewhere. Several of the lumbermen saw the handwriting on the wall and began to investigate timber on the Pacific Coast. The quarries had closed, the last one in 1900. Frederick Prentice, the owner of the principal ones, was not easily convinced that his business was doomed. For several years thereafter, caretakers stayed at the sites to keep the machinery in order, and to act as watchmen.

The Island View Hotel in Bayfield closed its doors in 1900. The last meals served were forlornly placed before the guests by a small staff of aged colored men who, by their manner, implied that they had waited upon much more important people in the past. The parqueted ballroom was available for some years thereafter for dances and occasional banquets. Parts of the building were moved to other locations, and the remainder was wrecked in 1913 for its lumber.

The Chequamegon Hotel endeavored, with poor success, to maintain its former dignity. Parts of the building were closed off in the interests of economy. There was a deterioration in the type of clientele, with frequent changes in management. It, too, finally experienced dissection, the last part being moved away in 1913 to make room for the Ashland County Court House. This last portion was rebuilt, occupied first by the Hotel Culver and later by the Menard Hotel. This building burned in January, 1957.

The whalebacks were rarely seen. They had been retired to calmer waters to serve, in some instances, as oil barges. The Mesabi Range had come into production, with its increased demand for larger vessels. The new design of ship was proving safe and reliable. It possessed higher freeboard and straight sides, but retained the whaleback's feature of the wheelhouse well forward and the engine room far aft. The higher freeboard provided more carrying capacity, and allowed the use of larger hatches. Most of all, the pilot and engine houses were placed out of reach of ordinary high seas.

The first of these ships was three hundred feet long, but they were increased, by one hundred foot increments, to a total of six hundred. Only the size of the locks at the Sault prevented them from becoming larger.[1]

While the era of wooden ships and iron men was being superseded, in part, by that of iron ships, there were still plenty of iron men remaining on the lakes. These waters, naturally, cannot match the Atlantic in size of waves, but this condition is partially offset by short and choppy waves coupled with the lack of sea room in which to maneuver. With autumn storms battering at their ships, with lee shores nearby, the captains and wheelsmen display their skill and hardihood.

Nowhere else in the world will be found ships of this size brought up to docks without one or more tugs herding them into position, all as a matter of routine. At times they negotiate the Sault locks with scarcely two feet of side clearance, with the captains appearing to lean nonchalantly against the bridge rails.[2]

---

[1] The modern ships, as well as the locks, are longer. The Davis and Sabin locks are each thirteen hundred fifty feet long. The latest, MacArthur, lock is eight hundred feet long but is about seven feet deeper than the others, having thirty-one feet of water over its sills. (Author's note.)

[2] Tugs are occasionally used in Cleveland and similar ports where docks are located on small rivers, to assist in turning. Also, at rare times, ocean vessels dock in New York without tugs. At such times much publicity is given the event. (Author's note.)

In 1896, the post office at La Pointe had been restored through the volume of wedding invitations sent out by the Thomas G. Grassie family upon the marriage of one of its daughters. The restoration provided a means of travel during the navigation season, via the mail boat.[3] This was a small Mackinaw-rigged schooner which left La Pointe in the morning and returned about noon – provided there was enough wind. At times one might make the trip in fifteen minutes. At others, one might enjoy the delights of a calm for two or more hours. This length of time was somewhat dependent upon the energy of the skipper in his use of scull or oars. Plate 30.

With the turn of the century, the incoming summer residents were a bit perturbed by a widespread rumor which soon developed into *fact*. This related to the disappearance of Steamboat Island, westernmost of the Apostles. It had been composed of glacial boulders and drift. In its exposed position it had been subjected to heavy wave action. It had finally been washed away, in exactly the same manner that Little Manitou is gradually disappearing today. (1957).[4] The alarmists spread the fact that the island had sunk, and that the same fate was in store for the rest of the group. The summer visitors began to fear that they had come to a dangerous place.

In 1901, the sixty-year-old Catholic Church at La Pointe, built by Father Baraga, was totally destroyed by fire. His much prized bell was melted down in the conflagration, although the remaining metal, with that of some silver chimes, was recovered, to be sent and re-cast into the present bell. It was suspected that a lumberjack, inflamed by drink from the nearby *Bowery*, had committed the crime.[5] Another rumor was that some person had stolen the *priceless* paintings housed therein, and had fired the church to cover his deed.[6]

[3] Transporting the mail between La Pointe and Bayfield, is let out by Government contract. Some prestige is connected with the position of mail carrier (Author's note.)

[4] The date of Steamboat Island's disappearance has not been exactly determined. The U. S. Lake Survey of 1902 showed no land, per letter of Corps of Engineers, U. S. Army, United States Lake Survey, dated January 16, 1957. In 1903 a narrow ridge six inches out of water was reported. In 1904, no island was visible save in low water or in rough weather. *Bulletins of the Great Lakes*, (#13 for 1903 and #14 for 1904). Local sources claim the island disappeared in 1898. The fluctuations in lake levels evidently accounted for the phenomena. (Author's note.)

[5] The so-called Bowery was a combination saloon and dance hall. Through the years, it had acquired an evil reputation from the many fights which had occurred there, accompanied by several knifings. The Bowery was located on Rice Street, not far from the church. (Author's note.)

[6] A rather classic example of typical eye-witness accounts was displayed over the event. One thoroughly honest man, claiming to have arrived on the scene in the early stages of the fire, and peering through the flames, said that the pictures were

Certain valuable and irreplaceable vestments and candle sticks were destroyed. These had been presented to Baraga in Austria, at the time of Emperor Franz Joseph's marriage on April 24, 1854.[7] The loss of these was probably responsible for the many legends surrounding the more or less valuable paintings in the church. One widely accepted story was that Father Marquette had built the church in 1670, and that one painting had been executed by him. Another was that it contained the original of Ruben's Descent from the Cross, presented by the same priest. Plate 31.

A painting which was displayed in 1898 had an attached placard which recorded that the picture had originated in Spain in the 16th century, traveled by caravel around Cape Horn, and landed in Peru. After seeing service there for some years, it was taken to one of the California missions. Its next step was to New Orleans, conveyed thither on the backs of Indian servants over the blazing sands of Arizona. How long it remained in New Orleans was not recorded, but its next trip was to La Pointe, via the Mississippi, St. Croix and Bois Brule Rivers.[8]

To deflate somewhat cruelly these flights of imagination: the Descent from the Cross was a rather crude copy of the original which hangs in the Sistine Chapel. It had been brought from Austria by Baraga. At the same time he had transported a portrait of the Holy Family in St. Joseph's carpenter shop. This had been painted in Laibach by an artist named Lang, under Baraga's supervision.[9]

During the winter of 1900-1901 the old Protestant Church in the village had been purchased by Edward P. Salmon, and moved over the ice to the Old Mission grounds. It was placed toward the top of the hill south of the Mission, and near the old cemetery which the missionaries

missing. Another, equally reliable, villager said that he saw the pictures drop into the fire. (Author's note.) *Records of the Justice Court of La Pointe*, (1895 et seq), 6–7. In Madeline Island Historical Museum.

An entry before Thomas Stahl, Justice of the Peace, recorded that on June 20, 1901 at 5.00 p.m. action was taken against John Felt, charged with having burned the church building. Felt was found guilty and bound over to the next term of Circuit Court of Ashland County. Bond was set at $500.00, in default of which he was committed to the County Jail.

Up to date, there is no record on Felt having been tried in Circuit Court, and the presumption is that the case was dropped. Neither is there any record to show that he had been "inflamed by drink."

[7] Antoine Ivan Rezek, *History of the Diocese of Sault Ste. Marie*, (Houghton, Michigan, 1906), 1:108. Also Joseph Gregorich, *The Apostle of the Chippewas*, (Chicago, 1932), 80. At this time, Baraga was given other valuable presents. Som of them he sold in Austria, and used the proceeds for his missionary work.

[8] The attending priest was not backward in fostering some of these old tales. (Author's note.)

[9] Rezek, Ibid, 1:72.

had established and consecrated. It looked out over the mission grounds to the bay and the distant mainland. Plate 32.

Here, in 1915, Almon Whitney Burr ("Papa" Burr to his Beloit College Academy students) spent many hours lining the interior with carefully selected squares of birch bark. Many of the pieces had lichens and fungi growing on them in all manner of natural patterns, and Burr arranged these in a most pleasing and effective style. This treatment completely concealed the old and shattered clay plaster. In the summer months, when guests were at the Old Mission, church services were held every Sunday, announced by the shallow peals and clanking mechanism of the old original bell.[10] Many ministers of note conducted the meetings, using a Bible, on the front leaf of which was written, "Lyman Warren, July 10, 1834." Numerous flies also attended.[11]

These years saw a small but steady growth in the summer colony. George F. Thomas revamped and opened Treaty Hall as a small summer hotel.[12] It operated for about four years, but Thomas finally abandoned the project, and devoted more of his time to the sale of his property. The modest influx of summer residents served to revive the old village. Men found employment as caretakers and gardeners. Agricultural pursuits expanded, with dairies and truck gardens.[13] Altogether it appeared that the island might experience some of its former importance.

Recreational life of the time was fairly simple. There were walks in the woods, with the latter's profusion of ground pines and other characteristic flora of the latitude. There were berrying trips to local districts and other islands for gathering wild strawberries, blueberries and raspberries. The fishing enthusiasts traveled to the mainland to whip the small rivers for brook trout. There were sails and expeditions with Captains Charles Russell and Daniel Angus. Plate 33. Some of these cruises consumed several days in the waters of the adjacent archipelago, convincing the visiting city dwellers that they were truly experiencing pioneer life. The novelty of sleeping on sandy beaches which, before morning, converted themselves into beds of unyielding concrete, vividly confirmed this belief. And to spend a foggy night in the whistle house of a lighthouse station! The fog horn, blaring on a definite time schedule,

[10] Both bell and Bible are in the Madeline Island Historical Museum. (Author's note.)

[11] So did the author.

[12] Board and room $8.00 to $10.00 per week! (Author's note.)

[13] Excellent vegetables were raised for a number of years until the gardeners became discouraged at the forays of deer which the Conservation Commission allowd to overrun the island. The deer not only destroyed vegetable gardens but also have practically wiped out all new growth of white pine and cedar. (Author's note.)

could prove as irritating as waiting for drops of water to fall on one's face. The event was impressive, the memory enduring.

Some of the more venturesome experimented with Indian birch bark canoes, a few of which were still in existence. One of the more popular amusements was the annual hayrack ride to Big Bay, on the eastern side of the island, and about seven miles from the village. These were conducted under the auspices, and beneath the clouds, of Peerless cut plug smoke issuing from the pipe of Thomas Stahl — *King* Stahl! A lively debate always ensued as to whether the smoke attracted or repelled the mosquitoes. The discussion was sure to be interrupted by the hayrack's negotiation of a stretch of corduroy road which also set up an alarming cacophony amidst the picnic's collection of pans and bean pots.

Another pastime, which probably claimed more attention, was the annual clam bake, conducted by the Badger Clam Bake Club of Ashland. This organization was fortunate in having a man who was an artist in this field. Robert W. Parsons normally conducted a completely stocked tobacco store in Ashland, but clam bakes were his avocation.[14]

The day before the big event, Parsons would arrive at Madeline Island with all the accessories, and prepare the pits for the occasion. The details of his arrangements are lost in the obscurity of time, but the results were a triumph. There were clams, lobsters, green corn, bluefish, chickens and sweet potatoes, all steamed over the seaweed-covered coals.

This was a momentous event, not only for the members of the club, but also for the youth of the island. The moppets showed as much interest and excitement as at the arrival of a circus.[15] On the appointed day, the club, whose membership had been augmented by friends and relatives from miles around, chartered the steamers "Skater," "Mary Scott" and "Lucile." Their approach was heralded by the sound of band music on board the boats, and the entire village turned out to watch the arrivals disembark and stream up the dock — and to count the kegs of beer. The latter were conveyed to the Bowery by King Stahl and his dog team. Plate 29.

If Parsons was ever mystified by possible shortages in his viands, he never displayed any great concern, even though the village lads, re-enforced by certain summer urchins, mingled with the crowd and enjoyed a novel repast.[16]

[14] Parsons not only boasted the largest tobacco shop outside of a large city, but also owned the most magnificent wooden Indian which graced the front of his shop. With a distinct feeling of grateful nostalgia, we have noted that this Indian has been carefully preserved, and now stands inside the entrance of the Ashland County Court House. (Author's note.)

[15] The modern lad will probably never experience this event.

[16] The author was one of the urchins.

An outing of considerable interest to the summer visitors was a trip on the Booth Fish Company's "S. B. Barker."[17] This boat made daily rounds of the islands' fish camps to collect the catches of the fishermen. While on these trips it was possible to see all of the Apostle Islands. The "Barker" was an old vessel which had been a tug in the service of the Barker & Stewart Lumber Company of Ashland, named after one of its owners. A superstructure had been added, and sides enclosed for the accommodation of passengers. She entered the Booth service in 1901. In addition to her regular crew, she carried a cook whose fame for frying fish was widespread. The anticipated blueberry pie might turn into custard after the flies had been scared off, but this was forgotten in the memory of the succulent fish.[18]

Another drawing card of the "Barker" was her skipper. Captain Okay J. Vorous (generally called "Okay jay") was not only a most accommodating man, but he also had built up a local reputation of infallibility in the piloting of his boat. In a fog, he would blow the ship's whistle and then listen for the echo. From long experience among the islands he was able to determine his exact whereabouts.[19]

An event of no historical importance, but one which caused considerable local comment was the appearance in 1902 of the first bath-tub on Madeline Island, the property of one of the summer residents. Cries of "Snob," "Down with the rich" and "Untrue to the customs of Madeline" were hurled at the owner. The son of the family groaned, inasmuch as there was no running water and he knew that the task of filling the tub would fall to him, involving many trips to the lake with his buckets. Saturday was a very busy day for him.

Within a few years after the opening of the Old Mission, increased custom brought about additions to its facilities. Two so-called dormitories were built as sleeping quarters for additional guests, followed, very shortly, by the addition of a large dining-room, connected to the old building.

The dormitories added little to the aesthetic appearance of the mission grounds. Since they were of rather primitive construction, the slumbers of a first floor occupant might be audible to a second story guest. This condition was solved, in part, by a fire which destroyed the Upper Dormitory in 1905, an exciting and locally sensational conflagration.[20]

[17] This company was then known as the A. Booth Packing Company. It was the predecessor of the present Booth Fisheries Corporation, and came to Bayfield in 1880. (Author's note.)

[18] To those culinarily curious, the fish was cooked by the deep-fry method. (Author's note.)

[19] The forerunner of radar?

[20] Rumor stated that the fire was caused by the upset of a kerosene lamp which was being used to heat an old fashioned curling iron. (Author's note.)

A short time later, the Lower Dormitory was halved, and each portion remodeled into more attractive quarters.

The increase in the number of summer residents brought about an improvement in the mail and ferry service between Bayfield and the island. The refinement of the internal combustion engine was also a factor in making the trips faster and surer. The carrying of the mail does not seem to be especially hazardous, and at La Pointe the summer visitor rather envies the man who can spend his hours on the water in that service. Upon the advent of winter, however, the picture changes. Generally in December the ice starts to form. If it were not an omen of bitter days to come, its arrival might please the artistic eye. Ridges of ice, in freak designs, appear on the shores. The sides of the docks collect it from the wash and spray of the waves, until a valance of glittering blues and whites is built up. A period comes when the boats can no longer plow through it, and when it is not strong enough to support the weight of a man. During these periods La Pointe was isolated for a time varying from a few days up to two weeks.[21] Plates 34 & 35.

The same condition exists, in reverse, in the spring. Upon one of the latter occasions, Captain Charles Russell, the current mail carrier, left the island in a row boat with a number of companions. The little group safely reached Bayfield, after making its way through the open channels in the floe-ice. Upon its return, these channels had shifted, frequently balking the men in their attempts to thread their way home. At last, when they were about one-half mile from the Madeline shore, they were apparently trapped in the grinding ice. One of the group stood up to push aside an ice cake with his oar. Through some accident, he lost his balance, capsizing the boat. The ice was not strong enough to support a man's weight, and the five men climbed onto the bottom of the over-turned boat, hoping that help might come. The trapped air inside the boat gradually leaked out, allowing the little craft to settle lower and lower in the water.

With the icy water creeping up their bodies, the men became more and more helpless. One would slip off his precarious perch, to be painfully pulled back by his companions. At last, none was able to offer this assistance, and one after the other, three of them slid off and perished. In the meantime a rescue party was being organized on the island. It too had trouble in working its way out to the survivors. At long last the task was accomplished, and Captain Angus and William Johnson were rescued. In this tragedy, Captain Russell, Chauncey Wright and Nelson Teigen lost their lives on April 12, 1915.

[21] In recent years this isolation has been overcome with planes and so-called wind sleds. (Author's note.) Plate 35A.

The isolation of the island was somewhat relieved in 1915 by the installation of telephone service to the mainland in conjunction with the formation of the local Madeline Island Telephone Company. The latter, through its purchase of second-hand instruments of the vintage of 1895 (which, incidentally, were still in use in 1957), along with the stringing of wires supported by many trees, instituted a rudimentary communications system. Like many other rural party lines, where central was the clearing house for all local news, it was possible, by a violent twisting of the crank, to learn that Mrs. Jones, with whom one wished to speak, had gone to Bayfield and would return on the 4:00 p.m. ferry.

Through the years, the fishing industry has played an important part in the economy of the region. The American Fur Company, but for unforeseen events, might have built it up to considerable proportions. In later years, local companies had entered the business, with varying results. The Booth Fisheries Corporation has been a prominent factor in the market. With its nation-wide distributing facilities, it has had a steadying influence on prices, and has provided local fishermen with an outlet for ther catches regardless of general economic conditions. It has done much to encourage the fishermen by financing them when they went into business, and tiding them over when storms destroyed their nets and boats.

It has been a far cry from the days when the Indians used bone fish hooks, or nets crudely fashioned from bark fibers, to the modern methods of long gangs of linen or nylon nets; from their use of canoes to gasoline and diesel powered boats.

Through the use of these newer techniques, more fish have been caught than the lake could steadily provide. By 1920, under prevailing conditions, the industry seemed doomed. At that time, by means of legislation limiting net meshes and seasons, and by cooperation between the three affected states, and with hatchery propagation, the catches were improved. In recent years, with the arrival of more fishermen and their use of the finer thread nylon net, catches are again on the decline. In spite of these decreases the Bayfield County catch for 1949 amounted to 5,430,000 pounds, with a value of $628,606.09.[22]

These conditions do not appear to have disturbed the November run of lake herring. At this time of year all normal activities in the region are suspended for the usual take of this fish. The regular fishermen are

[22] *Ashland Daily Press*, June 20, 1950. The Bayfield County figures include virtually all fish caught among the Apostle Islands, most of which are in Ashland County. The alarming raids which the lamprey eel has made upon the fish of the lower Great Lakes, have thus far (1957) not been as serious on Lake Superior, although fishery experts believe the industry is doomed unless some method is devised to eliminate or control this parasitic pest. (Author's note.)

joined by many men from the surrounding neighborhood. The latter leave otherwise steady employment for the excitment and high wages of *herrin' fishin.'* Bayfield is a hive of industry. Many women find employment in the fish houses. During the war years, schools were dismissed so that the older children might take the places of the absent men. Hundreds of tons of the fish are brought in to be processed — cleaned, packaged for freezing, and salted down in kegs. It is nearly Christmas time before the aroma of herring leaves the town.

Another kind of fishing proved to be a very important business for a number of years but since 1950 has fallen off to a marked degree. This was the trolling industry, catering almost entirely to the summer tourist. The center of this was the City of Bayfield, and it was an extremely valuable adjunct to that city's economy. Approximately thirty boats purveyed to the vacationer. Often times these craft were reserved for months in advance by enthusiastic amateurs. The captains were very consistent in taking fishermen to places where they might make a catch. It was the exception when a party returned without some evidence of its prowess.

The boats started early in the morning for the fishing grounds which lay from ten to thirty miles distant, depending on the season and the fancies of the captains. The fishing was done by means of a plug or spoon attached by a leader to a woven wire copper line. Each captain had his own type of lure by which he swore. Upon reaching the fishing grounds, the boat was slowed down to trolling speed, the plug was thrown over, and the captain's favorite, and oftimes secret, course was held.

To the average inlander, the experience of hooking a large trout and landing it was one of great excitement. If the lake happened to be a bit rough, he returned home and recited in great detail his bravery in venturing on the stormy waters of that famous sea, and of his skill in landing his fish. To the experienced angler, who loved to play his game on light tackle, this kind of fishing held no great lure, but the fact that a large number of boats were kept busy, and that hotels and all available rooming houses were filled to capacity with budding Izaak Waltons, bespoke the popularity of the sport. The amateur who landed a thirty or forty pound trout could not be convinced that he was not an angling genius.

While the region catered to these fishermen, it was and still is especially indifferent in serving the true expert in the matter of that elusive and sporty aristocrat of fish— the brook trout. The State fish hatcheries annually plant a large number of these speckled beauties, along with rainbows and German browns, but the local fishermen seem to have the idea that the stocking is done for their benefit only. They turn out in large numbers on the opening day of the season to catch all they can. Since the season is set too early for the summer vacationer, he finds little or nothing left, with the result that he by-passes the region and goes to Minnesota or Canada where he may test his skill. This condition is in marked contrast to that existing on the Bois Brule River in the late 1870s. An observer then remarked, "In these [tributary] lakes are the breeding grounds of the vast numbers of brook trout that inhabit the upper waters of the Brule. I have seen them, upon a clear day – as thick as minnows in a common pond, – It has been truly said that this is an angler's paradise. One may capture in a small time all that he can carry."[23]

In line with changing scenes and faces, another landmark was destroyed in 1923 with the burning of Treaty Hall at La Pointe. A small cottage nearby had caught fire, and this had spread to the old building.

Another indication of time's transitions was the closing of the Ashland blast furnace in 1924. James Burnside, the last foreman of operations, with all the exactitude of the old timer, consulted his little black book and stated that the furance shut down at 11:00 p.m. on December 16 of that year.

A number of factors were responsible for this cessation: one was the exhaustion of the hard wood in the immediate area; another was the policy of the owners in concentrating their operations in the Upper Michigan Peninsula, near Escanaba. The market had also changed, because the coke fueled furnaces, under chemical control, could produce an iron comparable to the Lake Superior grade at a lower cost. The furnace stood idle for about twenty years. Some of the buildings were then torn down, and others were put to various uses. The only evidences remaining today (1957) are two tall chimneys and a pervasive odor of creosote from the sites of the charcoal ovens.

In 1924, the last sawmill in the region closed down. After the death of Captain Pike in 1906, his mill was sold to the Wachsmuth Lumber Company in 1907. In spite of a disastrous fire on September 5, 1908, which spread through the storage yard and burned about ten million feet of lumber, the new company prospered. In 1914 it had purchased the Bayfield Transfer Company's railroad to Red Cliff, and some of the right-of-way of the old Bayfield Harbor and Great Western Rail-

---

[23] E. T. Sweet, *Geology of Wisconsin*, Ibid, 3:321. In the author's opinion, the only economic future for the northern one-third of the State of Wisconsin, besides growing a crop of wood, is the development of the summer resort business. Unless the state authorities can make it more attractive by the planting of larger numbers of game fish, and by nurturing other summer activities, that portion of the state may become an inert and backward area.

road beyond. It extended the rails to reach uncut timber on the hills back of Bayfield, which was sufficient to keep the mill running for about ten years. Contrary to usual custom, the mill was dismantled instead of having the more or less 'judicious' fire.[24]

The closing of the mill left Bayfield to seek other means of support. The fishing industry remained as a small but consistent backlog. The city began to serve an increasing number of farmers who had moved in to take up cut-over timber lands. It began to feel the missionary efforts of William Knight who, for nearly thirty years, had been preaching the value of the Bayfield Peninsula for fruit culture. This neck of land, surrounded on three sides by Lake Superior, enjoys the most equable temperature of any for miles around and has the longest growing season for agricultural products. Knight had fathered the many apple orchards of the region. He had been instrumental in the cultivation of strawberries which today command premium prices in the Duluth and St. Paul markets.

A cannery has been built for processing string beans. In the opinion of many summer visitors, these beans also are of superior quality. The cannery is encouraging farmers to raise other crops which it may handle. The younger generation has commenced the construction of a ski camp, Mount Ashwabay, in the hope of filling in the winter low spots of the tourist trade.[25]

All of northern Wisconsin was agog in 1928 when it was learned that President Coolidge was to spend his summer on the Bois Brule River. For the first time, the roadside from the small Village of Brule was to be lined with hot dog stands, erected by expectant vendors. The local newspapers went all-out in proclaiming his advent.

The President occupied the large summer home of Henry Clay Pierce on the Brule, and between his official visits to Superior, where his summer offices were established, whiled away his hours in fishing for the wily brook trout for which that stream was famous. It was whispered that he used *worms* for bait.[26]

During his vacation he visited Devil's Island in the spacious cabin cruiser of Frank Woods of Lincoln, Nebraska and La Pointe.[27] After his trip, he inspected the old Protestant Church and other points of

[24] The term 'judicious' was a colloquialism of the era. By having his mill burn after the timber was cut, the owner was considered very judicious, especially when insurance was involved. (Author's note.)

[25] The Mount's name is a coined one, made up from ASHland, WAshburn and BAYfield. (Author's note.)

[26] Dr. Arthur T. Holbrook, *From the Log of a Trout Fisherman*, (Privately printed. Plimpton Press, Norwood, Mass., 1949) 105.

[27] Frank Woods was the second of six children of Colonel and Mrs. Frederick M. Woods. (Author's note.)

interest on Madeline Island, ending his tour with a reception at the Hunter Gary summer home, where an enthusiastic movie fan caught the chief executive in an un-presidential and grinning struggle with a a stubborn caramel.

In addition to the providing the region with an aura in which it basked for a number of years, the Coolidge visit was the means of supplying a passable highway from the Bois Brule to Superior — something which had been needed for many years.

A touch of the modern reached La Pointe in 1929 when the laying of a submarine cable brought electric power from Bayfield. It lessened the charm (and the fire hazard) of the candle-lighted summer homes, and possibly ended an era of the pioneering movement, but it eased the problem of housekeeping, and solved the difficulties of procuring water. It eliminated the quaint old trolley and windlass contrivance by which one hauled water from the lake, but it did save many an aching back. Diagram B.

Another link with the past was broken in the spring of 1943. The Protestant Church, on the hill near the mission, emulated the fate of the Deacon's One Hoss Shay and collapsed in a thousand pieces. Borers had riddled the ancient sills, and more modern neglect had weakened its foundations.

At the time it had been moved, it had seemed especially fitting that its new site should have been near the burying ground where a few of the wives and children of the missionaries had been buried. Here, too, were the graves of the Warren brothers, the last of whom had died in 1947. An infant daughter of Dr. Borup was also buried here. Her epitaph on one of the six extant tombstones, might lead one into discussions of birth in absentia.[28]

[28] The epitaph:

To the Memory
of
Marion Margareth
Daughter of
Charles W. & Elizabeth
Borup
Born 20th March
1843
Died 6th July
1843
in the absence of both her parents.

W. E. Peters, Detroit.
Suffer little children to
come unto me and forbid them
not; for of such is the
kingdom of Heaven.

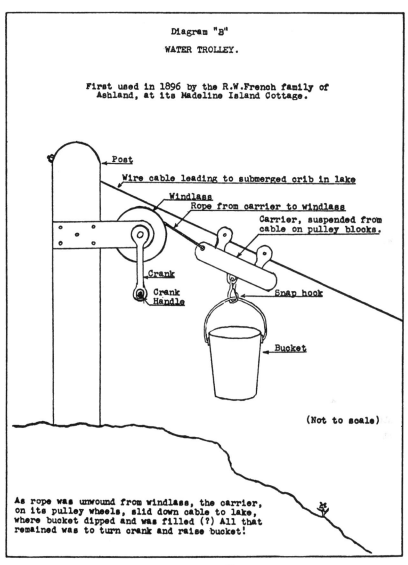

Diagram "B"

WATER TROLLEY.

First used in 1896 by the R.W.French family of
Ashland, at its Madeline Island Cottage.

Post

Wire cable leading to submerged crib in lake

Windlass
Rope from carrier to windlass

Carrier, suspended from
cable on pulley blocks.

Crank

Crank
Handle

Snap hook

Bucket

(Not to scale)

As rope was unwound from windlass, the carrier,
on its pulley wheels, slid down cable to lake,
where bucket dipped and was filled (?) All that
remained was to turn crank and raise bucket!

B. Water Trolley.

175

Another epitaph, expressing great pathos, appears on the marker of Mary M. Sibley. She had been the wife of Thomas P. Sibley who had settled on the Marengo River in 1854. She had died on July 15, 1865 at the age of 39 years. This epitaph reads:

Asleep in Jesus, Far from me
My kindred and their graves may be.
But mine is still the blessed sleep
From which none ever wake to weep.

The cemetery near Baraga's first church was no doubt meant to receive all who died in the Catholic faith, but inasmuch as no white persons had been buried there, it has since acquired the name of The Indian Cemetery. Aside from the quaintness of the small structures over the Indian graves, there are stone markers of historical interest. Among the latter is the head stone of Michel Cadotte. Another covers the grave of an infant daughter of Lyman Warren. He had been a Presbyterian but he had deferred to his Catholic wife in the baptism of the child.[29] Still another, no longer in evidence, marked the grave of an Indian who had been Struck by Thunder.[30]

The graveyard near the present Catholic Church contains the last resting places of historic characters as well as those of persons who had gained a measure of fame in later days. Here, too, is an interesting epitaph which has been widely publicized.[31]

At the extreme southwest end of the island (Grant's Point) is an unmarked and unsung burying ground containing the graves of many Indians. No authentic explanation has ever been advanced either for its location or why this number of Indians were buried there, unless it bears out Warren's statement that the principal Ojibway settlement of 1490–1610 was at this end of the island, and the sand beach offered a convenient burying place. The shifting sands of the point, at times,

[29] The child died May 6, 1824. The Indian cemetery probably was not established until 1836, after Baraga's arrival in 1835. It is the writer's belief that she had been buried originally toward the south end of the island, near where the Village of La Pointe was located at the time. After Baraga's cemetery had been consecrated she had been moved to it.

[30] The author saw this many years ago.

[31] This epitaph reads:

To the Memory of
Abraham Beaulieu
Born 15 September 1822
Accidentally Shot
4th April 1844
As a Mark of Affection From
His Brother.

unearth some of these graves, exposing bones, relics, arrowheads and tomahawks. One legend avers that certain unbaptized natives had been interred at the spot. Another, linked with an incident which occurred in 1900, might furnish the answer.

In that year, the Old Mission Inn was staffed by a number of Beloit College students who, impressed with the historical background of the locality, and hearing of the possible archeological trove, decided to investigate the area. Many skulls and artifacts were unearthed, and the budding scientists were jubilant over their finds. In the midst of their attempts to classify and sort their loot, they were waited upon by a delegation of La Pointe French-Ojibway. They were asked if they would like to have outsiders appear and disinter *their* ancestors. When Joseph Neveaux, the leader of the committee, delivered his Parthian shot of, "Besides, they all died of the smallpox," the amateurs quickly re-interred their finds, and hastened to be vaccinated.

About two miles from the village, and on the eastern side of the island, is the more modern Protestant cemetery which, as yet, has not accumulated the patina of age. It was originally called the Black Thorn cemetery, but at the request of a former pastor it was changed to the less imaginative one of Greenwood.

The grave of Chief O-Shaka can scarcely be rated as another cemetery but it still remains as an item of interest.[32] The chief had died in December, 1853, at the age of fifty-one. His grave is located near the entrance to the mission grounds, concealed by four sentinel evergreens. Map 24.

He had been the chief speaker of the Ojibway on Lake Superior, and had been a personage of considerable importance. He had been baptized a Catholic, but in later years had become a Protestant. He could not be buried in the Catholic cemetery, but because he was a

[32] O-Shaka was also known as O-Shoga and Little Buffalo, and was the son of Chief Great Buffalo. The latter's Ojibway name was Bezhike, but he was also known as Kechewaishkeenh — the latter with a variety of spellings. Bezhike's tombstone, in the Indian cemetery, has had the name broken off. The original epitaph was:

BEZHIKE
PRINCIPAL CHIEF OF
THE CHIPPEWAS
LAKE SUPERIOR
DIED
Sept. 7, 1855.
Aged 96 years.

Much litigation took place in later years in regard to Bezhike's land holdings. His heirs claimed that a Government treaty ceded to him the real estate now occupied by the business section of the City of Duluth. While the heirs apparently lost their case, there are rumors that the matter will be re-opened. (Author's note.)

notable chieftain he could not be consigned to a potter's field. The Protestant mission had closed at the time of his death, and his Catholic friends and relatives would not bury him in that graveyard. Thus, a small plot was chosen, approximately half way between the two cemeteries. We do not know whether any particular significance may be attached to this solution of the problem, but at least it would appear that someone had possessed the gift of compromise.

We have brought our Village Outpost to modern times. The underlying urge to set down a chronological story was initiated by the author's interest in, and affection for, the village and its present inhabitants. To this extent the importance of the village has probably been over emphasized.

Although the magnificent forests of Madeline Island and the Bayfield Peninsula are gone; although the fishing boats, with their quaint sails and sturdy hulls, have been replaced by busy and clamorous gasoline or Diesel craft, and although the lumber hookers, with all sail set, no longer pass our door, yet these inroads of so-called civilization cannot rob the region of its glorious sunsets; cannot lessen the mysterious animation and chromatism of the Aurora Borealis; cannot fade the reddish cliffs with their cappings of greenery, nor diminish the unparalleled blueness of the lake.

Neither can they take away the fairy land of autumnal foliage nor the experience of cruising along the beaches and into the wave-worn caves of the headlands in a small boat, and drinking in their ineffable charm and beauty. Like Michel Cadotte, we may still gaze at the play of shadows on the opposite hills, and watch the ever-changing colors of the lake.

Glossary of Related Ojibway Names

NAME	TRANSLATION	IDENTIFICATION
Aminikan	Fishing Ground	Amnicon Bay at northeast end of Madeline Island Also Amnicon River, east of Superior, Wisconsin
Ashuwaguindag Miniss	The Further Island	Hermit Island
Bawatig	Rapids in the River	Sault Ste. Marie
Bishegokwe Sibi	Woman-Who-Has-Been-Abandoned-by-Her-Husband River	Three Mile Creek, east of Ashland, Wisconsin
Bugadabi Miniss	Hook and Line Island	Michigan Island
Eshkwegondens Miniss	Small Island at End of Larger	Little Manitou Island
Gachiishquaguindag Miniss	The Furthermost Island	Outer Island
Gagwadjiw	Porcupine Mountains	Porcupines of the Upper Michigan Peninsula
Ga-Kashkikawangag	Steep Sand Hill Going Down Toward Lake	Sand Bay. On mainland opposite Sand Island
Ganitagekweiag	Mourning Squaw Bay	Squaw Bay. On mainland next east from Siskiwit Bay
Gegawewamingo (or) Gegawewauindag Miniss	Burnt Wood Island or Almost an Island. (Meanings uncertain)	Stockton Island
Gawassidjiwang Sibi	Where There is a Strong, Foamy Current in the River	Montreal River. Wisconsin-Michigan Boundary
Gemananosi Miniss	Island of Ironwood Trees	Ironwood Island
Gete Odena	Old Town	Superior, Wisconsin (Waikwakitchigaming probably preferable)
Giashko Miniss	Gull Island	Gull Island
Gigig	Heaven	Heaven
Gigito-Mikana	Council Road	Washburn, Wisconsin

179

NAME	TRANSLATION	IDENTIFICATION
Gigito-Mikana Sibi	Council Road River	Vanderventer Creek, near Washburn. Now known as Thompson Creek
Gigonsi Sibiwishi	A Small-fish Creek	Fish Creek. At foot of Chequamegon Bay
Gogibic	He Dives into the Water	The Gogebic Range. (Probably derived from Lake Gogebic where the allusion to water originated)
Gogogashagun Sibi	River Crossed on a Fallen, Swaying Tree	West branch of Montreal River. Its path through the Penokee Range now called Rocking Chair Gap
Jigagawanjikani Sibi (Probably Baraga's Spelling)	Onion River	Onion River, south of Bayfield. So called because of its wild onions
Joniia Sibing	At Silver River	Silver Creek. Between Ashland and Mellen
Kakagan	The Home of the Wall-eyed Pike	Applied to the Kakagan River and slough
Kagagiwanjikag Miniss	Island of Hemlock Trees	Cat Island. (Locally called Hemlock)
Keweenaw	The Way Made Straight by Means of a Portage	Specifically, the portage across the Keweenaw Peninsula
Kitche Ajawew	On the Other Side of the Island	The Old Fort, the first American Fur Company post
Kitchibinikanensi	Big Sucker Creek	Bono's Creek, between Ashland and Washburn. Mistakenly named Bonus Creek by Wisconsin Highway Commission
Kitchi Gami	Big Water	Specifically, Lake Superior
Kitchimokomen	Long Knife	Ojibway name for an American
Kiwideonaning	Where a Boat Goes Around a Point	Point Detour. The north-ernmost end of the Bayfield Peninsula
Makadassonogoni	Bear Trap River	A tributary of the Kakagan River
Mako Miniss	Bear Island	Bear Island
Manitou Miniss	Spirit Island	Manitou Island
Matchimanitou Miniss	Evil Spirit Island	Devil's Island
Mashki Sibing (or) Mushkego	Swamp River	Bad River
Mekatewikwanaie	Black Robes	Priest
Menabosho	See Nanabazhoo	
Mesabi	The Giant	The Mesabi Range
Metabikitigweiag	Meaning uncertain but possibly Small River Running into a Larger	South Fork, a tributary of Fish Creek

NAME	TRANSLATION	IDENTIFICATION
Michilimackinac Miniss	The Island of the Great Turtle	Mackinac Island
Minikan	Blueberry	Blueberry
Mikominikan Miniss	Island of Raspberries	Raspberry Island
Miskwabimijikag Miniss	Island of Willow Trees	York Island
Mitigominikang Miniss	Acorn Island	Oak Island
Moningwunakauning Miniss	The Island of the Golden-Breasted Woodpecker	Madeline Island. (See Waugabame)
Moningwana Neiashi	Golden-Breasted Woodpecker Point	Grant's Point, southwest end of Madeline Island
Mushkego Miniss		See Mashki
Nabikwana Miniss	Boat Island	Eagle Island
Namakagan	Home of the Sturgeon	Namakagan Lake or River
Nanabazhoo	Demi-God	Fabulous Ojibway Demi-god
Namebinikanensi	Little Sucker Creek	Boyd's Creek, between Ashland and Bayfield
Nadobikag (or) Nidobikag Sibiwishen	Creek From Which Water is Fetched	Bay City Creek, in Ashland
Neiashibikang	A Rocky Point of Land Extending into the Lake	Houghton Point, at entrance to Chequamegon Bay
Nemadji Sibing	The Left Hand River	Nemadji River, at Superior, Wisconsin
Nesakee	The House at the Foot of the Hill	Protestant Mission on Madeline Island
Netawagansing	Little Sand Bay	Sunset or Kapunky Bay on Madeline Island
Nigig Miniss	Otter Isalnd	Otter Island
Nontounagon (or) Tonagan	I Have Lost my Bowl	Ontonagon. Named according to legend, by a girl who had lost her wooden bowl in the river
Odena	A Town	Specifically, Odanah, Wisconsin
Ojibway (or) Otchipwe	Puckered up.	Taken either from the Indians' design of moccasin or from their custom of sewing their victims into a hide before burning. The heat puckered the hide and squeezed the victim. The word Chippewa was introduced by the English.
Omakakakaning	At the Place Where There are Many Frogs	Frog Bay, first bay west of Red Cliff Point, on the mainland
Opini Sibi	Potato River	Potato River, a tributary of the Bad River
Oshki Odena	A New Town	Bayfield, Wisconsin
Passibikaning	At the Place of the Steep Cliff	Specifically, the Red Cliff Indian Reservation

NAME	TRANSLATION	IDENTIFICATION
Shabominikong	At Gooseberry Place	Chebomnicon Bay, on Madeline Island
Sibiweiang	At the Creek	Five Mile Creek, east of Ashland
Sinsibakwado Minnising	Maple Sugar Island	Rocky Island
Siskawekaning	Place Where the (fish) are Caught	Siskiwit Bay, on which the Village of Cornucopia is located
Shagawaumikong	Soft Beaver Dam	Chequamegon Point
Totogitiweiag	The River is Muddy	Totogatic River, a tributary of the Namakagan River
Wababiko Miniss	The Island of the White Rock	Sand Island
Wabaso Miniss	Rabbit Island	South Twin Island
Wabi Sibing	White River	White River
Waikwakitchigaming	At the End of the Big Lake	Superior, Wisconsin
Waugabame (or possibly Waubagame)	Meaning uncertain Possibly The Sorcerer of the Lake	A rarely used name for Madeline Island
Wigobic Miniss	Basswood Island	Basswood Island
Wikewade Sibiwishen	Bay Creek	Another name for Fish Creek
Wikwedawangag	Sandy Bay	Specifically, Middle Fort
Wikwedong	In a Bay	Ashland, Wisconsin
Wikweiang	There is a Bay	Buffalo Bay, on which the Village of Red Cliff is located
Winnboujou	See Nanabazhoo	

Most of the above words and names have been taken from Verwyst's Glossary, and were checked against Baraga's dictionary.[1] A few, which do not appear in Verwyst's list, were taken from Baraga or Warren.[2] One may possibly question Baraga's spelling of some of the Indian words. However, when one remembers that Baraga and Verwyst were of Slavic and Teutonic descent, respectively, and when one considers the difficulties which these nationalities have in the pronunciation of both French and English, it is reasonable to presume that they might have had the same trouble when they came to "English" the Indian words.

Baraga had a tendency to substitute the French J for the English SH and for the French CH. In his dictionary he explained the substitution on the ground that, to him, the Indian pronunciation more nearly approached the French J. He did this with the words Chequamegon

[1] Chrysostum Verwyst, "A Glossary of Chippewa Names," *Acta et Dicta* (St. Paul, 1916), 4: #2, 253–274.
[2] Warren, Ibid, 5: Various.

and Chebomnicon. Although, to the author, the Indian pronunciation has always sounded like SH, he pleads ignorance in the field of languages, and bows to Baraga's superior knowledge and experience. However, where Warren has given different spellings, they have been used in preference to Baraga's.

ENGLISH-OJIBWAY GLOSSARY

ENGLISH	OJIBWAY
American	Kitchimokomen
Amnicon	Aminikan
Ashland	Wikwedong
Bad River	Mashki Sibing or Mushkego
Basswood Island	Wigobic Miniss
Bay City Creek	Nadobikag Sibiwishen or Nidobikag Sibiwishen
Bayfield	Oshki Odena
Bear Island	Mako Miniss
Bear Trap River	Makadassonogoni Sibi
Blueberry	Minikan
Bono's Creek	Kitchibinikanensi
Boyd's Creek	Namebinikanensi
Buffalo Bay	Wikweiang
Cat Island	Kagagiwanjikag Miniss
Chebomnicon	Shabominikong
Chequamegon	Shagawaumikong
Chippewa — See Ojibway	
Devil's Island	Matchimanitou Miniss
Eagle Island	Nabikwana Miniss
Fish Creek	Gigonsi Sibiwishi or Wikwade
Five Mile Creek	Sibiweiang
Frog Bay	Omakakakaning
Gogebic	Gogibic
Grant's Point	Moningwana Neiashi
Gull Island	Giashko Miniss
Heaven	Gigig
Houghton Point	Neiashibikang
Hermit Island	Ashuwaguindag Miniss
Ironwood Island	Gemananosi Miniss
Kakagan	Kakagan
Kapunky Bay (Sunset)	Netawagansing
Keweenaw	Keweenaw
Lake Superior	Kitchi Gami
Little Manitou Island	Eshkwedondens Miniss
Mackinac Island	Michilimackinac Miniss
Madeline Island	Moningwunakauning Miniss
Manitou Island	Manitou Miniss
Mesabi	Mesabi
Middle Fort (Sandy Bay)	Wikwedawangag
Michigan Island	Bugadabi Miniss
Montreal River	Gawassidjiwang Sibi

ENGLISH	OJIBWAY
Namakagan	Namakagan
Nanabazhoo, Menabosho & Winneboujou	Nanabazhoo
Nemadji	Nemadji
Oak Island	Mitigaminikang Miniss
Odanah	Odena
Ojibway	Ojibway, Otchipwe
Old Fort	Kitche Ajawew
Old Mission	Nesakee
Onion River	Jigagawanjikani Sibi
Ontonagon	Nontounagon or Tonagan
Otter Island	Nigig Miniss
Outer Island	Gachiishquaguindag Miniss
Point Detour	Kiwideonaning
Porcupine Mountains	Gagwadjiw
Potato River	Opini Sibi
Priest	Mekatewikwanaie
Raspberry Island	Miskominikan Miniss
Red Cliff	Passibikaning
Rocky Island	Sinsibakwado Miniss
Sand Island	Wababako Miniss
Sand Bay	Ga-Kashkikawangag
Sandy Bay	Wikwedawangag
Sault Ste. Marie	Bawatig
Silver Creek	Joniia Sibing
Siskiwit Bay	Siskawekaning
South Twin Island	Wabaso Miniss
Squaw Bay	Ganitagekweiag
Stockton Island	Gagawewamingo or Gegawewauindag Miniss
South Fork (of Fish Creek)	Metabikitigweiag
Superior (City)	Waikwakitchigaming or Gete Odena
Three Mile Creek	Bishegowke Sibi
Totogatic	Totogitiweiag
Vanderventer Creek	Gigito-Mikana Sibi
Washburn	Gigito-Mikana
West Branch (Montreal River)	Gogogashagun Sibi
White River	Wabi Sibing
York Island	Miskwabimijikag Miniss

Bibliographical Note

ORIGINAL SOURCES

American Board of Commissioners for Foreign Missions, Papers of the, 1831–1835. "Relations to Ecclesiastical Bodies," *Memorial Volume of the First Fifty Years of the American Board of Commissioners for Foreign Missions,* Fourth Edition, Published by the Board. Boston, 1861.

"Calendar Of the American Fur Company's Papers," *Annual Report of the American Historical Association for the Year 1944.* 2 and 3. Grace Lee Nute, Collator and Editor. Washington, 1945.

Armstrong, Benjamin. *Early Life Among the Indians.* Ashland, 1892.

Baraga, Frederic, Otto Skolla and Angelus Van Paemel, *Liber Baptizatorum Missionis S. Josephi in loco dicto a la Pointe du Lac Supereur,* 1831–1854. Negative photostats at Wisconsin Historical Library.

Baraga. *A Dictionary of the Otchipwe Language.* Montreal, 1878.

———. Journal and Letters, 1831–1868. Photostats and Microfilms from National Archives, Marquette, Mich.

Bayfield, Lieutenant. Maps of Lake Superior, Henry Wolsey. Photostats at U.S. Engineers Office. Sault Ste. Marie.

Bayfield County Press, 1870 et seq. Bayfield, Wis.

Beeson, Harvey C. *Marine Directory for the Northwestern Lakes.* Chicago, 1915.

Bowditch, Nathaniel. *American Practical Navigator.* Washington, 1905.

Cadillac, Lamothe & Liette, Pierre. *The Western Country in the 17th Century.* Milo M. Quaife, Editor, Lakeside Classics. Chicago, 1947.

Calendar of Canadian Archives, 1888.

Cadotte, Michel, Journal 1793–1818. Privately Held.

Chamberlin, Thomas C. *Geology of Wisconsin,* 4 Vol. Madison, 1880.

James Chapman Journal, 1857–1863. Madison.

Charlevoix, Pierre. *History of New France,* John Gilmary Shea's Translation. Madison, 1866.

Copway, George. *Life of Kah-ge-ga-gah-bowh, The Traditional History of the Ojibway Nation.* Philadelphia, 1847.

Franchere, Gabriel. *Voyage to the Northwest Coast of America.* Milo M. Quaife, Editor. Lakeside Classics. Chicago, 1954.

Gagnon, Ernest. *Essai de bibliographic canadienne.* Montreal.

Hall, Sherman. *Papers, 1833–1840.* Copy in Minnesota Historical Society.

185

Hennepin, Father Louis. *A New Discovery of a Vast Country in America.* R. G. Thwaites, Editor. Chicago, 1903.

Henry, Alexander. *Alexander Henry's Travels & Adventures,* Milo M. Quaife, Editor. Lakeside Classics. Chicago, 1921.

Holbrook, Dr. Arthur T. *From the Log of a Trout Fisherman.* Private Printing. Norwood, Mass., 1949.

Jefferson, Thomas. *The Writings of Thomas Jefferson.* Andrew Lipscomb, Editor, Monticello Edition. Washington, 1904.

Jerrard, Leigh P. Map of Bois Brule River. Privately held.

———. *The Brule River of Wisconsin.* Chicago, 1956.

Kellogg, Louise P., Editor. "Memoir of Duluth on the Sioux Country," *Early Narratives of the Northwest.* Scribner's. New York, 1917.

Kent, Robert E. *Kent's Mechanical Engineers' Handbook.* New York, 1923.

Kohl, Johann Georg. *Kitchi-Gami. (Wanderings Around Lake Superior.)* London, 1860.

La Pointe, Minutes of the Town Board, 1857 et seq. La Pointe, Wis.

La Pointe Mission Church Records, 1832–1866. Chicago Historical Society.

Mackinaw Roman Catholic Parish Register. Mackinac Island.

Marin, Joseph de la Margue, Sieur. *Journal de Monsieur Marin, Fils.* Loudoun Papers. Huntington Library, San Marino, California.

Martin, Lawrence. *The Physical Geography of Wisconsin.* Madison, 1916.

Masson, Louis R. *Les bourgeois de la compagne du nord-ouest.* Quebec, 1889.

McKenney, Thomas L. *Sketches of a Tour to the Lakes,* Baltimore, 1827.

Minnesota Historical Collections. St. Paul.

National Archives. Washington.

Neilson, Charles. *Burgoyne's Campaign.* Albany, 1844.

New York Colonial Documents. Albany.

Nute, Grace Lee. *Caesars of the Wilderness.* New York, 1943.

———. Editor. *Mesabi Pioneer.* St. Paul, 1951.

———. "Marin Versus La Verendrye," *Minnesota History,* 32, #4. St. Paul, 1951.

———. "American Fur Company's Fishing Enterprises on Lake Superior," *Mississippi Valley Historical Review,* Milo M. Quaife, Editor. XII. June 1925–March, 1926.

Owen, David Dale. *Geological Survey of Wisconsin, Iowa and Minnesota.* Philadelphia, 1852.

Perrault, Jean Baptiste. "Narratives of the Travels etc." *Collections of the Michigan Pioneer and Historical Society,* J. Sharpless Fox, Editor. Lansing, 1909–1910.

Radisson, Pierre E. *Voyages of Pierre Esprit Radisson.* Peter Smith Edition. New York, 1943.

Ritchie, James S. *Wisconsin and its Resources with Lake Superior.* Philadelphia.

Sagard-Theodat, Gabriel. *Histoire du Canada* (Reprint). Paris, 1866.

———. *La Grand Voyage du Pays des Hurons* (Reprint). Paris, 1865.

Schoolcraft, Henry Rowe. *Narrative Journals of Travels in the Year 1820.* New York, 1824.

———. Narrative Journals of Travels in the Year 1820. Menlor L. Williams, Editor. Lansing, 1953.

———. Narrative of an Expedition Through the Upper Mississippi. New York, 1834.

Skolla, Otto. "Father Skolla's Report on his Indian Mission," *Acta et Dicta*, Grace Lee Nute Editor. VII, #2. St. Paul, 1936.

Sproat, Florantha. "La Pointe Letters," *The Wisconsin Magazine of History*, 1 & 2. Evansville, 1932.

Jedediah D. Stevens Papers, 1827–1876. Minnesota Historical Society.

Albert Stuntz Diaries, 1858–1864. Wisconsin Historical Society.

Sulte, Benjamin. "Jean Nicolet," *Wisconsin Historical Collections, 8*. Madison.

Thwaites, Fredrik T. *Sandstones of the Wisconsin Coast of Lake Superior*. Madison, 1912.

Thwaites, Reuben Gold, Editor. *The Jesuit Relations and Allied Documents*. Cleveland, 1896–1901.

———. "The Story of Chequamegon Bay." *Wisconsin Historical Collections, 13*. Madison, 1895.

United States Census Records of La Pointe for 1840. Minnesota Historical Society.

———. For 1850, 1860 and 1870. Wisconsin Historical Society.

United States Lake Survey Office. *Bulletins of the Great Lakes*. Number 3 & 4. Detroit, 1903–4.

United States Survey Records, 1852. Ashland, Wisconsin.

Van Hise, Charles R. and Charles K. Leith. *The Geology of the Lake Superior Region*. Washington, 1911.

Vaughn, Samuel S., Warehouse Records. Wisconsin Historical Society.

Verwyst, Chrysostum. "A Glossary of Chippewa Names." *Acta et Dicta*. #4, 2. July. St. Paul, 1916.

Wallace, W. Stewart. *Documents Relating to the North West Company*. Toronto, 1935.

Warren, William. "History of the Ojibways," *Minnesota Historical Collections*, 5. St. Paul, 1885.

Weidman & Shultz. *The Water Supplies of Wisconsin*. Bulletin XXXV. Madison, 1914.

Wisconsin Historical Collections. 20 Volumes. Madison.

Wisconsin Historical Proceedings. Madison.

Wisconsin Public Service Commission Records. Madison.

Woods, Frederick M. *Memoirs of Colonel F. M. Woods*. Privately printed. 1926.

SECONDARY SOURCES

Andreas, A. T. *History of Northern Wisconsin*. Chicago, 1881.

Baker, General James H. "History of Transportation in Minnesota," *Minnesota Historical Collections*. 9. St. Paul. 1901.

Biggar, H. P. *Early Trading Companies of New France*. University of Toronto Series. Toronto, 1901.

Burnham, Guy M. *The Lake Superior Country in History and in Story*. Boston, 1930.

Butler, James D. "Early Shipping on Lake Superior," *Wisconsin Historical Proceedings*. 42nd Meeting. Madison, 1895.

Campbell, Father Thomas J. *Pioneer Laymen of North America*. New York, 1915.

Chapple, John B. *The Wisconsin Islands.* Ashland, 1945.

Davidson, John N. *In Unnamed Wisconsin.* Milwaukee, 1895.

———. "Missions on Chequamegon Bay," *Wisconsin Historical Collections.* 12. Madison.

Drummond, William H. *The Habitant.* New York, 1904.

———. *Johnnie Corteau.* New York, 1901.

———. *The Voyageur.* New York, 1910.

Dugmore, Radclyffe. *The Romance of the Beaver.* London.

Folwell, William W. *A History of Minnesota.* 1. St. Paul, 1921.

Gagnieur, William. "Indian Place Names," *Michigan History Magazine.* #2. Lansing.

Gregorich, Joseph. *The Apostle of the Chippewas.* Chicago, 1932.

Havighurst, Walter. *The Long Ships Passing.* New York, 1942.

Hebberd, Steven S. *Wisconsin Under the Dominion of France.* Madison, 1890.

Hunt, John Warren. *Wisconsin Gazeteer.* Madison, 1853.

Irving, Washington. *Astoria,* Home Library Edition. 2. New York, 1882.

Jamison, James K. *By Cross and Anchor.* Paterson, N.J., 1948.

Kellogg, Louise P. *The French Regime in Wisconsin and the Northwest.* Madison, 1925.

———. *The English Regime in Wisconsin and the Northwest.* Madison, 1935.

La Boule, Joseph S. "Claude Jean Allouez," *Parkman Club Publications.* Milwaukee, 1897.

Lathrop, Stanley E. *The Old Mission.* Ashland, 1905.

Legler, Henry E. *Leading Events in Wisconsin History.* Milwaukee, 1901.

Lewis, Janet. *The Invasion.* Denver, 1932.

Macalester Historical Contributions. St. Paul.

Madaline Island Resort Company. Brochure. Milwaukee, 1887.

Margry, Pierre. *Decouvertes et Etablissments des Francais dans l'Ouest et dans le Sud l'Amerique Septentrionals.* Paris, 1879–1886.

Marshall, Albert M. *Brule Country.* St. Paul, 1954.

McKay, Douglas. *The Honourable Company.* Toronto, 1938.

Means, Philip A. "Preliminary Survey of the Remains of the Chippewa Settlements on La Pointe Island, Wisconsin," *Smithsonian Miscellaneous Collections,* 66, #14. Washington, 1917.

Morse, Richard F., M.D. "The Chippewas of Lake Superior," *Wisconsin Historical Collections,* 3:338. Madison.

Murdock, Angus. *Boom Copper.* New York, 1943.

Neill, Edward D. *History of Minnesota.* St. Paul, 1885.

———. *Neill's History of Minnesota.* Minneapolis, 1873.

———. "Explorers and Pioneers of Minnesota," *The History of Ramsey County.* Minneapolis, 1881.

Nute, Grace Lee. *Lake Superior.* The American Lakes Series. Bobbs-Merrill, 1944.

———. *Rainy River Country.* St. Paul, 1950.

———. *The Voyageur.* St. Paul, 1931.

———. *The Voyageur's Highway.* St. Paul, 1945.

Osborn & Osborn. *Schoolcraft-Longfellow-Hiawatha.* Lancaster, Pa., 1942.

Parkman, Francis. *A Half Century of Conflict.* Boston, 1894.

———. *Count Frontenac and New France Under Louis XIV.* Boston, 1894.

———. *The Jesuits in North America in the 17th Century.* Boston, 1894.

Quaife, Milo M. *Lake Michigan.* The American Lake Series. Bobbs-Merrill, 1944.

Ratigan, William. *Soo Canal.* Grand Rapids, 1954.

Rezek, Antoine I. *History of the Diocese of Sault Ste. Marie and Marquette,* 2 Vol. Houghton, 1906.

Smith, Henry E. *History of Wisconsin,* 3. Madison, 1854.

Twaites, Reuben G. "The Story of Chequamegon Bay," *Wisconsin Historical Collections.* 13. Madison, 1895.

Thomas, George F. *Picturesque Wisconsin.* Milwaukee, 1899.

———. *Pen & Camera Sketches of Old La Pointe.* Milwaukee, 1898.

Turner, Frederick J. "The Character & Influence of the Fur Trade in Wisconsin," *Wisconsin Historical Proceedings.* Madison, 1889.

Turner, Lura J. *Geography Handbook & Gazeteer of Wisconsin.* Burlington, Wis., 1898.

Upham, Warren. "Groseilliers & Radisson." *Minnesota Historical Collections.* 10. St. Paul, 1905.

Verwyst, Chrysostum. *Life of Bishop Baraga.* Milwaukee, 1900.

———. "Missionary Labors," *Wis. Hist. Coll.* 10.

Williams, J. Fletcher. "Memoirs of William W. Warren," *Minnesota Historical Collections.* 5. St. Paul, 1885.

Winsor, Justin. *Cartier to Frontenac.* Cambridge, 1894.

———. *Narrative and Critical History of America.* Cambridge, 1889.

Chronology

1362   Norsemen in Minnesota?
1453   Indians mined copper on Ontonagon River.
1490   Ojibway came to Madeline Island. (Legendary)
1492   Columbus discovered America.
1535   Cartier discovered the St. Lawrence River.
1608   Champlain founded Quebec.
1610   White men on Madeline Island. Ojibway flee from Madeline Island. (Both events legendary.)
1615   Etienne Brule explored Lake Superior. (Questionable)
1620   Pilgrims landed at Plymouth Rock.
1642   Montreal founded.
1659   Radisson and Groseilliers arrived at Chequamegon Bay and built a cabin.
1661   Father Menard arrived at Chequamegon Bay.
1665   Father Allouez founded mission on Chequamegon Bay.
1668   Allouez left Chequamegon.
1669   Marquette came to Allouez's mission.
1670   Marquette left Chequamegon. Hudson's Bay Company formed in London.
1671   Cadeau arrived at Sault Ste. Marie. (Father of Jean Baptiste Cadotte.) French traders reported to have built a stockade on Madeline Island. (Questionable)
1679   Duluth arrived at Chequamegon and spent winter.
1689   King William's War. (French-British)
1690   Traders may have built fort on end of Chequamegon Point. (Unconfirmed)
1693   La Sueur built fort on south end of Madeline Island.
1698   Le Sueur fort abandoned.
1718   St. Pierre arrived and built Middle Fort on Madeline Island.
1732   George Washington was born.
1755   Braddock defeated. Declaration of French & Indian War.
1759   Quebec fell to General Wolfe.
1760   Montreal fell to General Amherst. End of French regime.
1762   Peace between France and England.

1763 Ojibway massacred English at Mackinac.
1764 Michel Cadotte was born. (Son of Jean Baptiste Cadotte.)
1765 Alexander Henry and Jean Baptiste Cadotte partnership.
1768 Grand Portage founded. (In present Minnesota.)
1773 Boston Tea Party.
1775 American Revolution.
1779 North West Company founded.
1783 End of Revolutionary War.
1793 North West Company, with Michel Cadotte as factor, opened post at La Pointe.
1796 United States occupied Mackinac for first time.
1803 Astor founded American Fur Company.
1809 Abraham Lincoln was born.
1811 Michilimackinac & North West Companies, with Astor, founded the South West Company.
1812 United States at war with England.
1815 End of war.
1816 United States barred foreign fur traders.
1818 Warren brothers came to La Pointe.
1821 Hudson's Bay Company absorbed the North West Company.
1823 Warren brothers purchased Cadotte's interest in American Fur Company post at La Pointe. Lieutenant Bayfield started survey of Lake Superior.
1830 Frederick Ayer arrived at La Pointe to teach school.
1831 Sherman Hall came to La Pointe to found Protestant mission.
1833 Astor sold American Fur Company to Crooks et al.
1835 La Pointe moved to present location. Protestant mission building completed. Father Baraga arrived to found Catholic mission. Truman Warren died.
1836 Baraga left for Austria. American Fur Company started fishing. Charles Oakes built Treaty Hall.
1837 Michel Cadotte died. Baraga returned.
1838 Baraga built second church.
1840 Protestant church built at La Pointe. American Fur Company in financial trouble.
1841 Baraga built church in the Village of La Pointe. The Leonard Wheelers arrived at La Pointe. Fur Company halted fishing.
1842 American Fur Company in hands of receiver. Discovery of copper made known on Keweenaw Peninsula.
1843 Copper rush. Baraga transferred to L'Anse, Michigan.
1845 Wheelers moved to Odanah. First steamer, "Independence," arrived at La Pointe November 1.
1846 War with Mexico.
1847 Lyman Warren died at La Pointe.
1848 Wisconsin admitted to statehood. Iron discovered on Gogebic.
1850 Fishing revived at La Pointe.
1853 Superior, Wisconsin founded.
1854 Ashland and Duluth founded. La Pointe mission closed.
1855 Sault locks opened. Elisha Pike bought sawmill near Bayfield.
1856 Bayfield founded.

1857 Panic.
1861 Civil War.
1863 Ashland depopulated to one family.
1865 Civil War ended.
1866 Robinson D. Pike built shingle mill at La Pointe. Wheelers left Odanah.
1868 Baraga died. Quarry opened on Basswood Island.
1869 La Pointe fire. New settlers in Ashland.
1871 Chicago fire.
1872 Leonard Wheeler died. Wisconsin Central Railroad started laying track south from Ashland.
1873 Panic. Wisconsin Central stopped work. Ashland Lumber Company founded.
1877 Wisconsin Central completed. Chequamegon Hotel opened at Ashland.
1883 Omaha Railroad built into Bayfield and Ashland. Island View Hotel opened at Bayfield.
1885 Milwaukee, Lake Shore & Western Railroad completed into Ashland.
1886 First Gogebic ore shipped from Ashland.
1888 Ashland blast furnace built.
1889 First whaleback.
1893 Columbian Exposition at Chicago.
1895 First summer cottages built on Madeline Island.
1896 Post office re-opened at La Pointe.
1897 Edward P. Salmon bought Protestant mission property.
1898 Old misison opened as an inn. First gasoline boat, Bayfield.
1899 Colonel Frederick M. Woods started his Nebraska Row on Madeline Island.
1900 Charles Russell started regular ferry service La Pointe-Bayfield. Sandstone quarries closed.
1901 Catholic Church at La Pointe burned. Protestant Church moved to mission grounds.
1902 La Pointe-Bayfield ferry propelled by gasoline engine.
1908 Bayfield lumber yard burned.
1910 Fishing boats all powered by gasoline engine.
1914 World War I started.
1917 United States entered war.
1918 End of war.
1920 First Diesel-engined fish boat.
1923 Treaty Hall burned.
1928 President Coolidge visited La Pointe.
1929 Electric power brought to La Pointe.
1939 World War II started.
1941 United States entered war.
1943 Old Protestant Church building on mission grounds collapsed.
1945 End of war.

Index

Index

Aitken, William, fur trader, 114, 120
Allouez, Claude Jean, Jesuit, 30, 31, 33, 43
Amherst, Gen. Jeffrey, 53, 58
American Board of Commissioners for Foreign Missions, 75, 97, 100, 101
American Fur Company, 70, 73, 78, 79, 80, 83, 87, 88, 91, 98, 101, 102, 104, 105, 109, 113, 118, 119, 120, 151,, 158
Angus, Captain John Daniel, 115, 116, 166
Apostle Islands, 10, 13, 52, 152, 168
Arrowhead Country, Minnesota, 88, 118
Ashland, Wisconsin, 114, 116, 118, 121, 122, 123, 130, 146
Ashland Lumber Company, 130
Astor, John Jacob, 69, 70, 74, 78, 79, 88
Aurora Borealis, 178
Austrian, Julius, trader and land agent, 119, 122, 151, 162
Ayer, Frederick, Missionary, 75, 77, 83, 87, 118

Bad River, Wisconsin, 45, 110, 129, 151
Bank of the United States, 99
Baraga, Frederic, Missionary, 88, 89, 91, 96, 97, 100, 103, 113, 121, 126, 127
Basswood Island, 127, 148
Bayfield County, Wisconsin, 114
Bayfield Harbor and Great Western R.R., 155, 172
Bayfield, Lieut. Henry W., 70, 120
Bayfield, Peninsula, 35, 64, 173
Bayfield, Superior & Minneapolis R.R., 155
Bayfield, Wisconsin, 64, 65, 115, 117, 119, 120, 130, 170, 171
Bayport. *See* Ashland
Bear Island, 65
Beaubassin, Pierre Hertel de, 53, 55, 57

Beaulieu, Bazil and Family, 96
Bell, John W., 122
Bell, Sarah. *See* George F. Thomas
Bellegarde, — Sieur, 34
Beloit College, 149, 152
Beloit, Wisconsin, 125
Bicksler, Benjamin, 121
Black River, Wis., North or small, South or large, 29
Blaisdell, James J., 149, 152
Blast Furnace, 146, 172
Bois Brule River, 7, 17, 19, 35, 45, 123, 133, 134, 173
Booth, A. — Packing Company. *See* Booth Fisheries Corp.
Booth Fisheries Corporation, 168, 170
Borup, Charles William Wulff, 78, 83, 95, 98, 99, 108, 109, 174
Boutwell, Hester Crooks (Mrs. William T.), 83
Boutwell, William Thurston, Missionary, 76, 83, 118
Boyd's Creek, 30
Braddock, General Edward, 53
Breckinridge, John C., 120
Brownstone quarries, 127, 131, 148, 149
Brule, Etienne, Explorer, 14, 16
Brule River. *See* Bois Brule River
Budgett, Samuel, 134, 135
Burgoyne, General John, 56
Burr, Almon Whitney, 166

Cadeau, Mons. — *See* Cadotte, Jean B.
Cadotte, Benjamin, 90
Cadotte, Charlotte, 73, 88
Cadotte, Jean Baptiste, 59, 61, 62, 72
Cadotte, Jean Baptiste III. 1830–1913, 158
Cadotte, Marie, 73

Cadotte, Michel, 62, 63, 65, 67, 69, 74, 96, 114, 176
Cadotte, Michel Jr.
Campbell, Mrs. John, 75, 83
Canada, 13, 56
Cartier, Jacques, 14
Catholic Church. See Missionaries
Cedar Bark Lodge, 154
Champlain, Samuel de, 14, 17, 18
Champlain Sea, 7
Charcoal, 146
Charcoal Iron. See Blast Furnace
Chequamegon, 10, 13, 25, 28, 29, 30, 31, 32, 34, 60, 131
Chequamegon Bay, 19, 20, 30, 33, 35, 43, 45, 59, 60, 64, 127, 128, 148
Chequamegon Hotel. See Hotel Chequamegon
Chequamegon Point, 11, 23, 33, 37, 40, 148
Chicago, St. Paul, Minneapolis & Omaha R.R., 137
China 14
Chippewa Indians. See Ojibway
Chippewa River, 29, 45
Civil War, 123, 124, 126
Clevedon, Wisconsin, 134
Cleveland Northwestern Lake Company, The, 102
Company, The — of the One Hundred Associates, 18
Congregational Church. See Missionaries
Cooke, Jay, 130
Coolidge, President Calvin, 173
Copper, 111, 120, 123, 134
Copper Harbor, Michigan, 109
Corcoran, William W., 120
Crawford, T. Hartley, 106
Crooks, Hester. See Boutwell
Crooks, Ramsay, 78, 79, 83, 98, 99, 101, 105, 109
Crooks, Colonel William, 109

Dakota Indians. See Sioux Indians
Dalrymple, William, 155
Dalrymple's Dream. See Bayfield Harbor & Great Western R.R.
Descent From the Cross, 144, 165
Detroit, Michigan, 67
Devil's Island, 65, 145, 173
Dickson, Robert, 69
Dodge, Henry, 106
Douglas, Stephan A., 120
Duluth, Daniel Greysolon, Sieur, 17, 34, 35, 37
Duluth, Minnesota, 7, 55, 115, 127, 173
Duluth, South Shore & Atlantic R.R., 143

East Indies, 14
Eclipse Wind Engine Company, 125
Ely, Edmund F., Missionary, 83, 87, 118
Equaysayway. See Michel Cadotte

Faffart, Duluth's Interpreter, 34
Fairbanks, Morse & Co., 125
Ferries, 127, 159, 169
Ferry, William, Missionary, 75
Fish Creek, 20, 23, 30
Fishing and fishermen, 149, 168, 170, 171
Flag River, 135
Flambeau, Lac du. See Lac du Flambeau
Fond du Lac, Minnesota, 45, 69, 84, 89, 110, 113
Fort Duquesne, Minnesota, 54
Fort Ramsay, 79
Fort Wilkins, 109
Fort William Henry, 55
Fox Indians, 11, 32, 49
Fox River, Wisconsin, 17, 32
Franchere, Gabriel, 89, 91
Freer, John M., 121
French, The, 13, 32, 53
French-Ojibway, 177
French, Russell W., 157
Frobisher brothers, Benjamin and Joseph, 62
Frontenac, Louis Buade, Count de, 34, 37
Fuller, General, Allen C., 158

Gage, General Thomas, 59
Gaudin, Louis, 90
Geology, 110, 128, 134
Georgian Bay, 14, 30
Glacial Lakes, Algonquin, Duluth, Nemadji, Nipissing, 7, 14
Gogebic Lake. See Lake Gogebic
Gogebic Range, 96, 110, 112, 115, 123, 143
Gordon. See Gaudin
Grand Lac du Nadouissou. See Lake Superior, 18
Grand Portage, Minnesota, 45, 61, 91, 95, 110
Grant's Point, 64, 102, 176
Grassie, Thomas Gordon, 149, 152, 164
Great Lakes, The, 7, 32
Green Bay, Wisconsin, 17, 32, 53, 54, 69
Greene, David, 97, 100
Grenolle, French explorer, 16, 17
Groseilliers, Medart Chouart, Sieur des, 19, 23, 25, 28, 30, 50, 115
Guerin, Jean, 28, 29

Hale, Herbert, 160
Hall, Elias Cornelius, 118

Hall, Harriet Parker, 76
Hall, Sherman, Missionary, 75, 77, 80, 83, 84, 86, 87, 97, 100, 101, 102, 114, 118
Hanley, John, 121
Harney, General William S., 120
Hastings, Minnesota, 54
Henry, Alexander, 59, 60, 61, 63, 72, 113
Hermit Island, 123, 148, 154
Highways and Roads, 135, 136, 137, 174
Hill, James J., 155
Hinkle. See Blast furnace
Hiroshima, 3
Hookers, 145, 153
Hotel Chequamegon, 131, 137, 163
Houghton Point, Wisconsin, 23, 148
Hudson Bay, 25, 28, 56
Hudson River, 7
Hudson's Bay Company, 28, 46, 49, 62, 73, 87, 88, 110, 118, 122
Huron Indians, 29
Huron, Lake. See Lake Huron

Indian agents, 91
Indian cemetery, 91, 102, 112, 176
Irish, 127
Iron Brigade, 124
Iron manufacture. See Blast furnace
Iron ore, 112, 172
Iron Ranges, 112
Iron River, Michigan, 143
Ironwood, Michigan, 143, 144
Iroquois Indians, 14, 32, 37, 149
Island View Hotel, 137, 160
Isle Royale, Michigan, 17, 50, 95

Jackson, President Andrew, 99
James, Woodbridge L., Missionary, 101, 102
Jesuits, 10, 18, 19, 28, 30, 31, 32, 33
Jesuit Relations, 18
Jogues, Isaac, Jesuit, 18
Johnston, John, trader, 63, 64, 65, 122
Jolliet, Adrien, trader, 28
Jolliet, Louis, explorer, 28

Kakagan River and sloughs, 37, 110
Kellogg, Louise Phelps, 58
Kensington Stone, 13
Kettle River, 7
Keweenawy Bay, 29
Keweenaw Peninsula, 4, 7, 17, 19, 63, 108, 110
Knight Hotel, 149
Knight, William, 173
Krakatoa, 3

Lac Court Oreilles, 20, 23, 52, 62, 73

Lac du Flambeau, 52, 62, 73, 77, 83, 96
Lac Tracy. See Lake Superior
Lafleche, — trader with Menard
Lake Algonquin. See Glacial Lakes
Lake Duluth. See Glacial Lakes
Lake Erie. See Glacial Lakes
Lake Huron, 14, 18, 51, 99
Lake Michigan, 17, 63
Lake Nemadji. See Glacial Lakes
Lake of the Woods, 55
Lake Ontario, 32, 37
Lake Owen, 20
Lake Superior, 3, 7, 17, 18, 19, 31, 32, 33, 34, 35, 37, 46, 51, 59, 65, 69, 80, 89, 104, 109, 111, 132
Lake Superior — Mississippi Canal, 134
Lake Winnipeg, 55
L'Anse, Michigan, 113, 118
La Pointe, 37, 43, 45, 46, 48, 50, 51, 52, 53, 54, 55, 56, 62, 63, 64, 67, 69, 70, 73, 74, 75, 76, 79, 80, 83, 84, 86, 87, 88, 89, 91, 95, 96, 98, 100, 101, 109, 111, 113, 115, 116, 118, 119, 122, 126, 127, 128, 132, 144, 145, 152, 153, 159, 164, 169, 174
La Pointe light, The, 115
La Ronde, Louis Denis, 57
La Ronde Island. See Madeline Island
La Ronde, Madame (Louise Chartier de Lotbibiere), 53, 57.
La Ronde, Philippe Louis Denis de, 50, 51, 52, 53, 57
Laurentian Mountains, 3
La Verendrye, Joseph Gaultier, Chevalier de, 54, 57
La Verendrye, Pierre Gaultier, Varennes de, 55
Lefevere, Bishop Peter Paul, 97
Le Gardier, Paul. See St. Pierre
Leopoldine Foundation, 88, 89, 104
Le Sueur, Pierre. French soldier and explorer, 40, 43, 46, 48, 49
Lincoln, Mrs., Abraham, 127
Linctot, Rene Godefroy, Sieur de, 50, 57
Lintot. See Linctot
Logging, 133
Long Island, 40, 65, 115
Long Lake. See Lake Owen
Louis, XIII, 16
Louis, XIV, 46, 53
Louis, XV, 58
Lumber, 132, 133, 145, 147
Lumberjacks, 133
Lusk, David, Ashland trader, 116

Mandelbaum, U. F., La Pointe trader, 122
McAboy, William, 121

Mackenzie, Alexander, 67, 69
Mackenzie, Sir Alexander & Co., 67
Mackinac Island, Michigan, 52, 58, 60, 65, 67, 74, 89
Madaline Island Resort Co., 144
Madeleine Cadotte. See Michel Cadotte
Madeline Island, 13, 16, 40, 43, 61, 62, 65, 67, 75, 88, 89, 114, 117, 120, 154, 159, 167, 170, 174, 178
Maistre, Sieur le, 34
Marin, Joseph de la Margue, Sieur, 53, 54, 55, 57
Marquette, Father Jacques, Jesuit, 32, 35, 78, 165
Marquette Range, 110, 112
Mattawa River, 14
Mauvais River. See Bad River
Menard, Father Rene, Jesuit, 28, 29, 30
Methodist Church. See Missionaries
Michilimackinac. See Mackinac
Michilimackinac Company, 69, 70, 79
Michigan, 3
Michigan Island, 117
Michipicoten Island, 50
Middle Fort, 48, 61, 62, 80, 90
Milwaukee, Lake Shore & Western R.R., 143
Mines and mining, 110, 112, 120, 123, 127, 134
Minneapolis, St. Paul & Ashland R.R., 160
Minnesota Mining Company, 113
Mission of the Holy Ghost. See St. Esprit
Missionaries and Missions, 75, 77, 80, 83, 86, 88, 97, 100, 102, 104, 110, 117, 118, 149, 152, 174
Mississippi River, 7, 17, 32, 45, 54, 69
Mohawk River, 7
Moningwunakauning. See Madeline Island
Montreal, Quebec, 11, 29, 32, 34, 43, 45, 49, 50, 51, 59
Montreal Island. See Madeline Island
Montreal River, 45, 112
Munising, Michigan, 63

Namakagan, Lake and River, 20, 45
Navigation, 163
Nebraska Row, 159
Nelson, George William, Missionary, 149, 152
Nemadji Lake. See Lake Nemadji
Neveaux, Corporal William, 124
New France, 28, 34, 46, 53, 55, 57, 58, 62
New North West Company, 67
Nicolas, Louis, Jesuit, 31
Nicolet, Jean, explorer, 17, 18, 48
Nipissing Great Lakes. See Glacial Lakes

Northern Outfit. See American Fur Co.
Northern Pacific R.R., 130, 137
Northland College, 149, 152
North West Company, 60, 62, 63, 67, 72, 73, 79
Northwest Passage, 14
North Wisconsin Academy. See Northland College
Norwegians, 149

Oakes, Charles, trader, 76, 78, 95
Oak Island, 64
O'Brien, Dillon, teacher, 122
O'Brien, John, 154
Odanah Mission, 149
Odanah, Wisconsin, 111, 114, 117, 125, 151
Ojibway Indians, 10, 11, 13, 16, 34, 40, 49, 52, 58, 59, 60, 86, 98, 102, 103, 114, 115, 176, 177
Old Abe, Mascot Eagle, 124
Old Mission and Old Mission Inn, 48, 158, 165, 168, 177
Oneota, Minnesota. See Duluth
Ontonagon boulder, 113
Ontonagon, Michigan, 112
Ontonagon River, 17, 50, 51, 60
Ore boats, 143, 147, 148
O-Shaka, 177
Ottawa Indians, 11, 14, 20, 23, 29, 30, 31, 32
Ottawa Lake. See Lac Court Oreilles
Ottawa River, 14

Parsons, Robert W., 171
Peerless, The. See Minneapolis, St. Paul & Ashland R.R.
Peet, James, Methodist minister, 122, 136
Penokee Range, 96, 110, 112, 115
Percival mine, 133, 134
Pewabic Range. See Penokee
Pictured Rocks, 63
Pig Boats. See whalebacks
Pigeon River, 61
Pike, Elisha, 119
Pike, Robinson Derling, 119, 123, 126, 129, 148, 176
Pike, R. D. Lumber Compony, 131, 132, 145
Pike's Creek, 119, 135
Pike's Quarry. See Brownstone quarries
Pine City, Minnesota, 53
Pirates, 151
Pointe de Froid, 80, 95, 126
Porcupine Mountains, 96
Port Arthur, Ontario, 4
Pratte, Bernard, trader, 80

Prentice, Frederick, trader and quarry owner, 116, 126, 148, 154, 162
Presbyterian Church. See Missionaries

Quarries. See Brownstone quarries
Quebec, 14, 18, 25, 31, 32, 50, 52, 58

Radisson, Pierre Esprit, explorer and trader, 18, 19, 20, 23, 25, 28, 30, 56, 116
Railroads, 123, 127, 130, 131, 137, 155, 156
Rainy Lake, 55, 111
Raymbault, Charles, Jesuit, 18
Red Cliff, Wisconsin, 116, 117, 122, 155
Rese, Bishop, Frederic, 89
Revolutionary War, 62
Rice, Henry M., 120, 121, 137
Rice's Island. See Rocky Island
Roads. See highways and roads
Rocky Island, 137
Rogers, Robert, 59
Roy, Vincent Jr., 111
Roy, Vincent III, 111
Royalton, Minnesota, 54
Russell, Captain Charles, 166, 169

St. Croix Creek, 35
St. Croix River, 7, 17, 45, 53
St. Croix, Upper — Lake, 35, 45
St. Esprit, mission of, 43
St. Lawrence River, 7, 10, 11, 14, 56
St. Louis Bay, 115
St. Louis, Missouri, 80, 99, 120
St. Louis River, 19, 45, 83
St. Lusson, Francois Daumont Sieur de, 59
St. Luc, Sieur Corne de, 55, 56, 57, 58
St. Mary's River, 18
St. Michael's Island. See Madeline Island
St. Paul, Minnesota, 120, 136, 137, 173
St. Pierre, Paul Le Gardeiur, Sieur de, 48, 49, 56, 57
Ste. Theresa Bay. See Keweenaw Bay
Salmon, Edward P., 158, 160, 165
Sand River, 155
Sault Ste. Marie, Michigan & Ontario, 11, 13, 16, 17, 18, 30, 51, 88, 89, 127
Sault Ste. Marie Locks, 119, 120
Sault Ste. Marie rapids, 18, 51
Saulteurs. See Ojibway Indians
Schoolcraft, Henry Rowe, 65, 77, 91, 101, 113
Shagowashcodawaqua. See John Johnston
Sibley, Thomas P., 116, 176
Shipping and captains, 119, 129, 130, 143
Shores, Eugene Arthur, 152

Silver Creek, 129
Sioux Indians, 11, 20, 29, 32, 37, 52
Sioux River, 135
Skolla, Father Otto, 87, 103, 104, 110, 122
Sleeping Giant. See Thunder Cape
Smithsonian Institution, 113
Snake River, 54
Soldier's Rock, 46
Soo. See Sault Ste. Marie
South Fork. See Fish Creek
South Shore, 158
South West Company, 70, 79
Spooner, Wisconsin, 137
Spooner, Miss Abigail, 101
Sproat, Florantha (Mrs. Granville T.), 97, 107
Sproat, Granville T., Missionary, 97
Stahl, Gabriel, 126
Stahl, Thomas, 167
Stanard brothers, Benjamin, A., Charles G., and John J., 109
Steamboat Island, 65, 164
Steamboats, 147
Stevens, Jedediah D., Missionary, 75
Stuntz, Albert, 137
Stuntz, George, 116
Superior, Wisconsin, 115, 121, 127, 147, 155
Swedes, 149

Tecumseh, 70
Terry, Alfred, Presbyterian minster, 151
Thomas, George Francis, 144, 145, 152, 154, 166
Three Rivers, Quebec, 50
Thunder Cape, 4
Tomkins, William Mawby, 161
Tonawanda, New York, 146
Trails. See Highways and roads
Treaty Hall, 117, 123, 166, 172

U.S. Government Surveys, Land and Lake, 72
Utrecht, Treaty of, 46

Vaughn, Samuel Stewart, 121, 127, 130
Vermilion Iron Range, 3
Vigne, Paul, de, 34
Vorous, Captain Okay J., 168
Voyageurs, 59

Wabogish. See Waubojeeg
Wachsmuth Lumber Company, 172
Warren, Lyman Marcus, 73, 74, 75, 76, 78, 80, 83, 87, 88, 98, 109, 112, 114, 174

Warren, Truman, Abraham, 73, 76, 80, 88, 174
Warren, William Whipple, 114
Washburn, Wisconsin, 137
Waubijijauk. See White Crane
Waubojeeg. See White Fisher
Wayne, General Anthony, 63
Welton, Junius T., 116
Wendat Indians. See Huron Indians
Whalebacks, 147, 153
Wheeler, Edward Payson, 149, 152. Leonard Heminway, 101, 118, 149. Mrs. Leonard H., 102, 125, 152. William Henry, 124, 152
White River, 20, 110, 116, 129, 130
White Crane, Chief, 65

White Fisher, Chief, 64
Whittlesey, Asaph, 124, 131. Colonel Charles, 115, 116
Willey, Charles N., 143
Wilson's Island. See Hermit Island
Wilson, William, 95, 122
Wisconsin, 3, 7, 17
Wisconsin Central R.R., 127, 129, 131, 137, 143
Wisconsin Monolith, 148
Wolfe, General James, 58
Woods, Frank, 173
Woods, Colonel Frederick M., 162, 163
Wyandotte Indians. See Huron Indians

York Island, 65